Cosmic

You Can be

Cosmic Ordering
You Can be Successful

$tephen Richards

First edition
Published in Great Britain
By Mirage Publishing 2009

Text Copyright © Stephen Richards 2009

First published in paperback 2009

A CIP catalogue record for this book
is available from the British Library.

ISBN: 978-1-902578-46-0

Mirage Publishing
PO Box 161
Gateshead
NE8 1WY
Great Britain

Printed and bound in Great Britain by

Book Printing UK
Remus House, Coltsfoot Drive, Woodston, Peterborough, PE2 9JX

Cover © Mirage publishing

Papers used in the production of this book are from sustainable
forests, thus reducing environmental depletion.

iv

For my Cosmic Friend, Chuka Agbasiere,
a real inspiration for us to aspire to be like.

Contents

Introduction

This guide is for those who thus far have not been able to find the time, means, inclination nor opportunity to delve far into metaphysical study, but who seek results. This is intended to be a hands-on guide, rather than a lecture in theories. Primarily it was written for those with a pressing desire for wealth; be it wealth of the pocket or wealth of the soul. However, I recognise that most people wish first to become rich and then philosophise about the Spirit.

In this book, I have forgone other considerations of theory in order to supplant simplicity and plainness of style, so that all readers might comprehend. The plan of action set to text herein is taken from the conclusions of a philosophical mind; it has been tested thoroughly, bearing the ultimate test of real-life experiment; put simply, it works. If you seek to harvest the fruits of my philosophies in practice, read this guide and follow the calls to action exactly as instructed.

Bearing in mind what is within here, it is my hope that you will place your faith in the fundamental facts presented herein, just as you would accept information about other laws of action.

The truth of the statements you find here will be proven of their own accord by your acting upon them without fear or hesitation. Anyone who follows these laws of action on faith will certainly find wealth; for the laws of action applied in this text are an exact science, making failure impossible.

There is a theory of the universe that claims in a monistic way that: everything is one. This theory of the universe, apparently, is that separate elements of the material world are actually manifestations of one Substance. This theory is of Hindu origin and has gradually won acceptance in Western thought over many hundreds of years.

The only power that can create tangible wealth from the formless essence is *thought*. All material things are made into matter from a substance that thinks. A thought of form made in this substance produces that form.

Each form and process you observe in the natural world is the observable interpretation of a thought occurring in original substance.

Original substance progresses by way of its thoughts. As the shapeless substance thinks of a form, it takes on that form; as it thinks of an action, it creates that action. This is how all material matter was created. We reside in a world of thought, which is a component of a thought-based universe. The idea of a moving universe reached throughout shapeless substance – progressed into the shapes of that thought – took the shapes of planetary systems, and continues to maintain those shapes.

Thinking substance becomes the shape and form of its thoughts, and progresses according to the shape of that thought. Bearing the notion of a rotating system of suns and planets, it takes on the form of those objects, setting them in motion as it thinks. Thinking of a slow-growing plant, it consequently progresses to produce the plant, although it may take eons to accomplish the task.

The formless appears to create according to lines of motion already established. That is to say, the idea of an oak tree will not result in the instant creation of a fully mature tree, but it sets in motion the powers that will eventually produce the tree, along the lines established for growth.

Each forming thought, kept in thinking substance, produces the creation of that form, but universally, or at least in most cases, along the path of growth and action thought has already created.

The idea of a business of a particular makeup, if the thought was affected upon formless substance, may not bring

Introduction

the instantaneous creation of the business. However, it would set into motion the creative energies that are already established in commerce and trade into such streams as to bring about the speedy establishment of the business. If no channels existed through which the original energy could labour, then the business would come about directly from the primal substance, not waiting for the slow progression of manifesting in the organic and inorganic world.

It is impossible that a thought of form would be impressed on the original substance and not result in the form being created. Humans are thinking creates and have the ability to originate thought.

Man cannot create any form without first thinking of that form. His hands do the work that his thoughts put into motion. Man cannot create or shape any object before he forms the idea of that object. Thus far, man has limited his attempts entirely to the labour of his hands. He has applied manual force to the forms of the world, attempting to alter or change forms already in existence. Man has yet to think of causing the creation of new forms by applying his thoughts to the formless substance.

When man comes up with an idea of form, he draws from material resources already found in the forms of nature and creates an image of the form he holds in his mind. At this juncture, he has made minimal to no effort in cooperating with the formless intelligence known as The Cosmos.

Man takes existing natural forms and alters or reshapes them using his hands – he has not considered the question of whether he might create material things from formlessness by impressing his thoughts upon it. I propose to show that man can do so – to prove that anyone has the ability to create from formlessness.

As our first step, we must apply some basic principles. To start with, we are the very the existence of what is called a single original formless substance from which all material things were and are created. All elements, while appearing separate, are only various manifestations of a single element.

11

Cosmic Ordering: You Can be Successful

The multitude of forms seen in organic and inorganic nature is simply an assortment of shapes, created out of the same stuff, what some call a thinking stuff. The amazing thing is that *any thought kept in this stuff will produce the form of that thought.* We then find that in thinking substance, thought causes shapes to form. We, as man, have the capacity for original thought. If we (man) learn to impress our thought onto the original thinking substance, we can bring about the creation, or formation, of the forms we dwell upon.

One might ask if I can give evidence of these statements, and without detailing the intricate workings involved, I tell you that I can prove my statements and do so by both logic and experience. Reasoning back from the phenomena of form and thought, I arrive at a single original thinking substance, and reasoning forward from this thinking substance, I come to man's power to bring about the formation of the things he thinks about. And by my own practical experiment, I have found the reasoning to hold true. This is my most powerful evidence.

In answer to this, I say:

If even a single person gains wealth from reading this book and following my advice, that then is the hard evidence to support Cosmic Ordering working, but if every person who follows what the book prescribes gains wealth, that is unshakeable proof that will hold until someone follows through the process without success.

Until the means of manifesting your desires fails, then this theory holds. Be rest assured, this means you CANNOT fail! Follow the advice in this book exactly and you WILL get rich.

I have held that people gain wealth by taking certain actions in a particular way. To be successful in this, people must learn how to think in a particular way. A man's methods for doing things results directly from the way he *thinks* about things.

If you want to do things in a certain way, it is necessary that

Introduction

you secure the ability to think in the manner you want to think. This is the first step in attaining great wealth. To think the way you want to think is to think the truth, without regard to the appearance of things.

Every one of us is given the natural and innate ability to think whatever we wish to think, but thinking without being influenced by appearances requires a great deal more effort than allowing thoughts to follow the suggestions of appearances. To think by following appearances is simple; to think true thoughts, without respect to appearances requires hard work and the spending of more energy than any other work man may be asked to perform.

Most people are willing to work very hard with their bodies, but shrink at the idea of holding sustained and consecutive thought. Controlling the mind and its thoughts is the most laborious work in our existence. Appearances make true thought even more difficult when they are contrary to the goals of man's thought.

Every appearance in the observable world has a tendency to create a form in the mind of the observer, reinforcing that appearance. Once can only prevent this by holding and sustaining the thought of the TRUTH.

Should you observe and dwell upon the appearances of poverty then it will only serve to produce the same forms in your mind, unless you can grasp and hold to the truth that poverty does not exist; there is only abundance.

To recognise there is only good health even when you are surrounded by the appearances of disease, or to think riches when the appearances of poverty are observed all around you, requires strength and power. Should you attain this power then you will become a *master* of the mind. A mastermind can defeat fate and can attain any thing or life situation that he or she wants.

You can only attain this power by taking hold of the fundamental fact, which lies behind all appearances, and understand that there is a solitary thinking substance out of which and through which all material things are created. You must then understand that through communicating your thoughts to the original substance, the substance progresses into form causing your ideas and thoughts to take shape and become realities.

When you come to realise this fundamental fact, it will be easy to let go of all doubts and fears. You will understand that you have the power to create whatever it is you wish to create, you can secure whatever you wish to obtain, and can become whatever you wish to become.

It is vital that you set aside any other ideas you may have about how the universe functions, and you must take these propositions and meditate on them until they become as certain and concretely as your own name, and have become a reflex in your thinking, rather than something you must always remind yourself of.

To do this, you should take time to read these statements repeatedly until they are solid in your memory. Be certain that you take time to dwell upon these concepts, until your belief in them is unquestionable and absolute. If you begin to doubt, remember that doubt is the obstacle to your personal wealth. Ignore arguments you might hear from others that are contrary to this idea. Avoid places or venues where ideas that conflict with these statements are espoused. Stay away from magazines and books that on the so-called 'logic' of taking action based on appearances because only your thoughts can create true change.

If you wish to attain wealth, these steps are vital because allowing doubt to mix up your understanding will bring all your efforts to naught. It is futile to ask why these laws hold true or to waste time speculating how they could be true. By simply accepting them on trust, you will ensure your success. It is important to realise that your old habits of acting on appearance have not thus far brought you the wealth you seek. Abandon the old principles and embrace wholeheartedly a new way of thinking based on the science of The Cosmos, which creates all things for you when you communicate your thoughts to it.

The scientific and certain approach to getting rich requires your complete and total acceptance of this. There is little point in gaining riches just to bask in the pleasures of triumph, to gain more knowledge, to satisfy your ambitions, to conquer others, to find fame. While each of these is a legitimate aspect of human life, you will never have a full life if you spend your time chasing after pleasures of the mind alone. You will never find satisfaction, no matter what level of wealth you attain. There is also no point in getting rich just to benefit others, losing yourself trying to save the world like a new saviour, just for the sake of sacrifice and philanthropy. These joys of the soul may feel pleasurable, but they are no more good or bad, despicable or noble, than any other part of life.

Getting rich can help you do more in your life. You may enjoy the pleasures of good food, drink and company at the proper times without regard to budget. Your eyes will always fall on objects of beauty, see lands far from home. Your mind will have a steady stream of new stimulations and you will be free to form your intellect as you please. You will have a chance to help the world know TRUTH. However, it is important to know that extremes of any sort should be avoided.

There is no more morality in excessive altruism than in extremes of selfishness. To bear too much of any given trait is a mistake. Banish the concept that you should sacrifice your life to benefit others or gain their favour. The Cosmos does not want or need sacrifice of any sort from you. The Cosmos, in its pure love, only wants that you grow to fruition the way it coaxes an apple seed into a tree. There is no expectation that the seed help other trees to grow. By being your optimal self, you benefit yourself and others. Just as the seed grows to a tree, simply by doing what it is designed to do, it fertilises other trees, helping them to bear fruit and flourish. You will help others by fulfilling your potential for your own desires, which will naturally benefit others with no conscious effort on your own part.

Becoming wealthy is the only way to reach your full potential. Understanding this fact makes it a moral imperative that you give your greatest efforts towards fulfilling the Cosmos' desires for you and acquiring wealth. Keep in mind that the desire for abundance is not limited or held especially for any individual. Movements always turn towards bringing more life to all creatures. The universe will not work towards lessening abundance to any individual, as it treats all equally in the search for wealth, life and abundance.

It is a mistake to believe that the intelligent substance might create wealth for you by taking it from some other person or source. Competition has no place in the attainment of wealth. Do not think of attaining what already exists, but focus on the creation of new wealth.

Riches secured by competition or taking from another's store will not endure, nor will they satisfy. Such methods bring wealth today and transfer that wealth to someone else the next day. If you wish to follow a certain and scientific path to wealth, it is necessary that you rise above competition and striving.

Never entertain thoughts of limited supply. If you allow thoughts that compartmentalise wealth into a limited supply, controlled by corporations and bankers, that you must make efforts to change laws or make other great changes in order to acquire wealth, you will sabotage your efforts.

The moment you view wealth as limited or controlled by human forces, you give away your inherent power to create wealth in your life. Doubts of this type can undo any creative forces that have already begun to work towards creating the wealth you seek.

You must KNOW that stored away from public eyes, countless wealth awaits the Cosmos' call. Wealth is stored in the earth, in deep caverns where gold can be mined. Even if this were not the case, know that the universe would create new wealth, whether it be from technology or new public desire for

Introduction

any given service or product. The thinking substance will create whatever market forces are necessary to supply the wealth you desire.

KNOW that all the money you could ever need or want is on its way. Never acknowledge the limits of the visible supply. What will be in the future is already there, waiting to be created. Always seek the unlimited resources stored in formless substance, and KNOW these resources are on their way to you, waiting for you to be ready to accept them. It does not matter if any one person hoards wealth from the world. Ignore the appearance of limited supply, since it cannot prevent you from creating and receiving what is already yours, waiting for you in the fullness of time.

Give no energy to thoughts of striving, the idea that you must rush to take action to secure your place in line. Ignore fears that those with great wealth and power will devour all the wealth of the world.

Do not fear that competition from others will steal your prize. It is impossible that anyone could take the riches that are waiting to be created for you because it is new wealth, not able to be possessed by anyone else.

Your thoughts will set in to motion the creation of wealth solely for you, without limits.

It was June 15, and in two days James would be turning thirty. James was insecure about entering a new decade of his life and feared that his best years were now behind him.

His daily routine included going to the gym for a workout before going to work. Every morning James would see his friend Nick at the gym.

Nick was seventy-nine years old and in terrific shape. As James greeted Nick on this particular day, he noticed James wasn't full of his usual vitality and asked if there was anything wrong.

James told him he was feeling anxious about turning thirty. James wondered how he would look back on my life once he reached Nick's age, so he asked him, 'What was the best time of your life?'

Without hesitation, Nick replied, 'Well, James, this is my philosophical answer to your philosophical question. When I was a child and everything was taken care of for me and I was nurtured by my parents, that was the best time of my life.

'When I was going to school and learning the things I know today, that was the best time of my life.

'When I got my first job and had responsibilities and got paid for my efforts, that was the best time of my life.

'When I met my wife and fell in love, that was the best time of my life.

'The Second World War came, and my wife and I had to flee Austria to save our lives. When we were together and safe on a ship bound for England, that was the best time of my life.

'When we came to England and started a family, that was the best time of my life.

'When I was a young father, watching my children grow up, that was the best time of my life.

'And now, James, I am seventy-nine years old. I have my health, I feel good and I am in love with my wife just as I was when we first met. This is the best time of my life.'

1

The Theory of
Cosmic Ordering

The Importance of Positive Thought

If you wish for wealth to come to you quickly, you must maintain a steadfast and continuous faith in the wealth waiting to be created for you. As you make only positive thought impressions on the formless substance, you will ensure the swift and ready deliverance of your desires. Doubts and negative thoughts will neutralise or delay the creative forces at work.

By keeping a strong image of your wants and maintaining faith and belief in your purpose, you create ripples in the pond of formless substance that continue without obstacle to far shores, potentially throughout the entire universe.

As these ripples of thought spread, all things are pushed towards the realisation of your thoughts. All life, all objects, and all that is waiting to be created is stirred and set in motion towards making your thoughts of wealth a reality. Just as those tiny ripples on the pond travel out and then return to the source, your thoughts will become realities that return to you.

Your thoughts set all forces into the direction of your desires and all things begin to move toward the creation of your desires. Your thoughts influence the minds of all people who act unconsciously on your behalf. If you doubt, you disrupt the flow of energy towards your desires and slow the fulfilment you await.

Just as certainly as unshakeable faith and positive thoughts set the forces of creation in motion, doubt is sure to slow or reverse the powers at work to create wealth for you. Those who fail to understand the obstacle that doubt presents fail to receive their desires. Each moment you waste on doubt or fear, every minute you spend fretting, distances you from your connection with the intelligent substance, disrupting your link of communication. The Cosmos promises all to those that believe, but only to those who believe.

This story is a prime example of the power of belief. There once was a wise sage who wandered the countryside. One day, as he passed near a village, he was approached by a woman who told him of a sick child nearby. She beseeched him to help this child.

So the sage came to the village, and a crowd gathered around him, for such a man was a rare sight. One woman brought the sick child to him, and he said a prayer over her.

'Do you really think your prayer will help her, when medicine has failed?' yelled a man from the crowd.

'You know nothing of such things! You are a stupid fool!' said the sage to the man.

The man became very angry with these words and his face grew hot and red. He was about to say something, or perhaps strike out, when the sage walked over to him and said: 'If one word has such power as to make you so angry and hot, may not another have the power to heal?'

And thus, the sage healed two people that day.

Because belief is so vital, you must take care to pay close attention to your thoughts. It is natural for human thought to be influenced by the visible world, so you must learn to retract thought energy from influences that can sow doubt. Use your innate power of will to focus on those aspects of life that serve to reinforce the attainment of your desires. To illustrate this, we will examine poverty in order that you can better understand how it related to understanding the attainment of riches.

It is pointless to put efforts towards traditional 'charitable' work. Charitable organisations seek to end poverty through means of striving and control. The futility of these endeavours

The Theory of Cosmic Ordering

is clearly seen as one observes the perpetual wretchedness of the people charity strives to serve. Charities have operated as long as man has understood the concept, yet poverty persists. These organisations accomplish nothing for their efforts. That is not to say you should turn your back on the poor and downtrodden. Quite the opposite is true. However, you must put to rest your old ways of thinking about poverty. Only by attaining wealth yourself can you truly help the poor, for your success helps them.

Change yourself, not the world. There was once a king who ruled a prosperous country. One day, he went for a trip to some distant areas of his country. When he was back to his palace, he complained that his feet were very painful, because it was the first time that he went for such a long trip, and the road that he went through was very rough and stony. He then ordered his people to cover every road of the entire country with leather. Definitely, this would need thousands of cows' skin, and would cost a huge amount of money.

Then one of his wise servants dared himself to tell the king, 'Why do you have to spend that unnecessary amount of money? Why don't you just cut a little piece of leather to cover your feet?'

The king was surprised, but he later agreed to his suggestion, to make a 'shoe' for himself.

There is actually a valuable lesson of life in this story: to make this world a happy place to live, you better change yourself - your heart; and not the world.

You should avoid dwelling upon poverty and images of the poor. This will retard the deliverance of your wealth. No amount of knowledge or understanding of poverty and its terrible affects on humankind will assist the poor in any way. Dwelling on poverty does nothing to prevent or cure it.

The best way to reduce poverty is to focus instead on wealth and plenty for all. By redirecting your thoughts away from the poor, you are not abandoning them, but abandoning poverty. Only when we enrich the minds of the poor to believe in their innate power to create wealth will we eradicate poverty. No amount of meditation by outsiders on the problem of poverty will accomplish this.

The poor are not in need of your charity, which is difficult to come by and quick to go. What the poor really need is your inspiration and your example. Teach them by fulfilling your potential for wealth, by leading with your example. Your inspiration will change their thoughts; teach them to rise above the misery of everyday life, as they have hereto known it. Show the poor how they can become rich by becoming rich yourself.

Poverty can only be banished from this world when you practise and spread the teachings in this volume. Competition does nothing to help the poor attain wealth. Only learning helps the poor rise from their poverty.

The poor often cannot escape poverty simply because they do not understand that wealth is available to them and you can best teach them through your own example, by living a life of wealth and affluence. Some are poor simply due to the lazy minds and lack of enthusiasm for life. You can best help these people by inspiring them with your own happiness and the lust for living that the truly wealthy enjoy.

Many remain poor because they become overwhelmed by the many potential avenues to wealth that they observe in the world. These people feel lost in a sea of possibilities often making a stab at one method or another to attain wealth, never truly understanding the scientific workings of the Cosmos. These efforts fail repeatedly because such persons are caught in an endless striving and fretting over money.

Your example is also the best remedy for this kind of poverty, which is essentially poverty of purpose. Show these people the way to wealth by reaching your true potential and sharing the methods you used to attain wealth. It is often said that an ounce of action is worth a pound of theory. By making the most of our self, you will be giving hope and affluence to the entire world.

The Theory of Cosmic Ordering

A straight line makes the shortest distance from one point to another. Follow the line of science, taking the simplest and straightest route to your goal. Lay all other plans aside, keeping them from your mind altogether. Do not deviate from the straight line by trying to alter or add to this simple plan.

Once you have acquired the wealth you desire, there is no reason you cannot study other means of gaining wealth. Focus only on optimism and good news, the things that resonate harmoniously with your image of a wealthy life.

Shaping Your Desires

'If wishes were horses then beggars would ride.' These words and others like it are sewn into our young minds as children. But can you imagine a world where kings would ride, where all you need to do is ask and your desires come true? Stop imagining and start believing because you can change the outcome of any event and create an abundance of joy, well-being and money in your life. It is easy to be sceptical considering such a statement, when we have been trained since children to take action, rather than use thoughts to attain our desires. While these lessons from our elders were well-meant, they failed to teach us the TRUTH: you can shape the results of all that you desire by changing your mindset to one of receptivity and openness.

The simple act of asking the universe to fulfil your desires is known as Cosmic Ordering. It may be that you have tried this before with limited success. Perhaps in prayer, what some consider a form of Cosmic Ordering, the universe answered with the outcome you desired. There is more power in Cosmic Ordering that you know and by now, you may be starting to understand the strength of your own thoughts.

The thoughts we transmit into and through the universe have the power to change that universe. When we put particular attention and focus on these thoughts, they begin to resonate with the frequency of the universe, like individual notes in a piano chord. When your thoughts strike the right tone, they become the chord, the reality you desire. Quite suddenly, you will notice new opportunities where before there was only despair. Good things begin happing all around you. You will begin to gaze in wonder at the beautiful simplicity of creating your desires through thought.

Just as there are five elements in the universe (ether, fire, air, water and earth), the human microcosm consists of five distinctive elements. An imbalance in these bodily elements results in disease or ill health. The five elements join to form a human life in birth and dissipate in death. Our health through life is dependent on maintaining balance among the five elements.

By examining the ancient Vedas of Eastern thought, we can see the origins of the five elements in human thought. The five elements in Vedas thought are each called *tattwas.* All elements are descendent from the principle ether or *akash.*

Ether is tied to sound, or rather the spaces that sound vibrations resonate through. Since sound resonates through all things, the ether is a reorientation of all things.

Fire is known as *tejas* and *vayu* represents air. *Apas* is the element of water and movement. *Prithivi* represents the earth and non-movement or heaviness. The cosmic element, or *akash tattwa*, gives rise to the remaining four elements and is the essence of all cosmic elements.

Because ether is tied to sound and all things, it is useful to understand this concept when thinking about communication. There are those communications that are transmitted to the Cosmos as well as those that are received. All communications to the Cosmos must travel through the ether element.

Einstein actually proved that matter is energy and energy matter. His famous theory, $E = mc2$, proves that all things are one; merely different manifestations of the same stuff, energy. The theory, which has held true for many years, shows there is no duality and that all things are connected.

Various manifestations of energy, or matter, take many forms. Dense matter like stone or metal has a slower frequency

The Theory of Cosmic Ordering

of vibration than other, less dense materials.

Sunlight, the fastest known energy in the universe, vibrates at an inconceivably faster rate or higher frequency. These different frequencies, when observed by human eyes, create the illusion of separateness.

When we look closer at these forms of matter and view them on a subatomic level, we find that the solid-appearing matter is mostly empty space, dotted with electrons rotating about atom nuclei.

When we look even closer, we find quarks and smaller particles that blink in and out of existence, sometimes behaving as matter, sometimes as energy.

The average mind cannot fully grasp the concept of energy. It is one of the most complex subjects one can contemplate. However, it is clear and undisputed that *all things are energy*. When you understand that your body and the thoughts emitted by your mind are both made of the same basic stuff, energy, you begin to access the power that lies dormant in your mind. This power will allow you to attain absolute abundance in your life in all things.

Energy vibrates, albeit at different speeds or frequencies. Since all matter is energy, all matter vibrates as well. No matter what makes these various forms of matter, they all are in a constant state of motion and flux.

When two vibrations resonate, the sound is amplified and strengthened. The vibration of your thoughts resonates similarly with the universe as it travels through the ether. The frequency of your thoughts is governed by the content of those thoughts. By thinking in positive and abundant frequencies, you are able to replicate the life circumstances of other people who think with the same frequency.

Positive thoughts are found at high frequencies and attract similar thought frequencies in your life. Lower negative thoughts will attract just the opposite. For this reason, you must raise the frequency of your thoughts, remaining positive and attracting like thinkers into your sphere of influence.

Cosmic Ordering: You Can be Successful

Understanding Cosmic Ordering

You can think of Cosmic Ordering as a means to use positive thought to create abundance and attract the things needed to make your life richer and more fulfilling. Bearing in mind the fundamental principles of frequency resonation, Cosmic Ordering is the process of using our intentions and affirmations to communicate with the universe and become open to receiving the Cosmos' responses, which are your thoughts manifested as reality.

Ordinary people tap into this universal power every day, creating abundance and wealth in their lives. Everyone has the potential to create the experiences he desires. One only needs to correct mindset and methods.

Cosmic Ordering: True or False!

Simply Rest and Wait for the Cosmos to Provide

That can happen; many books about Cosmic Ordering will offer advice that you do just that. However, thoughts without action can often result in a long wait or getting something a little different from what you wanted. There are times when some emotional work needs to be done.

You may need to change your personal attitudes or let go of resentments. Do not forget that the creation of abundance and wealth will need your input and attention.

Abundance creation begins with you as the co-creator of your reality. This book seeks to bring about the changes you desire more efficiently and directly. While you can sit back and wait, you may watch your lifetime pass away while you are waiting.

You Must Follow a Specific Programme to Benefit from Cosmic Ordering

This idea is a complete myth and fabrication. You need only the correct attitude and intentions to create the opportunities that will fulfil your desires.

The Theory of Cosmic Ordering

It Would have Happened Anyway

This is a half-truth. If you believe you are a lucky person by chance, good fortune will come. If you intend to become a lucky person and manifest that destiny for yourself, you will also have good fortune.

Understanding Cosmic Ordering

Remember that energy is energy. This means that you are a being of energy! If you wish to understand fully the forces at work in creating abundance, you must first look to yourself.

The atoms that comprise our bodies are fundamentally made of energy. Your body is simply a complex ordering of the same original substances and energy that comprise the vast universe. Pay attention to the word 'universe' since it holds a fundamental truth that you must grasp. 'Uni-verse' means 'one tune' or 'one rhythm'.

We communicate with this solitary gathering of energy by using the energy within us. Many different forces exist within you than can either attract or repel, just as a magnet attracts or repels. You may have noticed how your energy can sometimes seem to 'tune-in' to another person's energy so that you feel you are on the same wavelength. This same energy, with which you communicate and resonate with the Cosmos, can be tuned to the frequency of the Cosmos, which is seen in individuals who have attained enlightenment or possess psychic abilities.

The universal energy appears to be infinitely vast, making it a partner and co-creator with unlimited power. Once you accept that you are a being of light and energy, you can begin to understand the level of power you hold to connect with the universe and manifest your desires.

As you study these concepts and begin to appreciate the power within you and recognise your unending capacity for co-creating abundance, you may be astonished at the god-like power you possess. You may also begin to ponder some difficult and complex questions. For instance, how is it that humans have had access to this abundant creative energy for

27

thousands of years, yet remain in squalor?

It is true that this is ancient knowledge. Practitioners of Kung Fu in ancient China accepted and cooperated with this energy. Acupuncturists knew the benefits of original energy as well. The Western world has only begun to accept the truths these ancient civilizations understood and practiced for centuries. The Chinese understanding of 'chi' or initial energy and 'li' or universal energy has thrived in the unnoticed by Western eyes until recently.

Those who study alternative health therapies believe that the Chinese were among first civilisations to notice that humans possess the ability to influence energies to heal and strengthen the body, mind and spirit. Over the years, stories of seemingly miraculous healing and amazing physical powers have evolved. Despite the passage of centuries, these methods of manipulating energies for healing have remained stagnant amidst cultural traditions, remaining unexplored to their fullest potential. For all intents and purposes, we are like kindergarten children, learning the basics of social interaction and learning. The Western world's unwillingness to accept and explore these capabilities has been based in unsubstantiated scepticism, especially in the field of alternative medicine.

Eastern holistic treatments like acupuncture, reiki and reflexology work by manipulating the energy fields that reside within and surround the body. Despite the many successes in healthy complicated health problems, science fails to explain why these methods work. Quite often, this type of healing is dismissed by traditional medicine as palliative, only helping patients feel relaxed and comfortable. At best, Western doctors recognise that the relaxation and good feelings these treatments bring are only a small part of healing.

The Shaolin monks are an exceptional example of Eastern healing in practice. These men travel the globe, healing by means that are often dismissed as carnival tricks. Western medicine fails to grasp that the Shaolin have acquired super-human abilities through mastering chi.

The Theory of Cosmic Ordering

Feng Shui is yet another Eastern practice that has gained some popularity among Western civilisation, but only in the most commercial and wasteful way. Practices in the Western world as a form of interior decorating, Feng Shui is actually an art form, finding the energies of a location and altering the layout to allow for the harmonious and balanced flow of energy to optimise the benefit of those energies for those who dwell in the space.

This art incorporates all elements of a space including geography, objects, colours and spaces where energy flows. Feng Shui asserts that each of these elements has a direct impact on our lives. Whether subtle or drastic, changes made to our living spaces can enhance our overall well-being and health.

In the fullness of time, spiritual evolution will encourage the active exploration of creative energies, to learn not only the effect these energies have on our bodies and minds, but also how we can use these energies to further mankind's collective well-being. These discoveries are likely to change how mankind views the world in proving the importance of energy in reaching our full potential both as individuals and as a civilisation. We may begin to understand why it is that some people have seemingly super-human abilities, can commune with the dead or remotely see events that are occurring thousands of miles away. I fully expect we will be able to explain Cosmic Ordering through scientifically backed theories and evidence. Until that time arrives, there is no reason not to remain open-minded to the powers that can create abundance in our lives.

Think of the structure in your daily life. As a child, you needed structure to make you feel safe and loved. You learned to get up at the same time, brush your teeth, comb your hair, eat breakfast and so on with a regular routine each day. While routine is good and reassuring for childhood insecurities, too much routine can be confining for adults. When you practice your daily routine, there is no need to think about the actions you take. Your physical memory does all of the work for you while your mind frets about other things. While routine is good for maintaining your health, if you allow routine to fall into all aspects of life, you are not really living. I do not mean to say such a life is unacceptable, but it is up to you to determine if this life is acceptable for you. Clearly, if you are reading this book, you are looking for more. This means you will have to step from your comfort zone and make some changes. The mind-numbing affects of too much routine dull your thoughts so that they do not resonate with the Cosmos, wasting the power of your thought energy on low-frequency mundane thoughts. Until you decide to change your routines, you will not change your life.

Exploring the concept of comfort further, realise that comfort of the sort you experience now is illusory. Millions remain within the psychic boundaries they set for themselves for the sake of comfort based on appearances set by society and family. But the opportunities for abundance lie beyond these imaginary fences we erect. If you allow yourself the freedom to flourish and reach beyond the confines of your comfort zones, you will find a wealth of experiences and opportunities awaiting you.

The way you think has a direct affect on your life experience in this moment. Consider the situations in your life that you tolerate simply because it feels safer then the alternatives, yet you have not yet stepped outside your comfort to learn truly what those alternatives are!

Your experiences are the direct result of your moods, feelings, thoughts and reactions. How you respond to any stimulus will determine the thoughts and actions that follow your response. This may seem like a paradox as we consider seemingly chance events like earthquakes, floods and other world events. Do my thoughts and feelings create the devastation of an earthquake, killing thousands? Some texts on this subject will say *yes*, that our thoughts contributed to the outcome of the earthquake event. But more importantly, you must understand that YOU create YOUR experience. You may need to ponder this concept for a time to truly understand it. Your mental and emotional responses to events in your life actively shape and create your actual experience. The thoughts you process, from things that happen in your life, creates your experience.

Let us consider the example of the nightly news. How do you respond to the sensational news you see on television every day? You choose whether to be indifferent, horrified or disgusted. If you respond too sensitively, you could find yourself caught in a pattern of catastrophic negative thoughts, stress and worry. You are likely to become caught up in the stories you hear and take them on as your own experience.

Now, not only is there a mother across town grieving for her lost daughter, but you are now grieving as well for a child you never knew. It is important you alter your thinking when watching the news to reduce the emotional damage it can place on your psyche. It may be best simply to avoid news altogether, a common practice for those seeking to avoid unnecessary and counterproductive negative thoughts in their lives.

When we let ourselves react negatively to our life experiences and allow the resulting thoughts and emotions to consume us by dwelling too much on the negative experiences, we create a negatively charged energy field. Conversely, adopting a positive attitude and letting go of negativity we put ourselves in a position to react sensibly, objectively and without attachment. The resulting thoughts and emotions create a richer experience resulting in the positive energy necessary for abundance creation.

The field of energy that surrounds you is constantly in flux, so we are always changing and evolving. You are always a dynamic work in progress! This constant change and evolution allows you to change your life and harvest more fulfilling experiences from it. However, this also means you must always be vigilant in observing and monitoring your moods and thoughts. If left to their own devices, your thoughts can push you from the direct path to abundance you seek to take. Vigilance is needed because subtle changes can cause you to lose balance, even the influences of the energy fields of the people surrounding you can disrupt your synchronicity with the original substance.

Physical changes can also affect your connection with the Cosmos, such as hormonal changes or some distant solar flare disrupting the magnetic fields around you.

Infinite energies in our bodies, other people, objects, planets, even in the air we breathe, are in constant bombardment with the others, influencing your balance and equilibrium, and causing geopathic stress.

While our bodies seek to find this balance, known as homeostasis, without the necessity of active thought, our minds are highly susceptible to outside influences and must be constantly kept in check. The greatest challenge is to maintain balance of thought amid this sea of influences, while remaining flexible to the constant change necessary to receive the gifts offered by the Cosmos. All this points to the fact that abundance creation begins within you and it is vitally important that you monitory your thoughts and emotions, remaining aware of them throughout each day.

Limits to Manifesting?

There are absolutely no limits. However, if you want wealth to take a straight line to you, there should be a strong intention and purpose behind your request. You must KNOW without doubt what you want if the universe is to respond. Remember, always Order within the bounds of your capability. Naturally, it would be fruitless asking to be able to ballet dance if you are 'duck-toed' or to be able to sing in the Royal Opera if you are 'tone deaf'!

Is There Anything I can do to Start With?

Yes, there is something you can do to start off. There is

something I call a 'Step Order'. With this you first start by placing Orders for the mundane things, like a parking place, a seat on the coach, and so on. Then when you 'get the feel' for it is the time when you can expand to the mid-range Orders.

Step Orders are the best way to begin when seeking to manifest your desires. Accomplishing large Cosmic Orders often necessitates the creation of a series of smaller Step Orders. Several factors can cause difficulty for you getting started.

You have already heard the wisdom, 'For everything there is a season.' This basic truth of the Cosmos must be understood. It is often easier for those just learning to manifest to communicate small desires with the Cosmos each day that will eventually progress into the larger Cosmic Order you desire.

Can I use Other Methods to Place an Order?

Of course! I have something else in my bag of tricks that I call a 'Third Party Order'. How it works is like this, you get someone rooting for you by promising them something in return if a certain situation should happen for you.

For example, I rent properties out that I have bought for my rental portfolio and usually all of my tenants are people I have already known or they are referrals from current tenants.

Let's say I am looking to buy a particular property to rent out and synchronicity steps in when I get a referral for a rental property.

I tell the person seeking to rent a property which potential property it is I am looking to buy, and that if I secure the purchase of it that it will be their new rental property.

Of course, so long as it is in the area they are seeking and the rent is within their budget then they are now part of that Cosmic Order.

I might have placed an Order so that my offer for the property is accepted, and now I have the potential tenant sending out positive vibes, too!

Cosmic Ordering: You Can be Successful

What if I Order a Winning Lottery Ticket from the Cosmos?

Then you will get it. When you are focussed and intent on winning, your chances of doing so increase exponentially. There are prayers and Cosmic Orders coming from people everywhere for a winning ticket at any given time. The more specific, intent and on target your Cosmic Order, the more likely your chances of receiving. Be specific and communicate exactly how much you want to win. Do not consider this a game to see if you can win. This must be a serious certainty and KNOWING that you will win. Place your Order to the Cosmos and include the numbers you want to have a chance of winning you the lottery. Write the Order down, list the numbers and then when you connect to the Cosmos you will be able to recite the Order in your head.

If you ask people who frequently enter and win lotteries and other competitions, they will tell you luck had little to do with it. These people win cars, prizes, vacations and cash because they were positive thinkers who knew without doubt that they would win. The only action these people needed to take aside form the knowing was to enter the contest.

Of course, there are physical barriers that must be overcome, just as your mental barriers must be dealt with. It is often the case that several elements both physical and mental, originating from you and others, must fall into place for the corresponding reality message to return to you from the Cosmos.

How to Place Your Cosmic Order

Specificity and clarity of purpose are needed when communicating with the Cosmos. The Cosmos will not interpret or guess at anything for you. Vagueness will result in unresponsiveness, and I will discuss this in more detail later. The journey towards your desires begins with YOU. The properly focussed positive intent followed by the corresponding positive action will set in motion the realisation of your desires. Your will alone does not accomplish this. It is easy to forget that all people and all things are interconnected, part of one whole entity. We are fibres in the fabric of the universe, with matching energy signatures. When your positive, high frequency thoughts find resonance with the Cosmic frequency, your experiences begin to synchronise with those of the universal mind. You will notice a high instance of déjà vu and a greater abundance in your daily life.

Is there a Divine Being or Simply a Force of Nature?

Congratulations, you have stumbled on the biggest questions of all time. We are no closer than our ancestors were in understanding if there is a divine, intelligent listener, controlling our destinies and granting wishes. Although science has progressed enormously in decoding the universe and the energy / matter in it, the big questions remain a mystery.

However, there is no doubt that the Cosmos surprises humankind every day. Miracles and wonders abound. Just the fact that your heart keeps beating, that newborns take a first breath, that the earth does not stop spinning, each of these is a daily miracle. Is it too much of a stretch to believe that the energies that make these miracles happen can be accessed by each of us to create our own destiny? Does it really matter whether the source of that energy is a divine being or simply a force of nature?

What Evidence Exists to Prove Cosmic Ordering Works?

Thus far, these theories are unproven. It is important to note that even Einstein's famous $E=MC2$ equation remains a theory. In physical science, theories are judged not by the ability to prove them as such, but by the usefulness of those theories. So far, Einstein's theory explains observable phenomena in the universe very well. Until it fails to explain how and why the physical universe behaves as it does, the theory will remain. It is the same with the theory of abundance. It works; therefore, it is accepted as true.

Cosmic Ordering: You Can be Successful

In the same way, science has not been able to specify all of the exact elements that may influence the outcome of a Cosmic Order. However, abundance theory is based on evidence and observations in the universe that are widely understood and known to be true. Just as the idea of a radio would have seemed like magical nonsense to someone 1,000 years ago, the theories of Cosmic Orders are difficult for many to understand today.

Einstein's theories and studies in quantum mechanics and the energy surrounding, permeating and powering our universe have given inspiration to a generation of scientists. This generation has made great strides in the advancement of quantum theory, expanding the frontiers of human knowledge. The more these scientists learn, the more those facts support abundance theory.

Cosmic Ordering - New Age Fad?

Well, no it is not a New Age fad. The practice of manifesting abundance is ancient. Most people know this practice as prayer, but have never been counselled on how to make those realise those prayers. In actual fact, prayer differs to Cosmic Ordering. Communicating your desires to the universe is older than recorded history.

Ancient Pagan civilisations held rites and festivals designed to bring about their desires for abundant crops or offspring. Those attracted to New Age philosophies certainly have a strong understanding of Cosmic Ordering, but this is not a new theory originating in the New Age movement. Cosmic Ordering and the theory of abundance are ancient concepts that never entered the mainstream of public consciousness. Most of us are just discovering our potential as human beings.

Be Careful what You Wish For!

Cosmic Ordering is a very powerful means to acquiring your desires. The signals you communicate with the universe are so powerful that they can return to you ten times in strength. When negative signals are sent, Cosmic Ordering can bring great harm to your life!

The events shaping your life at this moment are influenced by your thoughts, attitudes and beliefs. Your future is shaped by the intentions and purposes of your current thoughts and actions. The past has no bearing on your presence or future. The past contains the illusions you have created based on appearances. When you become thankful for all that you have now, you change your life for the better. Thankfulness makes you receptive to the frequencies of abundance being directed back to you by the Cosmos. By maintaining positive thoughts and acting on them, you send out positive frequencies that resonate with the Universe, bringing you all that you wish for. This is why creating abundance can only start inside of you!

Consider that the possibilities in your life are the same possibilities available to anyone, no matter what station in life. What could you do with the wealth and wisdom of abundance creation? You can alter your present life situation to one of success and wealth. If you desire to be wealthy enough to spend all of your days on a warm, sunny beach, you will do just that. If you are searching for a career that makes you feel good every day of your life, no problem! If you want to be surrounded by luxury and good taste, you can. The thrills and adventure you seek are all available to you simply by asking.

Manifesting YOUR Desires is about Karma (action)!

There is nothing wrong with daydreaming. It is pleasant and relaxing to sit back and relax with dreams of your potential future. What a relaxing afternoon you could spend, simply resting and daydreaming about the life you want. This type of daydreaming is the hem of the cloak of abundance creation, but only offers a small glimpse into your potential. The difference between a daydreamer and one who realises his dreams is action. Daydreamers dwell on what could have been, as though there were no real possibility the dream could come true. But abundance creators understand that their daydreams are only realities waiting to come to fruition. They seize opportunities to create abundance in the present moment by implementing Cosmic Ordering in their lives. This willingness to act upon ones dreams requires a certain perspective.

Hopefully, at this point you understand the immeasurable power dormant within you and that the tools to create abundance need only to be taken in hand to begin the work. However, understanding the potential is not the same as putting your power into action.

You may be thinking that there must be some mysterious magical secret to this perspective. While some will see it as magical, it is really not so cryptic. The potential for abundance is available to all. No one is exempt. The simple change you need to make can be one of the most difficult. Although not complex, it requires strength of will, intention and action!

To create abundance, you need to shift from the daydreamer perspective to a positive 'I can!' thought process. You will need to release the habitual routines that rule everyday life. Your thoughts and feelings need to be closely monitored at all times, feeding them positive energy. Finally, you must believe that you have the power to co-create your future, changing and improving your life.

If you keep resilience and an open mind, this will be easy for you. Unfortunately, most of us are not so resilient or open-minded. You may find that changing the lifetime of habits and routines you have formed to be the biggest challenge to successfully manifesting abundance.

Just as New Year's resolutions often fade by the end of January, you may find it easy to commit to change now, while reading this book. It is not uncommon for the best of intentions to fade quickly, when the work involved in action becomes tiring. Do not be afraid to admit that you have made resolutions that faded, perhaps enduring a week or even a month, but then fell back into old habits. It happens to the best of us. Few actually implement the changes they desire for the long term. Living a more abundant life requires constant vigilance and action. It requires that you renew your commitment continually. The process of manifesting abundance becomes much simpler once you have mastered bad habits. Change takes time, so give yourself room to accept and become accustomed to our new habits of mind.

Here is a story that may help you to realise your goals.

I am hereby officially tendering my resignation as an adult. I have decided I would like to accept the responsibilities of an 8 year-old.

I want to go to McDonald's and think that it's a four star restaurant.

I want to sail sticks across a fresh mud puddle and make a sidewalk with rocks.

I want to think M&Ms are better than money because you can eat them.

I want to lie under a big oak tree and run a lemonade stand with my friends on a hot summer's day.

I want to return to a time when life was simple; when all you knew were colours, multiplication tables, and nursery rhymes, but that didn't bother you, because you didn't know what you didn't know and you didn't care.

All you knew was to be happy because you were blissfully unaware of all the things that should make you worried or upset.

I want to think the world is fair. That everyone is honest and good.

I want to believe that anything is possible. I want to be oblivious to the complexities of life and be overly excited by the little things again.

I want to live simple again. I don't want my day to consist of computer crashes, mountains of paperwork, depressing news, how to survive more days in the month than there is money in the bank, doctor bills, gossip, illness, and loss of loved ones.

I want to believe in the power of smiles, hugs, a kind word, truth, justice, peace, dreams, the imagination, mankind, and making angels in the snow.

So... here's my chequebook and my car keys, my credit card bills and my 401K statements. I am officially resigning from adulthood.

And if you want to discuss this further, you'll have to catch me first, 'cause...

...'Tag! You're it.'

2

The Importance of
Positive Thought

An Energising Phrase

'If only' is an energising phrase. It is the seed that sparks the growth of your dreams. 'If only' fuels new discoveries in science and progress in business. If you find yourself more likely to say 'if only' in everyday speech, you should examine the energy fuelling your inner and outer communications.

Your words convey your feelings and intentions. You may be conveying those thoughts to yourself or someone else. The words you choose have a direct affect on the energy in all things around you. Words carrying negative emotion create negative results. If your thoughts are positive, your words will carry positive energy, empowering your intentions to create abundance.

In the same way that 'if only?' gives the power of creation to your thoughts, helping to find solutions and answers to difficult questions, positive thoughts and speech give strength to your intention for abundance.

Sadly, many people struggle through life with the words 'if only'. These words deliver the negative energies of regret and sadness. They refer to the past, unfulfilled destinies and broken hearts. 'If only' admits defeat, encourages self-pity and wallowing. It is an unproductive expression that weighs heavy on the soul.

Believe, Believe, Believe!

All the prominent wealthy figures that come readily to mind,

The Importance of Positive Thought

anyone who lives a successful and shining life, has tapped into the Law of Attraction (this is the theory of Cosmic Ordering), whether they were aware of it or not. Call it what you will, abundance creation or the Law of Attraction is not such a mystifying process. You need no special qualifications, connections or religious affiliations. The only thing you need to manifest a meaningful and fulfilling life is YOU. If you can accept this, you are already on the way to discovering all the Cosmos can do for you!

While you may be influenced by other people and things, it is ultimately you and your responses to life that are responsible for your reality. You must believe in yourself and believe in the reality you seek to create.

Successful people attain their desires because they believe and KNOW it will happen. Admittedly, other factors influenced their careers; they worked hard, remained determined, were brave and sometimes brazen. Take some time to read the biography of a successful person that you admire. Artists, leaders of industry, actors and gurus will all detail thoughts of 'I can; and 'I believe'. They succeeded because their belief in their ability to succeed fuelled their actions

Next, consider your own beliefs. Do you fervently believe you can attain wealth or do you wonder if you can do it? To succeed you must be committed to the creation of wealth and abundance, leaving no room for doubt of any sort.

Faith really does move mountains. Believing energises your intentions and actions. Protect and nurture your belief, as it is the power behind abundance creation.

Attend to Your Inner Voice

If you moan about the disparities in life or make repeated negative statements, you are not ready to create abundance for yourself. Instead, you are creating poverty and unhappiness. It is vital that you catch yourself in these negative thoughts and statements and change them to positive ones. You must focus on the positive, give yourself positive feedback in your inner dialogue, and be willing and able to speak positively about yourself when speaking to others. If you do not believe in yourself, why should anyone else?

When assessing your readiness to create abundance in your life, listen to both your inner and outer voices. Your inner voice, while more subtle, influences your thoughts and your outer voice. Does your inner voice always look for negatives, make excuses or blame others? Does the voice complain or worry incessantly? Now hear yourself speak with others. Do you often make negative statements about yourself or others?

Create Positive Energy!

When you realise you are spending too much time dwelling on a negative thought, remember your intention is to create positive energy and switch back to positive thinking. Although it will take some time to gain skill at this, be patient with yourself. A lifetime of negative thinking is rarely changed in an instant. Simply be steadfast and persistent in your efforts. Pay attention to the thoughts in your mind and the feelings that arise. Pay attention to the words that leave your mouth and be careful to consider each word you say before you let it influence your energy fields. By being ever on the lookout you will begin to notice changes in your life's energy that open the gates leading to abundance.

Change Your Intention

Monitor your thoughts and speech. Choose triumph over defeat. Charge your intentions with the positive creative energy that hopes rather than despairs.

You can choose to emit positive energy and remove 'if only' from your vocabulary. Rather than, 'if only I could get a raise', find a thought that creates allows for a possible solution to the problem. Instead of 'if only', try, 'when I get a raise?' Your energy is now infused with hope and the possibility of a raise becomes more real. Changing your dialogue instantly transforms defeat into aspiration.

The Importance of Positive Thought

The answers to your problems are not difficult to find once you take on a positive attitude and emit the positive energy that will resonate with the universe and bring the reality you desire back to you. Dwelling on thoughts of self-pity erodes your connection with the Cosmos. We can all tap into the power of originating substance, but only if we can maintain open paths of positive communication with the universe.

The Mindset of Intention and Action

Mastering intention will put you in the right mindset to receive abundance, but following through with action solidifies and enhances your link with the Cosmos. Action energises intention, giving it power and force.

So be on guard for negative thoughts and transform them into positive powerful ideas by using the right words. Do not underestimate the power of your thoughts and words; make each word matter in creating the positive energy needed to change your life. Transform your thinking to include the right words and intent, and then follow them with the right action to put yourself on the path to abundance and success.

In *The* Now

When you consider which thoughts and statements you will use to empower your life, be careful to use statements that suggest you have already achieved your goal. Statements based on the future, like 'someday I will' or 'I hope' push what you seek farther away from the present. You are essentially telling the Cosmos that you do not want your wishes right now, but sometime in the future. Use words with present-tense qualities like 'I am' or 'I have' and you will see a shift in how quickly your desires are realised.

Psychic Sappers!

As babies and children, we are greatly influenced by our caregivers. We are small mirrors that reflect in our minds the attitudes of those who raise us. Like sponges, we soak up the

44

influences around us and become saturated with the thoughts and ideas we absorb.

Children are highly impressionable. They learn a set programme of learning that is taught uniformly for all. Some say we lose touch with our natural psychic abilities because learning is so inflexible. Children take impressions from events, news, and all events that we learn about as they grow. The kind of information that forms our childhood experiences determines if we are positive or negative thinkers. Some of us turn out to be very open-minded and others quite fixed in our ideas about how the world is.

Schoolteachers rarely spend time on the more mysterious aspects of the universe. Science is focused on easy to explain, black-and-white mechanisms without spending time on the powerful mysteries throughout our world and the universe. Teachers offer a narrow focus on what is possible or not. Little time is spent on theory or simply taking time to wonder about the miraculous fact that we are here at all. No room is left for creativity or exploration. Schools spend no time wondering about the universe or teaching any aspects of achieving life goals through abundance theory.

Schools do provide children with a great deal of useful information when it comes to navigating the world in a traditional sense. But no time is spent discussion the quality of that life. While the intentions of those who teach us as children are good, it is easy for children to believe solidly with no room for doubt that the world is just as it appears. Because the adults that teach us believe it strongly, so do we. However, the adults that teach us are not always right.

Abundance saboteurs can be found all around you in people you know and love. Whether they are well meaning or not, the negative influence of these people must be avoided. The only way to do this is to maintain an unshakeable faith in your own understanding of abundance creation. Trust yourself to be correct in your thinking. Trust in the Universe and your ability to follow the path to wealth.

The Importance of Positive Thought

Energy Drainers

People who put out negative statements like 'you can't' will limit your own ability to say 'I can'. These people will drain your positive energy if you cannot detach from their negative statements and influence. Such energy drainers can be thought of as energy vampires, feeding on your positive energy and sucking you dry. These energy draining vampires can be especially dangerous if your defences are low, adversely affecting your positive energy and connection with abundance.

Conversely, when you spend time with positive people who communicate at the same positive frequency, the signal resonates even more strongly than without that positive influence. Inspirational people fill your life with opportunities for abundance. Spend time with a positive thinker and you will notice your spirits rising and a more positive thought pattern in your own mind. When you respond to this person with positive energy, the mutual exchange creates an overflow of good feelings and happiness, increasing opportunities for creating abundance in both lives.

Take a look at the people around you every day. Do you have contact with energy vampires? Those who constantly bemoan their fate and seek too much support and counselling from you are eroding your connection with the Cosmos. This situation is unacceptable and must be changed. Because it all begins with you, you should first take a look inside yourself to see if you are attracting this type of person into your life with your own negative energies. Like begets like, so your negative energy could be attracting the same, sabotaging your efforts to create abundance.

You are not trapped under the influence of energy vampires. You can reduce the amount of time you spend with negative people. If you want to maintain the friendships you have with such people, there are steps you can take to defend your psyche from the negative influence.

Do not be afraid if your abundance potential has been damaged by abundance saboteurs. You have the power to change your life and any time is a good time to start. There is no such thing as 'too late'. It may take you time to change the negative energy that is stored within your spirit, but you can do it.

Gratitude

There is a single concept that has the power to transform your outlook in an instant: gratitude. Underlying gratitude are two basic ideas. First, believe in the intelligent substance, which is the source of all things. Second, know that the intelligent substance provides all things that you desire. From this follows a deep and profound thankfulness for these gifts from the Cosmos. You may think positive thoughts and send out positive energy, but without gratitude, it can come to naught. You may have received a gift from the Cosmos because of your positive thinking, but if you have no gratitude, your connection with the infinite is severed.

Gratitude brings you closer to the source of all things. Those who desire wealth will receive more of it if they are near to the source. Those who distance themselves through ingratitude will receive less.

When we are grateful, we intensify our connection with the universe. It creates a snowball effect where the more good things we receive, the more grateful we become and the more addition good things come our way. This happens because gratitude puts us in close proximity to the source of abundance, creating a direct path for good things to find their way to you.

If this is your first time thinking about gratitude and its importance in your life's happiness, take time to meditate on this idea. You will see the truth of the matter, that gratitude brings your mind into harmony with the Cosmos. Gratitude is a way of following the paths to which good things came to you, making a smoother and easier to travel path for more good things in the future.

Gratitude is useful in changing your thinking about supply and demand as well. It can help you to see that supplies are not

The Importance of Positive Thought

limited, that there is an endless abundance of wealth available to you. Gratitude is subject to certain laws and one of them is vital for you to understand if you are to succeed in creating abundance.

The law of gratitude can be defined as a natural law of the universe in which actions and reactions are equal and always travel in opposite directions. When you send out thankful praise to the Cosmos for the good things you have received, you expend energy and the Cosmos reacts by moving in the opposite direction, towards you.

The strength and constancy of your gratitude affects the extent of reaction by the Cosmos. When your gratitude is habitual, good things will always be moving toward you. Without gratitude, your manifesting power will be weak. The power to attract good things is rooted mainly in gratitude. However, there is more to the idea of being thankful than just its ability to bring more good tings to your life. It also helps to squash thoughts of dissatisfaction with life as it is now.

When you allow dissatisfaction to enter your thoughts, you begin to repel the Cosmos. If you become fixated on poverty, meanness and everyday negative forces, your mind is drawing more of the same to you. You will be sending out negative signals to the Universe which will send back just what you ordered: more meanness, poverty and everyday negativity.

Allowing your mind to dwell on the negative is just another way for asking for more negativity in your life. But turning your thoughts to positive and abundant creativity creates more of the same for you. As co-creator of your life, the images you send out are the images your life becomes.

Just like the intelligent substance, we are of thinking substance. The scientific law that thinking substance takes on the form of the things it thinks about will always hold true. Thankful minds become fixated on the joy and abundance of their lives find and receive more of the same.

You should also understand that faith comes from gratitude. Thankful thoughts create the expectation of more good things

48

to become grateful for, a faith in the constant delivery of abundance. Your mind responds to gratitude with faith and every grateful vibration that emits from your thoughts creates more faith. Without gratitude, your faith will wither and when faith becomes weak, your connection with the Cosmos weakens as well. We will discuss this further in following chapters.

Because gratitude sows faith, you must cultivate thankfulness habits in all things. For every thing that comes your way, be thankful. All things have helped to shape your success, so practice gratefulness for everything in your life.

Once upon a time, there was a farmer in the central region of China. He didn't have a lot of money and, instead of a tractor, he used an old horse to plough his field.

One afternoon, while working in the field, the horse dropped dead. Everyone in the village said, 'Oh, what a horrible thing to happen.'

The farmer said simply, 'We'll see.' He was so at peace and so calm, that everyone in the village got together and, admiring his attitude, gave him a new horse as a gift.

Everyone's reaction now was, 'What a lucky man.'

And the farmer said, 'We'll see.'

A couple days later, the new horse jumped a fence and ran away. Everyone in the village shook their heads and said, 'What a poor fellow!'

The farmer smiled and said, 'We'll see.'

Eventually, the horse found his way home, and everyone again said, 'What a fortunate man.'

The farmer said, 'We'll see.'

Later in the year, the farmer's young boy went out riding on the horse and fell and broke his leg. Everyone in the village said, 'What a shame for the poor boy.'

The farmer said, 'We'll see.'

Two days later, the army came into the village to draft new recruits. When they saw that the farmer's son had a broken leg, they decided not to recruit him.

The Importance of Positive Thought

Everyone said, 'What a fortunate young man.'

The farmer smiled again - and said 'We'll see.'

Moral of the story: There's no use in overreacting to the events and circumstances of our everyday lives. Many times what looks like a setback, may actually be a gift in disguise. And when our hearts are in the right place, all events and circumstances are gifts that we can learn valuable lessons from.

Everything we call a trial, a sorrow, or a duty, believe me... the gift is there and the wonder of an overshadowing presence.

3

Preparing to Place
Your Cosmic Order

'Cosmic Ordering gurus' abound, with claims to provide you with a system designed to provide you with your dreams for wealth, but none of them will tell you exactly how it is done. I will actually show you, step by step, how to connect with the Cosmos and reveal the entire Cosmic Ordering process. Here I will reveal the true, shortest and swiftest path to realising your desires.

The 17 Steps to Cosmic Success

1. Empty Yourself of 'Catastrophic Vibrational Negativity'
I have spent a great deal of time answering questions from Cosmic Friends and I have learned that some people have strong difficulties putting Cosmic Ordering into effective practice. Although I took pains to examine every possible scenario, these people still seem to bump up against obstacles that block their success. While this only happens to a very small percentage of the hundred of thousands of people I help, I have concerns that you may run into difficulty as well. Some of you may be able to manifest certain Orders but struggle with other Orders that should be possible to manifest.

The other aspect of this entails the spreading of positive or negative energy. These energies continue to influence your life until you alter them. When you create friction against others and emit negative energy in arguments, the energy continues to ripple through the universe, putting a load on your karma, the energetic loads you create.

FACT! The energy in the universe is neither positive nor negative; it is simply energy. All of the energy you emit have a natural tendency to return to the source, YOU. You may have sent out negative energy at a time when you were anxious or upset, tainting your karma. Although these energies are not physically 'negative', the word works as a good tool to explain the unwanted results of these energies.

Just as a small beam of light can be magnified into a laser by a magnifying glass, even subtle negative energies can sometimes create severely damaging vibrational negativity. Because energy cannot be created or destroyed, the energy must go somewhere. The 'bad' karma still exists, even though you have moved on into a happier state. That karma can have severe consequences for you or those connected with you, even when that connection is remote or fleeting. This is the strange behaviour of negative energy that perplexes me most.

Overcoming Catastrophic Vibrational Negativity

Luckily, there is a way to overcome and dissipate negative karma. Forgiveness is a vital component (among many others) in neutralising bad karma. You must choose to forgive the people who you may believe have wronged you. For some people, this may seem like an insurmountable task. For others it will be easy. Still, forgiveness must be approached with a sincere desire to resolve friction. If you decide to forgive for the selfish gain of making your Cosmic Ordering work, you will fail.

Forgiveness can be challenging, especially with those who have inexplicable desires to do you harm. But when you forgive these people unconditionally and universally, they change their behaviour towards you. These people will sometimes respond in kind. Other times, they will simple leave you alone. Kindness and forgiveness are confusing to those with harmful intentions. These people travel a wandering, aimless path and cannot tell good from bad. Such beings offer you practical lessons in learning to forgive all people without conditions or restrictions.

2. Be Non-judgemental (Judge not, Lest You be Judged)

You are not a judge. It is easy to become inflamed over hearing about those that harm children or commit genocide on their people. But your righteous indignation only creates bad karma for you and does nothing to help those who were hurt. You are not an all-powerful god with the full knowledge of all aspects of a situation. You have no right or power to judge any act. If you take on the role of judge, you choose to create painful karma. Just as you do not like to be judged, you should not judge others. It is simply not your place.

3. Only Focus on What You Want, not What You Don't

Spending energy dwelling on the things you do not want simply creates more of not wanting it. More of it will be created in your life so that you can continue to not want it. When you continue to do things you do not want to do, you engage in compulsive behaviour. Compulsions are reactive, behaviours that we engage in without thinking about what we are doing until the act is done. We then criticise ourselves for engaging in that behaviour, feeding and reinforcing the energy that brings more of the same. This results in a painful cycle of more compulsive behaviour and more self-criticism. The harder we struggle to end compulsive behaviour, the deeper our connection to that behaviour becomes.

4. Never Forget who You are

Do not forget your true self and the path you took to arrive at your current life situation. When you remember who you are and examine the processes used to reach the present you can learn to follow a new path that will bring us to a new, more abundant reality. Knowing yourself is the key to opening the emotional gateways to the happiness and abundance you deserve.

53

5. Jettison Emotional Blocks

Human minds do not like pain. The mind finds so many ways to avoid negative emotions through suppression or denial. Your emotions are like children, who will tug at your sleeve and make as much noise as possible until you acknowledge their needs. In severe cases, your emotions may become damaging to your body and spirit, aggressively seeking your attention.

Powerful emotions like anger and fear are difficult to face. It takes courage to face such emotions openly. If you fail to acknowledge and fully feel the emotions dwelling within you, they can ravage your health. All feelings need to be acknowledged and felt. You cannot go around them, you must go through them.

Walk Through the Emotional Block like Walking Through a Wall

When you fully experience and accept your emotions, acknowledge your doubt and fear, be present in your feelings, you experience your life fully. These feelings represent who you are. They are expressions of your true nature and eternal self. Embrace negative emotions just as you would embrace a child in need of your affection. Find the courage to embrace emotional blocks. This Emotional Clearing dissolves negative emotions before they can harm your physical and emotional health.

6. Don't Allow Negative Emotion to Give You a Negative Belief

Any time you observe negative emotions in relation to a given subject, you can be sure there is a negative belief lurking within you. Pay close attention to your feelings so that you can bring these negative beliefs into your awareness. Find the belief connected to the feeling to root it out. Your feelings are your emotional compass and should be trusted at all times. Your feelings will be better indicators of your position in life than your mind will ever be. While your mind is a pliable, easily influenced living organ, while your feelings are part of your eternal constant soul. The true you that always existed, even before the body you inhabit was born, will always steer you towards happiness. The two more powerful emotions are *fear and love*. All other emotions are small moons orbiting these two great planets of emotion. Love expands, encouraging you to be greater and stronger, removing limitations. Love is the antithesis of fear, which makes you jealous, angry and withdrawn.

A Native American grandfather was talking to his grandson about how he felt. He said, 'I feel as if I have two wolves fighting in my heart. One wolf is the vengeful, angry, violent one. The other wolf is the loving, compassionate one.'

The grandson asked him, 'Which wolf will win the fight in your heart?'

The grandfather answered, 'The one I feed.'

7. Be Fearless
Fear drains you - Fear is a limiting emotion. It sucks life energy and blocks you from forward mobility. Fear creates captivity, disease, blindness and death.

8. Don't Just Want Something... You must Crave it!
Wanting something vaguely has insufficient strength to create abundance in your life. You cannot be lukewarm, you must be hot! Your strong emotional desire for abundance is a feeling, part of your eternal constant soul. If you notice your mind is jumping from one want to another, always chasing after something else, then you are listening to your less dependable mind, not your feelings.

9. Pain is the Basis of Fear – Rid Yourself of It
Notice the pain underlying our fear anger and jealousy. Notice how much easier it is to become angry with yourself and other people than it is to feel pain. Recognising your anger is only the first step. You must also root out the underlying pain and

55

bring those feelings to light. Find those feelings that have been hiding from your conscious awareness because you were too afraid or ashamed to acknowledge them.

10. Challenge Your Emotion – Become Strong

Pay attention to the sensations in our body when particular fears arise within you. Notice the thoughts that result from these feelings. You will recognise old feelings that you pushed aside in order to avoid pain. This is how you can challenge your emotions and build emotional strength.

There is an old Chinese tale about a woman whose only son died. In her grief, she went to the holy man and asked, 'What prayers, what magical incantations do you have to bring my son back to life?'

Instead of sending her away or reasoning with her, he said to her, 'Fetch me a mustard seed from a home that has never known sorrow. We will use it to drive the sorrow out of your life.'

The woman went off at once in search of that magical mustard seed.

She came first to a splendid mansion, knocked at the door, and said, 'I am looking for a home that has never known sorrow. Is this such a place? It is very important to me.'

They told her, 'You've certainly come to the wrong place,' and began to describe all the tragic things that recently had befallen them.

The woman said to herself, 'Who is better able to help these poor, unfortunate people than I, who have had misfortune of my own?'

She stayed to comfort them, and then went on in search of a home that had never known sorrow. But wherever she turned, in hotels and in other places, she found one tale after another of sadness and misfortune.

The woman became so involved in helping others cope with their sorrows that she eventually let go of her own. She would later come to understand that it was the quest to find the magical mustard seed that drove away her suffering.

11. Try, Try and Try Again
Challenging painful emotions takes practice, you will not see all of your anger and fear disappear at once. You must continually challenge your negative emotions until you become stronger than the negative emotions. Use your free will to challenge the parts of you that you want to change.

12. Protect Yourself from Negative-Minded People
Just no one can give a gift to you if you do not open your hand to accept it, you must give consent to all things you receive. No one can hurt you without your permission, although it sometimes occurs on a deep subconscious level. When you refuse to give others permission to drain your energy, you stop the drain very quickly.

13. Remove Chakra Hooks
Chakras are energy centres located in and around your body. While the subject of chakras is vast and sometimes complicated, it is important you have a basic understanding of how chakras work. These energy centres have hooks that block energy. They should be removed periodically in order to free you from limitations. You should know that jealousy from others causes these hooks and can limit your speedy acquisition of abundance.

14. Clear, Balance and Charge Your Chakras
This vast topic is likely to put you off track with Cosmic Ordering, so rather than muddle your thinking with this vast topic, it is easier to refer you to a project I designed to do it all for you: *Cosmic Ordering: Rapid Chakra Clearing* (Audio on CD). I also designed a chakra clearing system with the use of an audio CD and a card deck, it was a limited edition simply called *Cosmic Ordering Chakra Clearing*. It was based on the use of colours and the resonation they put out.

15. Use Clean Language when Placing Your Orders

Many people email asking me to write a Cosmic Order for them when they are having difficulty manifesting a particular desire. There is really only one rule to writing a Cosmic Order. Keep it clean!

The Importance of Clean Language

Keeping it clean means avoiding negative words. So many people use negative words in their Orders, I wonder what I am doing wrong with my teaching. Negativity must be eliminated entirely from all Cosmic Orders.

Some examples of negative words to avoid are: can't, suffering, bad, isn't, won't, trouble, hardship, isn't, distress, torment. For instance, a Cosmic Order worded, 'I can't go on with this suffering, it's bad and won't go away. I want to get rid of this trouble that is causing me hardship. Make the torment that causes so much distress go away,' does nothing for you.

You are simply telling the Cosmos, 'This is my dismal life; send more of the same, please.'

The positive words you should be using include words like: thanks, can, good, is, come, wealth, calmness, serenity, care, good-fortune, healthy.

A good Cosmic Order would be worded like this. 'I can feel a calmness coming over me, the good that is happening to me is growing each day. My good-fortune leads to an even more healthy and peaceful time that I am already experiencing. Serenity comes to me in abundance, just like wealth.'

Clean language unlocks the door to Cosmic Ordering for you. Avoid negative words at all costs, replacing negatives with positives. Consider this negative Order: 'My life is so hard. I am so tired of the pain and suffering I endure. Please stop my pain and save me from this dismal life.'

Simply replace those negative words so that it reads: 'My life is getting better and good things are coming to me. Good things keep coming to me, in a safe and natural way. I create joy and satisfaction in my life now and always.'

Neutral words can also have a limiting effect on abundance creation, so try to use positive words in your Orders.

To illustrate with the same example, here is the Order written with neutral and negative words: 'My dismal life will be getting better. I hope good things will happen to me. Please help make good things happen to me to change my life.'

Not only is clean language important for your Orders, you should incorporate the same practice into your thoughts and speech.

With practice, you will be sending positive energy that will return to you tenfold. Just as positive words bring positive reactions, negative and neutral words bring mixed results at best.

Let's try a short exercise to help you practice your understanding of negative, neutral and positive words. Consider the following statement:

You can have good happen to you when using clean language. This is the best way to enhance the good that you are already experiencing.

Can you pick out which words are neutral? What words would you use to improve them. Below is the same statement with some of the neutral words in bold italics:

You can *have* good *happen* to you when using clean language. This is the best way to enhance the good that you are already experiencing.

To word the above so that it would be more positive, it should look like this:

Good things are happening now because you use clean language. Clean language enhances the good that you are already experiencing.

Cosmic Ordering: You Can be Successful

Respect

You should give the Cosmos the respect it deserves as the mighty provider of all things. Therefore, when you place a Cosmic Order, be sure to address the Cosmos properly. For simplicity, I have left off the salutation in Orders shown in this book. However, when you place your Orders, simply start with something like, 'Oh, Mighty Cosmos' or 'Dear Cosmos.'

Within the Order, be sure to mark the path you are seeking clearly by being highly specific. Specificity ensures your Order is not misunderstood like in, 'Oh, Mighty Cosmos, I have such beautiful jewellery, it is beautify. How I would like some more.'

And more will come, a lot more! So be certain to be clear and concise in your Orders. It may be best to mark out exactly what jewellery you want so you are not inundated with a flood of new sparkling treasures. Tell the Cosmos exactly what you want in this way, 'Oh, Mighty Cosmos, I have a beautiful diamond necklace. I want a pair of ½ karat diamond solitaire earrings to match.'

Always end your communication with the Cosmos on a positive note that expresses gratitude and offers positive energy, such as, 'I leave you with this in peace, thank you.'

There are occasions when negative words may be necessary in your Order. If something in your life is causing you harm, you may be forced to use a negative term to ask the Cosmos for help. Here is an example of how to use negative terms:

The relaxation I get from smoking is pleasurable. I enjoy smoking, but now ask that I can get the same pleasure and relaxation without smoking.

The negative word used here is 'without', but it is placed in such a way as to say nothing negative about your smoking habit. It does not reinforce the need to quit smoking. If you ask to quit smoking, instead, you will get more of needing to quit.

By asking for the benefits you get from your bad habit, you reinforce the positive and address your lack of need. This is the way negatives should be used to help you rid your life of unwanted elements.

Throughout the book, you will see this format on Orders. Do what you can to include them in your Orders. Remember to be as to the point and exact as you can and avoid rambling unnecessarily.

Safety

It is important that your Orders are manifested in a safe and natural way. So be sure to make use of this phrase when placing an Order: *in a safe and natural way.*

16. The Energy Spent on Worry is Wasteful

There are two days in every week about which we should not worry, two days which should be kept free from fear and apprehension.

One of these days is Yesterday with all its mistakes and cares, its faults and blunders, its aches and pains.

Yesterday has passed forever beyond our control.
All the money in the world cannot bring back Yesterday.

We cannot undo a single act we performed;
we cannot erase a single word we said.
Yesterday is gone forever.

The other day we should not worry about is Tomorrow
with all its possible adversities, its burdens,
its large promise and its poor performance;
Tomorrow is also beyond our immediate control.

Tomorrow's sun will rise,
either in splendour or behind a mask of clouds, but it will rise.

Until it does, we have no stake in Tomorrow,
for it is yet to be born.

This leaves only one day, Today.
Any person can fight the battle of just one day.
It is when you and I add the burdens of those two awful
eternities Yesterday and Tomorrow that we break down.

It is not the experience of Today that drives a person mad,
it is the remorse or bitterness of something which happened
Yesterday and the dread of what Tomorrow may bring.

Let us, therefore, Live but one day at a time.

17. Love Thyself

Show the universe that you are worthy of its attention by
loving yourself every day in every way. Your self love shows
you are worthy of love from others and the Cosmos, which will
in turn reward you with your dreams, goals and visions. When
you show neediness for love, acceptance and approval, you are
reinforcing the idea that you must strive to secure these things.
But you are worthy of love and it should come easily to you.

When you practice self love, you become independent of
the judgement of others. Circumvent these damaging
influences and reserve your energy for self love and
appreciation. The more you think loving and approving
thoughts about your self, the greater your manifesting power
becomes. The strongest powers to manifest thoughts into
reality come from the infinite source of Thought at the core of
your being, which is Absolute Love.

Love is the answer to every question. Why are we here?
Love. Where do we come from? Love. How do we create
world peace? Love. It may sound overly simplistic to the
modern   .
human being, since we are want to analyse and look for
complex answers to questions. We don't believe that life is

simple and the answers to its problems can also be simple: love.

In truth, what are anger, sadness, pain but the soul's desire for love?

If we learn to love ourselves without reservation, the answer is simple. It is impossible, when filled with love, to be aggressive or hate-filled or violent.

When we know that we are beautiful and wonderful, we see the world through those eyes. We see the beauty and wonder in all things around us.

We don't need to look outside ourselves for the love we seek. It has been there all along. It is the voice of our self-esteem. It is our anger saying, 'hey this is not right for me. I don't want this in my life any longer.'

Self-love is saying no to abuse and betrayal. It is wanting the very best for yourself and accepting only that in your life. It is healing the wounds that you have carried all your life.

Self-love is walking away from those who mistreat you, knowing that you deserve better. It is taking the risk to pursue the career that will bring you joy. It is listening to your own inner voice – the one that will always guide you to what is best. It is trusting in yourself completely.

Self-love is following that little voice within that says, 'ooh I want to do that today.' Sometimes it means ignoring the voice of 'shoulds' and 'have-tos'. It is believing that, when you seek what you desire and fill yourself with joy, you will also be spreading that joy to those around you.

Love will fill you up so you will know there is nothing missing in your life.

Love will lead you to every answer. Love is the answer to every question. Why are we here? Love. Where do we come from? Love. How do we create world peace? Love.

It may sound overly simplistic to the modern human being, since we are want to analyse and look for complex answers to questions. We don't believe that life is simple and the answers to its problems can also be simple: love.

In truth, what are anger, sadness, pain but the soul's desire for love?

If we learn to love ourselves without reservation, the answer is simple. It is impossible, when filled with love, to be aggressive or hate-filled or violent.

When we know that we are beautiful and wonderful, we see the world through those eyes. We see the beauty and wonder in all things around us.

We don't need to look outside ourselves for the love we seek. It has been there all along. It is the voice of our self-esteem. It is our anger saying, 'hey this is not right for me. I don't want this in my life any longer.'

Self-love is saying *no* to abuse and betrayal. It is wanting the very best for yourself and accepting only that in your life. It is healing the wounds that you have carried all your life.

Self-love is walking away from those who mistreat you, knowing that you deserve better. It is taking the risk to pursue the career that will bring you joy. It is listening to your own inner voice – the one that will always guide you to what is best. It is trusting in yourself completely.

Self-love is following that little voice within that says, 'ooh I want to do that today.' Sometimes it means ignoring the voice of 'shoulds' and 'have-tos'. It is believing that, when you seek what you desire and fill yourself with joy, you will also be spreading that joy to those around you.

Love will fill you up so you will know there is nothing missing in your life.

Love will lead you to every answer.

4

The Pineal Gland

The pineal plays an important role in Cosmic Ordering, as you will see. The pineal gland is a pea-sized hormonal regulator located in a small area behind and above the pituitary gland, just behind the nose and eyes. There are several functions assigned to the pineal gland. It converts signals from your nervous system into endocrine signals and regulates endocrine functions. Because it releases the hormone melatonin into your system, it is responsible for feelings of sleepiness. Melatonin is a derivative of an amino acid known as tryptophane and is released when we are exposed to dark and inhibited upon exposure to light. The gland seems to play a large part in regulating sexual development in human, metabolism, animal hibernation and seasonal breeding. It may be responsible for seasonal mood disorders.

The pineal gland works by communicating with other parts of the brain. A pathway known as the retinohypothalamic tract runs from the retinas to the hypothalamus. The tract delivers signals of light and dark to part of the hypothalamus referred to as the SCN (suprachiasmatic nucleus). After reaching the SCN, signals follow the pineal nerve in the sympathetic nervous system to reach the pineal gland. Light impulses then inhibit melatonin production. When the pineal gland receives fewer impulses, such as at night, melatonin is released. So the pineal gland releases melatonin, unless light signals tell it not to.

Research done on the retinas of hamsters' shows that the pineal gland is not the only source for melatonin in regulating sleep cycles. The eyes appear to have their own way of regulating rhythms, because scientists could still reset the circadian rhythm in these animals even when the SCN was destroyed. The retinal clock appears to stimulate melatonin products just as the pineal gland does. As yet, scientists have not determined why there are redundant systems in the body for circadian rhythms or where the circadian clock of the eye is located.

The human body is regulated as a whole by the pineal gland because it works to integrate the functions of all glands. Through its ability to react to light, the gland controls our biorhythms. The pineal gland collaborates with the pituitary gland in the throat, helping to moderate speech and body language. It works with the hypothalamus to direct sensations of hunger, thirst and even sexual desire. The hypothalamus is also responsible for regulating the aging process. The pineal gland is made of the same type of tissue as the eyes, which explains its use of light to control hormonal responses.

An adult pineal gland weighs between .16 and .21 grams. The largest pineal gland ever recorded was 1.0 gram. As we age, mineral deposits accumulate on the gland and cysts can form, increasing its weight. The surface can become finely puckered from the mineral deposits and cysts. Medical texts note that the pineal cells may have emigrated during evolution from deeper layers of the brain. Because some lower vertebrates use the pineal gland more actively as a light receptor, it is believed that the pineal gland is the precursor to the modern eye.

The pineal gland begins to degenerate early in life, often showing signs of aging in the seventh to twelfth year and advancing with age. The range of variation in weight for this organ is a clue to medical experts that the organ may have passed its evolutionary peak and may someday no longer be used by the human body. The gland starts out large in children, but it shrinks with the beginning of puberty. When puberty starts, the gland produces less melatonin. Whether this is why children sleep more, or if melatonin production slows because we sleep less as adults is unclear. It is believed that the high

The Pineal Gland

levels of melatonin in children are responsible for inhibiting sexual development until puberty.

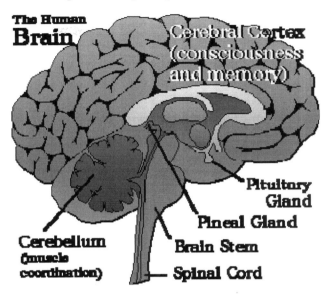

The Human Brain
Cerebral Cortex (consciousness and memory)
Pituitary Gland
Pineal Gland
Cerebellum (muscle coordination)
Brain Stem
Spinal Cord

Medical science has come a long way in explaining the physiological functions regulated by the pineal gland, but there are mystical traditions that remain in connection with this furtive organ. The relatively new discovery of the pineal gland has led to much speculation about its true function with some speculating that it is a 'third eye.' Its location in the centre of the brain suggests a link between the world of the physical and that of the spiritual. The pineal gland is seen as a strong centre for spiritual energy that is responsible for spiritual powers some humans possess.

The pineal gland's true function has been shrouded in mystery for ages and was even contemplated by philosophers in Ancient Greece. Some attributed the pineal gland as a spiritual connector to the Realms of Thought. The mystery surrounding the pineal gland has led some to associate it with the sixth chakra. Some say it is a dormant organ that may provide 'telepathic' abilities if awakened. It is considered a Spiritual Third Eye, responsible for our Inner Vision.

The awakening of the pineal gland has been described as giving a sensation of pressure at the brain's base. This sensation may also be experienced when your thoughts vibrate at a higher frequency. Head injuries have also been known to activate the pineal gland.

The pineal gland releases melatonin when we are very relaxed, such as with visualisation. Just as our bodies and minds were created by and respond to electromagnetic energy stimuli in the environment, the pineal gland responds in kind. The pineal gland is the telegraph of communication with the higher plan.

The pineal gland reaches up to meet with the crown chakra. This gland is a receptor for prana, or pure energy. With practice and diligence, one can separate the mind from the physical by raising the vibration level of the astral body.

The pineal and pituitary glands must work in harmonious resonance to achieve a higher level of perception, through the use of mediation and relaxation techniques. When these glands are aligned properly, a link is created with the personality (working through the pituitary gland) and the soul (working through the pineal gland), creating a magnetic field. The oppositely charged forces strengthen one another through resonance and form the 'light in the head'. When activated, this 'light in the head' allows you to astrally project, withdrawing yourself from your body and carrying the light with you.

Astral projection and similar special abilities related to the occult are linked to this 'light in the head'. To achieve this, one must first achieve physical relaxation and then focus on the pineal gland by visualising a point in the centre of the forehead. This activates the 'third-eye' properties of the pineal gland. Energy becomes focused between the centre of the forehead and the pineal gland, where consciousness becomes centred.

The Pineal Gland

By visualising the escape of the subtle body trough the door of the brain, the soul is set free. There may even be a sharp 'pop' sound in the pineal gland at the point of separation.

Because activating the 'third eye' begins with relaxation and visualisation, the first step is to practice visualisation techniques to direct our energy towards the 'third eye'. You can create the magnetic field surrounding the pineal gland by concentrating your mind at the point midway between the pineal and pituitary glands. Your creative imagination will visualise this and thought energy will animate the form.

Developing the 'Third eye', employing your imagination and using visualisation are all important parts in the various methods used to separate the soul from the physical body. You can also improve our intuition by developing your 'third eye'. Awareness and recall of the astral plane are not recorded in complete waking realisation until the intuition is strengthened. You may experience flashes of intuition more consistently when you learn to develop and activate your third eye more effectively.

By thinking at certain frequencies, we can erase the ego boundary that divides us from our eternal selves. This frequency, known as the theta state, lets us become deeply relaxed and rested while maintaining consciousness. In the theta state, your consciousness will pay less attention to your physical body. The active third eye will allow you to easily and naturally separate from the body. You can find several native traditions and mystical references to those who can 'see' or have awareness of high-level energy fields. This type of knowing is less concrete and more abstract than everyday ego consciousness, which is too absorbed in the self to look beyond the body's boundaries. The spiritual 'seeing' is the sight of the third eye.

When the pineal gland awakens, consciousness rises from an emotion-centred awareness to an illuminated awareness or enlightenment. For many, the still developing pineal gland must continue its evolution before such awareness can be attained. As a species, mankind will keep his mental energy intact when he can set aside ego and personality to become aware of the spiritual inner self. As a person, there are exercises you can perform to help you activate the 'light in the head' in this lifetime.

Cerebral Activity During Meditation

Electromagnetic energy is the fuel used by the brain to operate. Brainwaves can be seen and measured as electrical activity that emanates from the brain. Scientists have identified four types of brainwaves, ranging from high amplitude, low frequency delta to the low amplitude, high frequency beta. All humans produce the same characteristic brain wave patterns. All cultures and societies have the same experience.

During Meditation Brain Waves Change

Beta brain waves have a frequency of 13-30 cycles per second. These waves result from certain types of brain activity such as awaking awareness, extroversion, concentration, logical thinking and active conversation. Almost all of your normal daily activities, such as teaching a class or talking on the pone will produce beta waves.

Alpha brain waves carry a frequency of 7-13 cycles per second and are brought about by relaxation, non-arousal, meditation and hypnosis.

Theta waves, with a frequency of 4-7 cycles per second, are associated with day dreaming, dreaming, creativity, meditation, paranormal phenomena, out of body experiences, ESP, and shamanic journeys. If you are driving your car and realise you do not remember the last five minutes of the ride, you are just transitioning from the theta state back to beta. This can happen any time you are engaged in an activity involving muscle memory, where your brain is effectively on autopilot. Theta is considered a very positive mental state because the thoughts in the mind at that time are often free flowing, uncensored and unjudged by the ego.

70

The Pineal Gland

Delta brain waves are the slowest, at 1.5-4 or less cycles per second. This comes from a deep dreamless sleep.

Techniques for relaxing like mindfulness meditation work to train your ability to focus your attention for the purpose of gaining insight. These techniques create the opposite of attention deficit disorder, strengthening our attention span. With practice, you will become more aware during a situation and have the ability to respond in an emotionally objective way. This is highly useful when faced with morally difficult situations. You will be able to reach a responsive and creative awareness or 'flow' more easily.

In their study of this phenomenon, Daniel Goleman & Tara Bennett-Goleman (2001) suggest that the mechanism by which meditation works comes from the link between the amygdala (almond-shaped neuron groups found deep within the medial temporal lobes of the brain) and the prefrontal cortex. The theory can be simplified by saying that when presented with a situation, the pre-frontal cortex, which controls our inhibitions, first stops to think for a moment to logically decide how to act. The amygdala on the other hand, then takes on the job of determining how we should respond emotionally.

While the prefrontal cortex is a master at the tasks of planning and analysing, it is slow to respond, sometimes taking a long time to come to a decision. The amygdala is less complex both physically and on an evolutionary level. It can make snap decisions, impressing powerful emotional responses linked to our needs for immediate survival. This is associated with the 'flight or fight' reflex and allows us to respond quickly when presented with physical danger, rather than waiting for the prefrontal cortex to figure out how to respond.

The quick judgements made by the amygdala are highly prone to mistakes because of their reactive nature. They can sometimes respond to a perceived threat that is illusory. This is commonly seen in modern culture where we are more likely to feel or encounter social conflicts than physical threats of danger. The amygdala's emotional response can turn a harmless social difficulty into an emotionally dangerous situation, triggering fear, anger, anxiety and stress.

Meditation helps you to train your focus so that you can observe the responses of the amygdala without reacting to them emotionally. This gives you time to intervene between the event and the quarter second time it takes for the amygdala to order a reaction. The skill allows you to redirect the energy into more positive responses when appropriate.

The left side of the prefrontal cortex controls concentration, planning, metacognition (thoughts about the thoughts themselves) and positive feelings. Studies have shown that meditation practice can increase the level of activity in these areas and that the increase can be maintained over time, even when the practice of meditation stops. Similar studies on depression show a link between decreased activities in these areas and the onset of anxiety and depression.

New scanning techniques have helped neurologists to see how parts of the brain work more clearly. They have discovered that certain parts of the brains of Buddhists light up consistently, showing positive emotion.

Still more research, particularly that of Paul Ekman, at the University of California San Francisco Medical Centre, implies that mindfulness meditation actually calms the amygdala, which not only initiates the fight or flight response, but also acts as a centre for fear memories. Through his research, Ekman saw that long-time Buddhists had a lower propensity to react with shock, fear, surprise or anger.

In studying meditation, scientists have tried to learn more about the feeling of 'no space' experienced by Buddhist monks in their mediations. These studies have revealed that parts of the brain become inactive during meditation while other previously dormant parts awaken. With special brain imaging technologies, Dr. Newberg studied Tibetan Buddhist monks during one hour of meditation. The monks were instructed to pull a kite string when they reached the point of transcendental high in the meditation. This injected a radioactive tracer that allowed scientists to see which parts of the brain were active.

After meditation, brain imaging showed that the radioactive tracer had highlighted the active parts of the monks' brains, which were then compared to the ordinary state of consciousness. These scans showed that there was an increase in activity in the front part of the brain, the area that is activated when anyone focuses attention on a particular task.

A clear decrease in brain activity was noted in the parietal lobe, known as the part that governs orientation. This explained why special awareness was diminished during meditation.

Dr Newberg qualifies his work by saying, 'When someone has a mystical experience, they perceive that sense of reality to be far greater and far clearer than our usual everyday sense of reality. Since the sense of spiritual reality is more powerful and clear, perhaps that sense of reality is more accurate than our scientific everyday sense of reality.'

Life isn't about keeping score. It's not about how many friends you have. Or how many people call you. Or how accepted or unaccepted you are. Not about if you have plans this weekend. Or if you're alone. It isn't about who you're dating, who you use to date, how many people you've dated, or if you haven't been with anyone at all. It isn't about who you have kissed. It's not about sex. It isn't about who your family is or how much money they have. Or what kind of car you drive. Or where you're sent to school.

It's not about how beautiful or ugly you are. Or what clothes you wear, what shoes you have on, or what kind of music you listen to. It's not about if your hair is blonde, red, black, brown, or green. Or if your skin is too light or too dark.

It's not about what grades you get, how smart you are, how smart everyone else thinks you are, or how smart standardised tests say you are. Or if this teacher likes you, or if this guy/girl likes you. Or what clubs you're in, or how good you are at 'your' sport. It's not about representing your whole being on a piece of paper and seeing who will 'accept the written you'.

But life is about who you love and who you hurt. It's about

who you make happy or unhappy purposefully. It's about keeping or betraying trust. It's about friendship, used as sanctity, or as a weapon. It's about what you say and mean, maybe hurtful, maybe heartening. About starting rumours and contributing to petty gossip. It's about what judgments you pass and why. And who your judgments are spread to.

It's about who you've ignored with full control and intention. It's about jealousy, fear, pain, ignorance, and revenge. It's about carrying inner hate and love, letting it grow and spreading it.

But most of all, it's about using your life to touch or poison other people's hearts in such a way that could never occurred alone. Only you choose the way these hearts are affected and those choices are what life is all about.

5

Placing Your First Order

Now You are Ready to Place Your First Cosmic Order

For starters, it is important to get through the beginning sense of expectancy quickly and simply. For now, please simply follow my instructions.

The first ting to do is close your eyes and think through all of your dreams and desires. Brainstorm for everything you ever wanted, regardless of how attainable these desires may be. Do this now. When you are done, open your eyes and continue reading.

Now that you have an understanding of your greatest dream and desires, weed out the physically impossible so that you are left with those that are attainable. This is for the purpose of getting started. Later you will learn how to make even the most amazing things happen! For now, consider the attainable, such as a career change, rather than owning your own island.

Once you have whittled your list down to things that are more readily attainable, choose three goals that you believe are the most likely to be achieved. If you like, you can keep your eyes open for this part of the exercise. Already, the creative part of your mind is engaged. Consider the three goals you have chosen and list them in order of importance, giving you your target.

The next step requires that you find a quiet place to spend time thinking of nothing but the things you have set for your target. At this point, you only need to ask for what you want. Whether you ask with your inner voice, or speak aloud will not matter.

Cosmic Ordering: You Can be Successful

Do not forget to address the Cosmos with respect when placing your Order. Just like all things, there is a beginning, middle, and an end. Be sure you follow this universal arrangement in your Order. Address the Cosmos with respect such as, 'Dear Cosmos, I ask....' State exactly what it is that you want and address the advantages of having it. Do not forget to be polite and thank the Cosmos for its generosity.

Do not forget the importance of specificity. When you ask for that new whatever it is, be sure the Cosmos knows exactly what you want. Tell the Cosmos the exact details, options, etc. Let the Cosmos know exactly when it is you want that item and where it should be sent.

Once you have asked for your desires, help the Cosmos along by delivering an image, just as you would show a friend a cut out in a magazine of, say for example, the new dinning table you want. Visualise the table standing in your lounge. See yourself and your family sitting around the table.

Again, do not forget to thank the Cosmos. Remember that gratitude is the key to manifesting your desires.

So now that you have completed your first Order, you should have an air of expectancy. You may notice a bubbly excited feeling in your gut. You will have no doubts and KNOW the table is on its way. That is good, for you have tapped into an endless supply of wealth and happiness. Cosmic Ordering is more certain and secure than gold on the world money market.

There are times when your desires seem to run amok. You may wonder why your requests have not yet been fulfilled. In times like this, it is important to take stock of your inner landscape. Did you doubt? Did something go wrong with the Order and your new table is now your neighbour's new table? Be certain that you always think positively. Wishing for that new table is futile if you follow it with concerns and worry that can erode your connection with the infinite. Remember that you deserve the new table, it is yours, you earned and won it. In the same way that Einstein believed in his abilities to crack

76

the code of the universe, you should have an unrelenting faith in yourself to achieve your desires.

Doubt is not the only obstacle keeping you from your desires. Negative thoughts like jealousy will also corrupt your connection with the Cosmos. Simply picture your desires already fulfilled. A single request is all you need to make to the Cosmos, but small reminders, such as visualising your desires again, can help.

I can tell you of a millionaire who posted images of his desires onto his refrigerator door. Each of those things did eventually appear in his life. Such reminders help you to solidify your intent and keep from letting your faith wane.

Start by placing single Orders, and that way you can concentrate on placing your Order. If you take too big of a bite of the cherry then things could go pear-shaped. Slowly, slowly catchy monkey. Rome was not built in a day, etc.

Advanced Cosmic Ordering
Take the time to read through this process and become familiar with it. Practice runs may be helpful for you to help the practise be more effective. It is important that you remain relaxed, so do not strive or place intense effort into the process. Take heed: if you are tired or sleepy, choose another time to practice this exercise. Falling asleep during a Cosmic Order defeats the purpose. Take a moment to tell yourself that you will have full recall of this session and that it improves your life's well-being.

Step 1 – *Choose a quiet location*
The main characteristics of a good thinking place are only that the place is quiet and comfortable. Even if you are just waiting in your car for a half our or so, you have found a good place and time to begin your Cosmic Order. In fact, the Cosmos has arranged this for you, just so that you could have time to place your Order. Be sure the phone is turned off. Turn on some relaxing music. Be certain the temperature in your relaxing

place is comfortable. Avoid practicing at any location where you may feel vulnerable to being disturbed, since this can disrupt your peace. You should also avoid locations with strong electrical interference, like locations near electricity sub-stations or any other large electrical installation to avoid electro magnetic interference.

Step 2 – *Relax*
Relaxing does not come easily to most people these days. The modern world is a busy place, always pushing for greater effort and exertion. We have always been taught to try harder, so relaxing goes against the grain of our upbringing. Relax by sitting comfortable in peaceful surroundings. Remove any distractions, such as jewellery. Close the curtains to create a relaxed mood. Close your eyes and just let go of thought. Simply be.

Step 3 – *Become one with yourself*
There are two selves in every person. The true eternal self, tied with the infinite, and the false ego self that is tied with the body. Becoming one with yourself, means setting aside the ego self and becoming attuned to your inner eternal self. Make yourself comfortable by sitting or lying down. Wiggle a little to settle in and adjust any clothing that may distract you. Perform the following body scan, which involves simply feeling your body as it is:

> Quiet your mind . . .
> Still your thoughts . . .
> Relax your body . . .
> Feel your face . . . your jaw . . . relaxing . . .
> Feel your shoulders . . . your neck . . . relaxing
> Your arms . . . your hands . . . feel at peace . . .
> Your torso . . . your hips . . . letting go . . .
> Your legs . . . your feet . . . totally relaxed . . .
> Focus on your breathing.

Placing Your First Order

Inhale slowly and deeply through your nose . . .
Retain the breath as long as is comfortable . . .
Exhale through the mouth slowly and completely . . .
Repeat (inhale 1, exhale 2, inhale 3 . . . until you are comfortable)

Step 4 – *Visualise what you want, see yourself doing it*
Just as a picture is worth a thousand words, visualisation is a powerful way of communicating your exact desires in great detail. It also helps you to reinforce your faith, putting your mind in a state of believing what you want has already happened. It may help you to visualise yourself aiming a dart at a dartboard, imagine the dart carrying your Order to the board of manifestation. If you are more of a sedate type, instead imagine yourself cultivating a garden which is your metaphorical Cosmic Order. Then at harvest time you see yourself reaping the rewards. This will help you *establish your absolute faith in Cosmic Ordering*, instituting an air of expectancy.

Step 5 – *Eradicate negative thoughts*
It is vital that negative thoughts be erased from your mental landscape. Negative thoughts will rob you of your Orders. Use visualisation to send a battalion of helpers to subdue those robbing thoughts.

Step 6 – *Refocus your thoughts*
Sometimes during this practice, you may have difficulty staying focused. Fix this by switching gears. Stop and become quiet and take five minute to refocus. Eliminate distracting visual stimuli by closing your eyes. When thoughts race, focus instead on our breathing which is steady and constant. Stay with the steady in and out of your breath, which will slow your thoughts. Once you are calm again, redirect your thoughts to positive intention, directed towards your desires. Swim in the joy of the gifts you will receive before you continue.

Step 7 – *Cosmic Connection*

You are now ready to open your connection with the Cosmos. Do this by stimulating the magnetic field surrounding the pineal gland (Cosmic Eye) with focus directed at the point half way between the pineal and pituitary glands, deep within your brain, just behind the eyes and nose.

When you redirect your focus to this location, your mind begins to function more creatively without any direct orders from you to do so. Keep your eyes closed and maintain the focus on your pineal gland.

Without straining your eyes, but allowing it to occur naturally, stare at the point in the centre of your forehead. Simply think of it and let it occur. In the beginning, you may not notice the activation of the glad, but with regular practice, you will learn to recognise the feeling associated with this activation. A gentle pressure under the eyes is one sign of success.

You will find that your senses and physical awareness will begin to fade. Visualise intently the subtle body escaping from the brain. You will realise that time and space are meaningless illusions.

Let your requests find their way up the line of communication with the Cosmos. When you are in this state, all things are possible. You are no longer restricted by time or space. You can go anywhere and do anything. If you desire, visit the great pyramids. At this level of consciousness, time is meaningless so there is no sense of urgency. Your mind is free of all physical constraints.

Place your Cosmic Order and notice that it is already happening, so there is no cause for fear of failure.

With extended practice, you will learn to reach this level of consciousness without my guidance. You will be able to go there at will, finding your own pathways to the infinite.

Accelerated Cosmic Connection

As a certified clinical hypnotherapist, I have extensive

experience of having placed past clients in the hypnotic state. Hypnosis helped my clients to learn many things, receiving messages from other aspects of themselves, other dimensions of reality, the unconscious mind and even other entities.

I will teach you to fine-tune your skills of self-hypnosis to help you solidify and deepening your Cosmic Connection. This is merely an alternate method of connecting with the Cosmos as you did in the previous exercise.

Self-hypnosis can be a useful method for activating the Cosmic Eye because it allows for a smooth transition into higher consciousness without a sudden 'bang.' It will let you stay within your linear time line, rather than losing all connection with time and space. In addition, self-hypnosis can speed up the functioning of the Cosmic Eye without placing conscious effort on the task. It allows you to make good use of your subconscious while still remaining in controlled conditions. Self-hypnosis also stimulates other areas of brain functioning.

Let go of the preconceived notions you may have about hypnosis. You will have full control of yourself throughout the process. This is not a stage show or some cheap trick where people behave like chickens. You go into the hypnotic state without trying on a daily basis. You may have noticed this while brushing your teeth or performing other mundane tasks. You will learn now to create that state intentionally.

Some people will deny they have ever been in a trance or that they can even be hypnotised. These people are unwilling to let go of control, feeling they 'win' somehow by refusing a trance. But you win nothing by denying yourself the benefits of hypnosis. Still, there is no requirement that you find a trance state to accomplish your goals. If the preceding method worked well for you and you are uncomfortable with hypnosis, then by all means, stick with what works for you. You should know, however, that the self-hypnosis method has benefits over the meditation method, giving you a far better connection with the Cosmos. Understand that this guide is purely for the purpose of connecting with the infinite and is not meant to cure any illness.

Hypnotherapy works by bypassing the conscious mind to reach directly into the emotional body, or inner child, where we keep the emotional issues of our lives until we become ready to bring them out.

Before you begin, you should note that not everyone is ideal for hypnotherapy. Hypnosis requires the brain's natural capacity for producing deep relaxation. A hypnotic trance occurs in the alpha and theta states, but can potentially happen during any brainwave pattern. Please recall that there are four types of brainwaves, listed here from fastest frequency to slowest: Beta, Alpha, Theta and Delta. Hypnosis typically induces Alpha waves and deep hypnosis occurs with Theta waves.

Hypnosis creates a deeper state of relaxation in the mind than meditation. Hypnotherapy gives you the ability to explore past or parallel lives so that you can release blockages not apparent in the physical world.

Before we begin, there are a few things you should know. This session is intended to let you learn more about another method for connecting to the Cosmos. This method is highly efficient. You simply get to the state, take care of business and return to your normal state. The state is so easy to achieve, this can be accomplished whenever needed. To demonstrate, place your thumb just a few millimetres from the tip of your nose. When you stare at it, you allow yourself immediately to drift off into a light trance, as if in a daydream. It is that simple and easy.

The hypnotic state allows you to maintain awareness of your surroundings. Because you are fully aware, there is no need to worry about a knock on the door while you are practicing hypnotherapy. You simply move out of your trance and get up to answer the door. You will not lose your connection with reality at any time during hypnosis. At worst, you might fall asleep from fatigue. For this reason, you should practice self-hypnosis when you are well rested.

When you do come out of a hypnotic trance, it is helpful to remain in your relaxed state for a few moments to gather your thoughts.

I have provided you with some scripts that you might use while in the hypnotic state. You can say them in your head while in a trance. Pre-planning can be helpful.

Self-induced Accelerated Cosmic Connection

Step 1 *– Find a quiet, comfortable place*
As before, find a quiet comfortable place where you will not be distracted by a sense of vulnerability to disruption. Adjust your clothing or jewellery to ensure your comfort.

Close the curtains, if in a room, but leave the lights on low so as to help you to relax in the room's atmosphere and close your eyes. (The pineal gland loves light, so do not do this in total darkness unless you are confident that you can make a connection.)

Step 2 *– Become one with yourself*
Tune-in to your eternal self by simply being. Sit or lie down in a comfortable position and let go of the ego.

Step 3 *– Breathing*
Focus on your breathing by inhaling slowly and deeply through your nose. Hold the breath for a comfortably long pause, then exhale through your mouth slowly and completely. Do this for several breaths until you feel sufficiently relaxed.

Step 4 *– Relax your body (should take about two or three minutes)*
You may wish to try a relaxation CD which offers guided self-hypnosis. Becoming deeply relaxed is accomplished through the body scan as follows:

Start with your face . . . let your jaw drop . . . relaxing

83

Feel your shoulders sinking . . . your neck . . . relaxing
Let your arms go . . . your hands . . . feel at peace . . .
Your torso . . . your hips . . . letting go . . .
Your legs . . . your feet . . . your toes ... totally relaxed . . .

Tell yourself that you will have full recall of all that happens during your session and that it will benefit your well-being.

Step 5 – *Induction technique*
I am presenting you with only one of approximately 100 commonly used hypnotic induction methods. Remember that hypnosis in not sleep but a conscious state of deep relaxation. Choose either a comfortable chair or pick a comfortable place to lie down like a bed or sofa.

Imagine a spot above your head. Keep your head still while you look up at that spot with your eyes. Focus on this imaginary spot, being careful not to strain your eyes. Recite the following in your mind while maintaining the focus:

> 'I'm going to count down from 5. With each and every count, my eyelids will become heavier.'
> '5 ... So sleepy...' (emphasise the 's' sound), 'sssso tired'.
> '4 ... My eyelidsssss becoming heavier and heavier, ssssso sleepy, ssssso tired'.
> '3 ... My eyelidsssss beginning to clossssse all by themselvesssss, they are ssssso tired'.
> '2 ... And now my eyelidsssss closing, clossssing, clossssing, closing, clossssing, closing, clossssing, closing, clossssing them, close them, ssssso sssssleepy, ssssso tired'.
> '1 ...'

While your eyes will now be closed, you will still be

conscious and aware, but not asleep.

Step 6 – *Deepener*
Next, you will want to bring yourself down to an even deeper state of relaxation to allow your subconscious mind to pick up and control your Cosmic connection. Following from step 5, tell yourself the following:

> 'I am just like a leaf, falling gently from a tree, sinking, deeper and deeper. As I count down from five, with each and every count I am sinking deeper and deeper. I am sinking' (again, emphasising the 's' sound), 'floating down, deeper and deeper. 5 – Slowly sinking further and further down. 4 …'

Follow this deepening recital until you reach number '1'. Now you will find yourself in a deep state of hypnosis, where your subconscious has control of your conscious mind. It is a good idea to say to yourself, 'Should the need arise, I will come out of trance for safety's sake.' This ensures that your subconscious will respond to your senses and react appropriately should the need arise.

Step 7 – *Cosmic Connection*
Once in deep hypnosis, just have a gentle chat with your mind. Discuss the things that are going to happen, using words like, 'My Cosmic Eye is speaking to the universe. I want that connection to be made with ease.' Once you have connected in this way, you can then begin to approach your Cosmic Order. Again, images are especially effective. Visualise what it is you want and see it happening in your life.

The hypnotic state allows you to be aware of all things around you but in another way, not aware. The subconscious mind is paying close attention to your words while your conscious mind becomes deaf in its sleep. Even though your conscious mind is asleep, it can awaken any time it needs to.

Step 8 – *Coming out of the cosmic connection*

When you finish with your Cosmic Order and it is time to regain normal consciousness, speak to yourself with the following words:

> 'After the count of 1 I will awaken and feel completely refreshed.
> 3, I'm beginning to awaken.
> 2, I'm coming out of it.
> 1, awaken, my eyes opening slowly.'

At this point, you will be fully awake, in a normal conscious state. Rest for a few moments while you allow your mind to adjust to normal thinking. This is the equivalent of blinking your eyes when you wake up in the morning before getting out of bed.

With practice, you will begin to recognise signs of your improved skills in these techniques. When you have mastered it, you will simply know.

Once you have gained these skills, you will make major progress in your manifesting desires. Eventually, you will learn special tips and tricks specific to you that work best.

Understand that it is the nature of your unconscious mind to believe what it is told.

This is why self-hypnosis is so effective. By speaking to your subconscious directly, you instil absolute faith and trust in the Cosmos.

This faith and trust allow a higher vibrational level within you and this is when you are able to activate your pineal gland into making that Cosmic Connection.

Manifesting Your Desires

Manifesting requires that you have a clear image of your desires. In order to communicate what you want, it is vital you clearly know what it is you want. Forming a mental picture allows you to shape exactly what you desire and communicate the specifics to the Cosmos. Put simply, you must have it before you can give it. Many people fail to communicate clearly with the Cosmos simply because they have not formed a clear and specific image of what it is they want or wish to have happen.

Having a general idea that you want a better life is insufficient for creating an outcome. Wanting wealth so you can 'do good' is not enough either. These are the vague wishes of all people. This is akin to if I just wrote the letters of the alphabet on one page of this book and then I expected the reader to construct the text for the remaining pages himself out of these basic parts. When impressing your desires on the original substance, you must provide a cohesive clear picture of your desires.

Know exactly what it is you seek and be exact in your requirements. You will never become wealthy or initiate the power of creation by transmitting vague wants or wishes. That is like saying you want it, but it does not really matter to you. You must put forth the effort to clearly say what you want if you expect the universe to reflect that same effort and manifest your desires. Forming clear mental pictures of your desires helps the universe send back what you desire and helps you to clarify for yourself just what it is you want.

The mental image you form should be kept in mind continuously. Just as you steer your car in the direction you are going by keeping your eyes on the road, keep your eyes on that mental picture. You cannot lose sight of your desires any more than you could lose sight of the road and continue to drive.

Whenever you have time to spare, spend it meditating on your mental image. I have set forth methods in this book that require you to have a strong desire for riches. Your desire must be strong enough to overcome mental laziness if they are to work.

Delight in the details of your mental image. Study it as you would the face of a newborn baby or a lover. Memorise every shape, element, and substance. In going over your mental image repeated, it will be come more clear and defined in your own mind, reinforcing your desire and making it a better vehicle for communicating with the Cosmos.

You should know that there is a little something more needed than just having that clear image and desire. You must also have strength of purpose to realise your desires and bring about the tangible representation of your thoughts in this world. Behind this purpose in an unwavering belief that the thing you desire already belongs to you. It is yours. You own it. If you seek a new vehicle, spend time imagining yourself in it until the vehicle takes form around you in the material world.

You need not wait until your desires are realised to enjoy them. In your mind, delight in the achievement of your desires. See yourself living the life your desires will bring. Use your imagination to enjoy the future in the present. Meditate on your mental image and once it is clear and distinct, take a mental attitude of ownership for all the elements in your mental image.

By taking possession, I mean that you must fully recognise it already belongs to you. You must believe it absolutely. Keep unwavering faith and remember to be as grateful for the fulfilment of your desires now as you would be when they actually take the physical form. Sincerely thankfulness for those desires that you won within your imagination is the definition of true faith. KNOW you already have it, that you desires are in the process of taking shape in the physical real and you will achieve the wealth you desire. Your faith will cause the physical manifestation of your desires.

It is your job to mentally formulate what it is you truly want and to arrange your desires into a complete, cohesive and clear picture and then impress that image upon the original substance, which has all that is needed to bring what you desire.

This impression cannot be made with simple words. You must follow with a vision of purpose that is unshakeable and unwavering. While oral wishes are good and often effective at helping you to realise your dreams, this book is about my proven approach that will always yield results.

To become wealthy, you cannot simply place one Order and move on. You must hold the image of your desires fixedly in your mind. Be like a knight with a lance. Do not let go under any circumstances.

When the vision has been formed and you have the certain knowledge of what you desire, all that is left to do is to receive. Once your vision is formed, be sure to make a statement addressing your gratitude towards the Cosmos. Then start receiving. Be ready for your desires to manifest. Spend time in your mind doing all the things you will do with the wealth when it arrives. Make some travel plans since you will soon be able to afford it!

When you refer in your mind to your desires, always frame them in the context of present ownership. Secure an image of the environment you will live in and the financial state of your affairs as you desire them, then live all the time in this space until they appear in your life. This is nothing to play at. This is serious business. You are not simply daydreaming, you are CREATING. Maintain your FAITH by using the image of your desires and hold them in your PURPOSE to make them happen. The difference between the scientific process of manifesting and simple daydreams is faith and purpose. Understanding this, you will need to also understand the proper use of free will.

Here is a story which epitomises the above. Long ago in a small, far away village, there was place known as the House of 1,000 Mirrors. A small, happy little dog learned of this place and decided to visit. When he arrived, he bounced happily up the stairs to the doorway of the house. He looked through the doorway with his ears lifted high and his tail wagging as fast as it could. To his great surprise, he found himself staring at 1,000 other happy little dogs with their tails wagging just as fast as his. He smiled a great smile, and was answered with 1,000 great smiles just as warm and friendly. As he left the House, he thought to himself, 'This is a wonderful place. I will come back

89

and visit it often.'

In this same village, another little dog, who was not quite as happy as the first one, decided to visit the house. He slowly climbed the stairs and hung his head low as he looked into the door. When he saw the 1,000 unfriendly looking dogs staring back at him, he growled at them and was horrified to see 1,000 little dogs growling back at him. As he left, he thought to himself, 'That is a horrible place, and I will never go back there again.'

All the faces in the world are mirrors. What kind of reflections do you see in the faces of the people you meet?

Winning Willpower

You might think of *will* as control. The control over things both in and around you. However, you should know that only the Cosmos has the right to control anything outside of you. Free will is bestowed upon us only so that we may have power in our own lives. You have no right to control those things outside of yourself, which is why this path leads to frustration and pain. It is just as wrong to control or coerce others through force of will as it is to do so physically. The use of mental force to control others is no different than becoming a slave master. Thieves steal from others by physical force, and using mental force to do this is no different. The difference is a vital point to understand as amoral principle and physical fact.

Even if you think your force of will exerted on a person is for their own good, you are not so all powerful and all knowing that you should think you actually understand what is for someone else's own good. In the art of acquiring wealth through manifestation, there is no need to force your will on any person other than yourself. Any attempts to control others will only defeat your efforts and drain the mental energy you should be spending on yourself. When you become experienced and knowledgeable about Cosmic Ordering then that is the time you can consider helping others with it.

Exerting your will outside yourself in order to control

forces that have been keeping you from wealth is illogical. To attain wealth, you only need to exert will upon yourself.

Now that you have the knowledge of what you need to think and do, you should use your will to compel only yourself to think and do the necessary things. This is the only way your will should be used – to keep your eyes on the road and your vehicle travelling safely in the right direction.

Your will should be used to keep you on the right path, thinking and acting in the way necessary to manifest your desires. Focus your thoughts on your own mind and desires. This is where it does its best work.

For the creative visualisation of your desires, use your will to influence your mind to think in the right way. Saturate your thoughts with positive affirmations and imagery. Impregnate every nook and cranny of your conscious and subconscious thought with the result of your desires. These positive vibrations will increase your core vibration to the higher level needed to resonate with the Cosmos. The higher level will bring about many changes in your life; new experiences and people also vibrating at that frequency will gravitate towards you. This is when the positive changes will begin to appear in your life through the laws of vibrational frequencies.

Creative Visualisation

Think of visualisation as a gathering of words and thoughts, both spoken externally and internally, which creates a seemingly magical effect. It applies to anything you desire, whether it is to break a bad habit or improve yourself as a person. You imagine yourself in a situation and it just happens. To put it simply, 'creative visualisation' is your ability to imagine pictures in your mind and then make them come true.

When you add focus and emotions to your images, a powerful creative force is engaged that makes things happen for you. When used properly, visualisation will change your life. Your thoughts are the blueprints of your desires. Your focus and emotions are the tools to build your desires. Creative visualisation is much like Cosmic Ordering in that it alters your surroundings and life situation, making things happen, attracting wealth and all the things you desire. Use it in conjunction with Cosmic Ordering.

When you visualise an event or situation, even an object such as a new car, those things are attracted to us by Cosmic force. The desires you see in your imagination can be made to happen.

While it may seem like daydreaming and magic, there is no magic or dreaming involved. It is a natural force of the universe, just as warmth is a natural result of the nuclear reactions on the surface of the sun. Creative visualisation is a natural process resulting from the power inherent in our thoughts.

There are those who use this power unconsciously in every day life. They may be totally unaware of this power. They have no understanding that they are using the power behind their thoughts to visualise their goals in a positive way, attaining success. Whether they know it or not, all successful people are using this power to achieve success.

Manifesting Indulgence

You may see those touting an entirely new system for creating your own destiny. However, there honestly is nothing startlingly new. The underlying principles for Cosmic Ordering have been studied by sages and mystics for centuries. Even Socrates knew of them. These principles are older than most religions in practice today.

No matter what it is that you wish to manifest, the basic principles do not change. Because of the Law of Attraction, you will attract experiences in life that coincide with your belief system. As in quantum physics, the outcome of the event can be influenced by the observer. You are the observer, influencing the outcome of your own life.

Whether conscious or unconscious, your underlying belief system creates your experience. This makes it important that you become aware of your unconscious beliefs in your conscious mind. Carl Jung once said, 'Until you make the unconscious conscious, it will direct your life and you will call it fate.' Nothing could be truer.

In preparing to co-create the perfect life, be certain exactly what it is you want. Look at your desires and the motivations behind them. If your desires are selfish or manipulative, you should find another way to approach them. You will pay a hefty price for those desires born of ill will. Selfish desires should be reframed in a positive light.

Becoming clear on what you want is much more difficult than actually manifesting it. Manifesting is merely the process of visualising the specific and exact thing you want for a quiet moment each day. This process of creative visualisation is easy for anyone to do. It helps you to raise your core vibrational frequency by changing your core belief system.

Affirmations

Affirmations alone are ineffective unless you have already initiated the start of the change you desire in your subconscious mind.

Affirmations are effective at making you feel good, thereby increasing your vibrational frequency, but if they do not penetrate to your unconscious mind, only small changes will be seen in your reality. By regular use of creative visualisation, you will saturate your subconscious mind with those affirmations, altering your core beliefs and redirecting your life to a new positive direction. By deeply penetrating your full mind, both conscious and subconscious with high-frequency thoughts, you will attract positive people, experiences and things that also vibrate at that higher level, creating the positive changes in your life.

Creative visualisation is simply the capacity to use your imagination to create images of what you want in life. The high-frequency thoughts emitted during this process fuel the power of positive change. When you combine focus and emotion, the result is a powerful creative force that makes things happen for you. When used correctly, visualisation will change your life!

You can create an image of anything you desire, such as an event or an object. Perhaps you seek a new home or a car. What we visualise in our imaginations manifests in our lives. This is nothing magical, just the natural power of thought.

Let us take the example of someone who wishes to see the Egyptian pyramids. The first step is to relax. Perform the body scan as described earlier in this book and breathe deeply to relax thoroughly. Next, choose the image of the Great Pyramids that you are most drawn to. Be sure to include yourself standing at the base of the pyramid and feel the sense of joy that comes with being in this mystical and beautiful place. To have an image of the pyramid is not enough. You must also insert yourself into the image and FEEL what it is like to be there. Otherwise, you may get your reality to a lesser extent, such as receiving a postcard from someone in Egypt. Picturing yourself at the pyramid prevents any misunderstanding in what it is you want.

Picture your clothing and who is there with you. Add details that use your senses, like feeling the dry air and heat, smelling the dirt or hearing the hum of a crowd. Feel the hot wind in the back of your neck. Feel the weight of the sun hat on your head (articulated visualisation). Listen to the foreign dialects all around you.

Think about how you will feel at the base of that pyramid. Imagine your sense of wonder and awe gazing on the monumental structures. Think about your excitement in viewing them in person for the first time. Enjoy your sense of adventure, being a free traveller. Make it as real as you can.

Do not worry about how you will get to the base of that pyramid. The details approaching your realisation will be sorted out by the Cosmos. By interfering in the creative process, you could block your desires from reaching you. The Cosmos has its own ideas about how your goals will be accomplished. There are literally millions upon millions of possible realities awaiting you. Let the universe choose the one that fits best.

While that image remains in your mind, it is pleasant, but you must send it off to the Cosmos to get it working. When you finish your meditation, let the image go. To be sure you have done this, pick another activity after your mediation that will occupy your mind.

Now that you understand the process, it is time to give it a try. Before you begin, I should give you a brief warning. The technique is immensely powerful. Remember the adage, 'be careful what you wish for, you just might get it.'

To show you what I mean, let me tell you about a friend of mine. She mentioned how lucky one of her friends was to win a £100,000 settlement award from a personal injury case. Two weeks later, my friend was in an accident herself, suffering an injury to her back. She won a £50,000 settlement for her injury. I don't believe she felt the anxiety and pain from the injury were worth the money.

So that you do not find yourself in such a situation, be certain to close your meditation by ensuring you will manifest only those events or things that are to your benefit. Close with, 'If it pleases the Cosmos, then so be it,' or 'If this is for my highest good, then so be it.' This protection can save you from unintended negative consequences.

Finally, understand that physical action is often necessary in addition to the thought action. Once you have meditated on your desires, be certain to get out and go about your life as usual. Just be sure to keep open eyes and an open mind for the opportunities the Cosmos will be sending your way.

Rewarding Cosmic Ordering

What exactly is it that you want? How much do you want it? Before sending confusing signals out to the Cosmos, stop and take stock of your desires. Make sure you are certain of what you want and all the details connected with your desires.

Failing to take the time to get specific about your desires is a form of mental laziness that blocks abundance from entering your life.

You cannot get what you want if you do not first have a thorough understanding of what it is.

Most people float through life without ever realising even what they want, much less achieving success. This is why not everyone is a superstar. Vague notions of what a happy life could be are simply entertainment for such people. They drift along like leaves caught up in a storm, letting the wind decide for them how their lives should be. Part of this may be the natural balance sorting itself out.

Finding happiness with your lot in life is a blessing, but many are not content with the simple pleasures of the sun rising and setting each day. Many need more substance to their lives to give it meaning and purpose. When you have found exactly what it is that you want, Cosmic Ordering does the rest.

Mind Power

Mind power has a measurable effect on material objects. If powerful enough, thoughts can travel between minds. When we concentrate on the same thought, those around us also perceive the same thought and act upon it.

Although often the response is unconscious, these people will contribute to the furthering of the material realisation of your desires.

Morality may consist solely in the courage of making a choice. Wickedness is always easier than virtue, for it takes a short cut to everything. But over time you learn, you can not make wrong work.

There are always two choices, two paths to take. One is easy. And your only reward is that it is easy. You cannot do wrong without suffering wrong.

Work joyfully and peacefully, knowing that right thoughts and right efforts will inevitably bring about right results.

You can never lose anything that really belongs to you, and

you cannot keep that which belongs to someone else.

You always experience the consequences of your own acts. If your acts are right, you will get good consequences; if not, you will suffer for it. Sooner or later everyone sits down to a banquet of consequences.

The changes in your thoughts and mental imagery will actually change your reality. The illusions of the material world fall away. There is nothing magical or supernatural about it. It is a scientific process resulting from the power of your thoughts.

Instead of exerting force on material objects, we only exert force on our own thoughts, which have the power to make changes in the material world beyond anything our hands can ever do.

This is akin to finding yourself in a real-seeming dream, then switching to another dream that you prefer. You do not wake up, you just change the dream. Ponder this a while. Consider that you choose which reality you reside in, just as you can choose which dream you prefer.

Have confidence that you can use creative visualisation even if you think the idea is unrealistic, difficult to understand or overly complex.

Still, understanding and acceptance of what I have explained to you, at least in theory, while hasten the results you seek to achieve.

There is great power in creative visualization for those who can change their thoughts and minds. You may have difficulty making some of these changes right away.

Understand that the great power in creating visualisation is only found in the limits of your mind, not the technique.

You can Make it Happen

History abounds with tales of experts who were convinced that the ideas, plans, and projects of others could never be achieved. However, accomplishment came to those who said, 'I can make it happen.'

97

Cosmic Ordering: You Can be Successful

The Italian sculptor Agostino d'Antonio worked diligently on a large piece of marble. Unable to produce his desired masterpiece, he lamented, 'I can do nothing with it.' Other sculptors also worked this difficult piece of marble, but to no avail. Michelangelo discovered the stone and visualised the possibilities in it. His 'I-can-make-it-happen' attitude resulted in one of the world's masterpieces - David.

The experts of Spain concluded that Columbus' plans to discover a new and shorter route to the West Indies was virtually impossible. Queen Isabella and King Ferdinand ignored the report of the experts. 'I can make it happen,' Columbus persisted. And he did. Everyone knew the world was flat, but not Columbus. The Nina, the Pinta, the Santa Maria, along with Columbus and his small band of followers, sailed to 'impossible' new lands and thriving resources.

Even the great Thomas Alva Edison discouraged his friend, Henry Ford, from pursuing his fledgling idea of a motorcar. Convinced of the worthlessness of the idea, Edison invited Ford to come and work for him. Ford remained committed and tirelessly pursued his dream. Although his first attempt resulted in a vehicle without reverse gear, Henry Ford knew he could make it happen. And, of course, he did.

'Forget it,' the experts advised Madame Curie. They agreed radium was a scientifically impossible idea. However, Marie Curie insisted, 'I can make it happen.'

Let us not forget our friends Orville and Wilbur Wright. Journalists, friends, armed forces specialists, and even their father laughed at the idea of an airplane. 'What a silly and insane way to spend money. Leave flying to the birds,' they jeered. 'Sorry,' the Wright brothers responded. 'We have a dream, and we can make it happen.' As a result, a place called Kitty Hawk, North Carolina, became the setting for the launching of their 'ridiculous' idea.

The question was once asked of a highly successful businessman: 'How have you done so much in your lifetime?'

He replied, 'I have dreamed. I have turned my mind loose

to imagine what I wanted to do. Then I have gone to bed and thought about my dreams. In the night I dreamt about my dreams. And when I awoke in the morning, I saw the way to make my dreams real. While other people were saying, "You can't do that, it isn't possible," I was well on my way to achieving what I wanted.'

As Woodrow Wilson, 28th President of the US said: 'We grow great by dreams. All big men are dreamers.

'They see things in the soft haze of a spring day or in the red fire on a long winter's evening. Some of us let these great dreams die, but others nourish and protect them; nourish them through bad days until they bring them to the sunshine and light which comes always to those who sincerely hope that their dreams will come true.'

So please, don not let anyone steal your dreams, or try to tell you they are too impossible.

Finally, as you read these accounts under the magnificent lighting of your environment, consider the plight of Benjamin Franklin. He was admonished to stop the foolish experimenting with lighting. What an absurdity and waste of time! Why, nothing could outdo the fabulous oil lamp.

Thank goodness Franklin knew he could make it happen. You too can make it happen!

Creative Visualisation is Creative Energy
By thinking of and focusing on the good things you want to happen on a daily and regular basis, you will put into use a positive creative energy.

This energy will then take on the physical forms in the material world to fulfil your desires.

You may have experienced this power in your life subconsciously in one of the following ways:

> 1.	You answer the phone and the person on the other end was someone on your mind who you were just about to call yourself.

99

2.   You learn about a new book and think, 'I'm going to read that', then you do.

3.   You notice that you repeatedly attract bad romantic partners in your life.

There is more to creative visualisation than positive thinking. Through the creative visualisation process, we learn more about ourselves, who we are deep down inside. We begin to know and understand our eternal selves. We start to see patterns in how we feel and react to ourselves and what attitudes and behaviours have been keeping us from success. Recognising these views is the first step to changing them and improving your life!

Creative Visualisation for Manifesting
Creative visualisation is not difficult. Like other forms of manifesting desire, you must first relax. Find a comfortable sitting or lying position and exert your will on your consciousness. Try to feel each part of your body in a body scan, which will relax you by increments. Start with your toes and notice how each part of your body feels until you reach your head.

Take deep slow breaths as your body relaxes even deeper. In a few minutes, you will feel a sense of deep relaxation. This is very similar to mediation discussed in more detail later this book.

Next comes the work. If you have difficulty creating your mental picture at first, do not let it concern you. Once you are fully relaxed, create mental images of things in your every day life, to 'prime the pump'. Then you can change these images to those that you wish to manifest.

Practice
Imagine yourself doing things you enjoy. Perhaps you can imagine yourself at your favourite park or sitting with someone you love. Practice runs help you ready your mind to do the real

thing when the time comes. Beginners may wish to try practice runs several times before trying their first real visualisation. When you are ready to perform creative visualisation for real, there are a few things you should do.

Take the time to decide what it is that you want. Perhaps there is something you want to change about yourself, like finding a better job. Choose your goal, preferably one that is emotionally easier for you to believe you can attain. When you become better at this, you can choose any goal at all.

Next, imagine the goal you wish to achieve or object you wish to attain exactly as you want it. See yourself having accomplished the goal or using the object. See every detail very clearly. You might wish to draw the scene to reinforce the visualisation in your mind, though this is not a necessary step.

Now that the image is fixed firmly in your mind, think of it often. You do not need to be meditating to think of it, just be sure to come back to your mental image several times throughout the day. In doing this, you are sending our positive energy to the universe. Send as much positive energy as you can whenever you can since the energy you send comes back to you as reality.

Finally, you should have absolute faith that the object is already yours. It belongs to you and you alone. If you have any doubts about this, you are sending negative energy that can block the reality from appearing. And when your desires do materialise, it is vital that you give thanks to the Cosmos and to yourself for making it happen.

Make it Happen

You might think that Cosmic Ordering needs nothing to help it along. This impression can easily be picked up from many books on the subject that suggest you only need to decide what you want and wait for it to manifest.

While some people do have success getting just what they want this way, it does not always work that perfectly for everyone. It is quite possible that you have read about Cosmic

Ordering before and tried it without success.

You may have heard of the Christian saying that 'God helps those who help themselves.' Well, part of this saying is absolutely true.

To tune into the proper frequencies for manifesting abundance, you will need to make some changes for the better. Many have emotional obstacles that must be dealt with before they can see abundance working in their lives.

It could be that you need to learn a few things about life before the process can work for you.

Know What You Want

Prepare a list of the things you want and take your time about it. These are just things you think might make life happier or more meaningful. Getting rich is often high on many peoples' list of wants because it provides a level of freedom in life.

Now take the time to jot down WHY it is you want these things. Take time to reflect and be honest with yourself about your reasons. Journal the real reasons you want those things, including the logical and illogical emotional reasons.

Those things that you want for your own pleasure and happiness are true wishes, but if your motives lie in competition or the desire to control others, be cautious. Wishes fuelled by negative emotions tend to backfire. You may get what you wanted but the Cosmos will be sure your experience of it is not as pleasing as you would hope.

Select those goals with positive reasons underlying them. If you want a sports car because they are fun to drive, great! The universe wants you to enjoy life. If you want one because your neighbour just got one, not so good.

When you spend time reflecting on the true motivations behind your dreams, you will learn much about yourself. You might find that some of the reasons you once had for wanting something no longer make sense. Such wishes can be removed from the list. If you find the thing is really wanted to substitute something else missing in your life, cross it off and instead

102

write what it is that you really need.

Once this is done, you will have a clear list of those goals that are important to you in life. These things will give you a happier, more satisfying life. Now grab that pen again to add details to your wishes. Do not be surprised if you ask for a new car, without putting in details, and end up with something that is not quite what you wanted.

If it is a new job you want, write down what job title you want. Where will you work everyday? Imagine yourself in the process of doing the job. Indicate the salary you seek. If it is a new home you want, describe exactly what it will look like, how many bedrooms, bathrooms, etc. Write down the size of the yard, if it has a garage, how big that garage should be. Include the house's location, whether it be city or country. Create the image in your mind of exactly what the house should look like, room by room. These details will build the foundation work for the realisation of your goal. You will transmit this blueprint to the Cosmos.

Journaling – Cosmic Ordering Wish Book

An abundance journal is an excellent way to track your wishes and keep focused on them. Just as writing down your Cosmic Orders helps you know what it is you want, journaling helps you reaffirm those desires. Writing it down turns it into a solid contract between you and the Cosmos.

It is a good idea to keep your abundance journal private, simple and detailed. Each day you should set out your wishes to reaffirm and reinforce them. As your desires change, you can easily make changes. Perhaps you need to revise details or better yet, one of your goals become real and needs to be removed. Do not forget to thank the Cosmos in your journal!

I give those attending the two day workshops I hold a nice spiral bound book, it has ruled pages and a nice cover with the title on it. However, a blank notebook will suffice for this, although something more robust might last. You can write in it, stick things in or even actually type up and print out forms and sheets and stick them in, the choice is yours, and it is YOUR book.

The point of these pages is to help you get clear about what you really want and enable you to give thanks that it is now on its way to you. Once your book is set up you can begin filling it. Begin with small Orders first and watch your confidence grow as you achieve them. Write your Order as if you were Ordering it from a catalogue i.e. 'A new digital camera', 'Good health always', etc. Then put the date you wish to receive it. Remember, that you are asking for 'This, or something better' so the universe may decide to send your Order sooner or later than you requested. Do not worry about this. Just put your approximate date.

Do not begin by Ordering too much at once, otherwise you will get confused and it will seem like a lot to have happen. Just stick to a few simple things to start with.

Terms & Conditions
The actual Orders you might like to hand-write in as you go along. At the front of the book on the inside left, you could stick in a sheet, which can be called my 'Terms & Conditions'. Here you could put 'I ask that all these things or better come in wonderful ways and for the benefit of all.' This allows for something even better than you had imagined coming along, allows it to come in wonderful ways, and also ensures that everyone will benefit from your Orders. Of course, you can create your own 'Terms & Conditions'.

On the front right and the next few pages, you might want to create tables with three columns each. The first (widest) column could be labelled 'Order', the second column could be labelled 'Send By' and the third column could be labelled 'Order Received'.

In the first column, write your 'Orders' i.e. 'a new mobile phone with all the whistles and bells'. In the second column, write a date when you would like to receive the Order by (usually just the month and year, or 'ASAP' if it's urgent.) The third column, only fill in when your Order has been delivered. Put a short date in there and a lovely glittery star or heart sticker to acknowledge receipt of your Order after it's arrived.

Gratitude Sheet
In the middle of the book, perhaps you might want to create something like a 'Gratitude Sheet'. On it you could put: 'I willingly accept all of these wonderful things with a grateful heart and give thanks for the good they bring and for their presence in my life.' You could write your own 'gratitude statement'.

Orders Fulfilled Table
You could create another table, an 'Orders Fulfilled' table. This one only has two columns, 'Item' and 'Date Order Received'. In here, write whenever something wonderful or unexpected happens or when you receive an Order. Sometimes wonderful things come about which we haven't even Ordered and it is lovely to acknowledge and be grateful for those too. If you did not have these 'gratitude' pages, you would not have anywhere to write them.

At the back of the book, you could write a couple of pages about your main Order. Write it as if it were already manifested and write down all the reasons you feel excited, happy, etc, and what you are doing now that you have fulfilled your dream. You could use this section to describe the kind of life you want to live, or the main relationship in your life, or even describe yourself in the best of health. Remember to phrase it positively. You want to be asking for what you want, not what you do not want, otherwise the universe will simply deliver that.

Remember, this Ordering is not just for 'goods'. You can ask for information, guidance, even help with relationships or health. If you are having doubts, you could always ask for faith in the process or even that your Cosmic Ordering should always be successful! If you make your book really beautiful you will enjoy looking at it each morning and evening and this will help to reinforce your intentions and remind you of your Orders.

Some authors say we should just place our Order and forget it, but how, I wonder, will we know if our Orders are being fulfilled, if we have forgotten we Ordered them in the first place?

When an Order 'arrives' put a bright sticker or big tick next to it and then add it to the gratitude table. Also add any other lovely things that happen to you there. When you read this through, you will feel good knowing that great things are happening for you and it will reinforce your ability to allow things into your life and enhance your Ordering potential.

Manifesting Board

Writing things down neatly in the Cosmic Ordering Wish Book appeals to your left-logical brain, but you might also wish to use a cork board and stick on it, write, and draw or print out pictures of your desires too. That way, you are appealing to your right-intuitive brain as well. That side of your brain, which loves colour and imagery.

The 'manifestation board' I use sits in front of my desk so that when I am working, I can look up at it and imagine myself receiving/using the lovely things on it. That way, I am constantly aware of how the universe is working for me to help bring my desires into my life. Perhaps you could create a manifestation board, too...

Now leaf through your Cosmic Ordering Wish book once or twice a day, look at your board, and you will have a constant reminder of all the good the universe is sending you. Try and get the 'feeling' that what you want is on its way. Become excited at the prospect. It is the 'feeling' that helps create your desires as much as anything.

The universe may also require some help from you to fulfil your Order. Once you have placed your Order, be willing to act on any 'hunches' or ideas you have. These may lead you to the fulfilment of your Order. A general rule about this is, if it feels good and right, do it.

It is not really ideal to 'pretend' that you already have your Orders, because, somewhere deep in the back of your mind, you will be saying 'rubbish!' and this will work against you. It is better if you just take the attitude that it is coming to you now.

Please do not give up. Too many people wait ages for things, then, just when the universe is about to deliver, they give up and proclaim, 'This stuff doesn't work.' Well, you can probably tell me what happens next! Yes, you are right. It does not work! If you can take the attitude that the things in your life now are a result of your past thoughts and that, from today, you will gradually begin to change your thoughts and ideas to more positive, uplifting ones, you won't go far wrong.

As each 'Order' manifests itself for you, you will become more and more positive and happy, which, in turn, will create more and more positivity and happiness. Oh, and remember to always Order within the bounds of your capabilities.

Focus on Your Wishes
Now that you know what it is you want and have formulated a clear and detailed image, find another sheet of paper so that you can make your wish more personal.

Affirm what YOU want. Before each wish, put down the words 'I am' or 'I have'. Using the Cosmic Ordering system successfully means communicating in the present tense.

What about Dates?
You may have heard advice suggesting it is best to write down the date by which you want your wishes fulfilled, but others find that this too suggestive of a potential future, rather than a reality that has already formed but not materialised. If you must have something by a certain date to attain happiness, then still keep words in the present tense.

Do not worry about grammar. Try something like, 'I have a new car by 8 March'.

Cosmic Ordering: You Can be Successful

Dates can create differences of opinion in Cosmic Ordering. While some believe time varies, sometimes moving swiftly and sometimes slowly.

Trusting in the universe requires that the universe knows when the best time is for you to receive your wishes. It could be that there remains some internal work to be done before your wishes can find the path back to you.

Remember that so many potential futures exist for you right now, waiting to be realised. By giving your absolute focus on the one you want, that reality become more likely to materialise. In abundance creation, you are cultivating the future.

Meditation

Meditation is not just for yoga practitioners or for when you are in a retreat. It requires no special posture, physical technique or distant location to be successful. Meditation just needs a little time every day, about ten minutes, fit anywhere in your time schedule that works for you. Meditation is important in forming abundance-creating positive energy and a relaxed mindset.

The process of meditation creates an inner journey, helping you to find yourself. It is a gift you give to yourself, a moment of peace and space for the daily grind. By practicing stillness of mind, you free up energy to act on abundance creation. Meditation creates a direct link with the Cosmos by letting you focus and tune in to the proper frequency.

Meditate in a quiet place, away from noise and distraction. Create a space in your home that is specifically designed for your meditation. Turn off the phone and put up a 'do not disturb' sign. Be sure you make the space comfortable. By making time and space for meditation, you are investing in yourself and your well-being.

Remember to start a meditation with relaxation techniques. Close your eyes and feel the tension release as you perform the body scan. When you reach a state of deep relaxation, focus on the natural flow of your breath, in and out. Whether your mind is still or if thoughts are swirling, you only need to acknowledge that state. See the thoughts, notice them, and let them go. Accept random thoughts as part of the workings of your mind, which you are here to witness, not to control or change. With practice, you will learn to find and maintain the still spaces in your mind that reside between thoughts.

The idea of sitting and not thinking might bore you. You can try Tai Chi instead, which is a form of moving meditation. Walking meditations also work to calm the mind with motion. When you become accustomed to the route you walk, you can let your mind shut off while your body takes over. Some even choose to mediate during a massage or during a reflexology treatment.

Mind Chatter

Silencing your mind long enough to experience meditation is the most difficult hurdle to meditation. Some people might say it's the only hurdle. Regardless of how long you have meditated, there are still frustrating days when you just can't quiet yourself enough to reach a meditative state. It helps to have a suite of tools you can use to calm mind chatter.

Over the years I have accumulated a large collection of 'mind' tools. I learned correct breathing techniques (pranayama) during a Himalayas trip.

When silencing the mind chatter, try out different techniques and find which one works best for you.

I find pranayama exercises to be very effective in quieting my mind. Not only that, I will often drop into a very deep meditation without even realising it. It costs nothing and it can be done anywhere. There is a lot to like about using pranayama to silence the mind before entering meditation.

Sometimes, no matter how hard you try, you just can not shut your mind off from thinking regardless of what breathing techniques you try. This is why I am developing my own guided meditation audio CD. Okay, you might say it is lazy to just want a meditation technology CD to do all the work for you, but perhaps you might have a specific meditation application that requires a guided meditation script read to you by your favourite mentor.

There are many meditation paths and techniques, try out the pranayama techniques that follow. I would suggest attempting them more than once if they do not work at first try, but it is your path – do as you wish!

Ujjayi (pronounced oo-AH-gee) is the breathing used during ashtanga (pronounced ash-TANG-gha) yoga and for many pranayama exercises. To perform Ujjayi breathing, prepare by opening your mouth wide, stick out your tongue, and start to take a deep exhale.

While still exhaling, put your tongue on the roof of your mouth and then close your lips. Notice that the air is bypassing your mouth and flowing up your throat and out your nose. Keep your tongue position and lips closed while you inhale.

The reverse sensations will be noticed while the air flows back in through your nose and your throat into your lungs. That is the Ujjayi breath. It can be somewhat noisy but if it is, that is an indication of a strong Ujjayi breath.

If that does not work for you, deep breathing with your mouth open might provide a somewhat less appealing alternative. Add these pranayama techniques that follow into your meditation tool kit for silencing the inner chatter of your mind.

First Pranayama Technique

Simple focused inhale and exhale. Close your eyes while doing Ujjayi breath. Inhale at a natural comfortable pace while focusing your attention on following the air flow. Feel it hit your nostrils, back of nose, down throat, into lungs, expanding stomach.

Exhale naturally and feel belly lower, air comes up from lungs, flows past back of throat, up and out of nostrils. Continue doing this without any counting or anything else until you no longer feel like doing it.

Sometimes you can be off into a deep meditation just from this technique. If not, move on to the next technique.

Second Pranayama Technique

Inhales and exhales with paused delay. In this pranayama technique, you will breathe as you did in technique #1. However, your inhales and exhales will be a 5-count in length. Count as follows 1001,1002,1003,1004 and 1005 while inhaling and exhaling. This may take some practice to correctly measure out your breath.

Once you are able to focus on your count while breathing, add a 3-count hold of your breath at the top of your inhalation. So in your mind, you are now counting while deep breathing as follows: inhale 1001,1002,1003,1004 and 1005, hold 1001, 1002 and 1003, and exhale 1001, 1002, 1003, 1004 and 1005.

This will become methodical and rhythmic. Now add an additional 3-count breath hold at the bottom of your exhalation. Breathing is now: inhale 1001,1002,1003,1004 and 1005, hold 1001, 1002 and 1003, exhale 1001, 1002, 1003, 1004 and 1005. Hold 1001, 1002 and 1003, inhale…keep repeating.

You can get lost in this one for quite some time. Perhaps use a timer or an alarm clock and try technique #1 for 5 minutes and technique #2 for 10 minutes.

The state of your breathing is closely linked with your mind state. If you breathe from a lower space in your body and at a slower pace, you will gain more control of your mind, making your thoughts easier to hear. Learning to relax with your breathing will put you in a state that makes you more open and available to receiving your desires. You can practice this by paying close attention to your breathing, being sure to breathe more slowly and more deeply throughout the day. When you learn to slow your thinking and to control your breathing and body movements, your mind will eventually pause, creating a space of infinity. This is where you can find the infinite Source. Here you will make contact with your internal supernatural power.

When we spend the day in a state of relaxation, at a peaceful pace, we learn to truly utilise the power and intelligence of the eternal now. This week, experiment with doing everyday activities like walking, eating and talking at a slower pace. When talking, pay attention to how you enunciate your words. When driving, realise the speed limit is a maximum, not a minimum. Slow down and enjoy the drive. By practicing living at a slower pace, you will create a deeper sense of relaxation, awareness and joy.

Decelerate Mind Chatter
Because it is vital that we still the constant chatter of the ego to manifest our desires, a daily meditation practice becomes essential in training the mind and decelerating mind chatter. Practice meditating every day by focusing on your breathing to quiet and strengthen your mind. You will learn to have more control over your thoughts with regular practice. Once you teach yourself to be master over your mind, manifesting happens for you instantly. The better you become at remaining focussed on your breath, the more quickly your desires become realities. There is a direct proportional relationship between the time you spend meditating on your desires and the speed at which your desires are manifested. Remember, you are made of the same beautiful consciousness as the infinite universe. Learn to master your thoughts so that you can be a closer companion to the seat of universal consciousness within you.

6

Cosmic Ordering Principles

Once you become skilled at manifesting anything you desire, what will you create? Getting into a manifesting routine will help you acquire this skill more quickly. The routine is a set of actions you perform to increase the energy frequency of your thought vibrations. By thinking positively and feeling as though you are an unstoppable manifesting machine, amazing things will happen.

Everyone has the innate ability to manifest their desires. You are biologically and spiritually wired to co-create your life. However you focus your thoughts, they return to you as reality. Your everyday thoughts, feelings and attitudes are always attracting their content.

The science of manifesting is thousands of years old. This ancient practice will show you the way to opening an Unlimited Source of Energy sleeping inside you. In fact, the only reason you are not manifesting at this moment is because the power is dormant, waiting to awaken.

Your mind is like a communications tower. It is always sending signals of different frequencies, which travel out from your brain into the entire universe. Working together, your thoughts and feelings create the direction and propulsion energy to bring the signal of your desires out into the Cosmos. That vibration is reflected back to you by the universe in the form of physical realities in your life.

It is important for you to understand that Cosmic Ordering has nothing to do with 'blaming the victim'. It is about changing your life so that you get good things back from the universe. Cosmic Ordering is based on the idea that each person can communicate with the Cosmos to communicate his or her desires, making them become realities.

You may have heard some twisted versions of this theory which have arisen in recent years. Some even go so far to suggest that horrific events occurring in your life are a result of the Law of Attraction. This law states that both your conscious and unconscious thoughts dictate the reality of your life, even when you are not aware of it. This law alleges that you only need to truly believe in something to achieve it. It says that by putting strong focus and thought on something you do not want will make that happen. This 'blame the victim' mentality is unkind, incorrect and can lead to dangerous consequences for those who have contracted serious illnesses.

It is wholly unfair to claim that those suffering from serious illness or mental disorders chose such a situation for their lives. How can anyone say that infants born with a defect brought it on themselves from some past life? Such absurd reasoning should be squashed with haste. Although the Law of Attraction is one of the theories that underlie Cosmic Ordering, Cosmic Ordering is an actual practice that rejects the idea of victims being to blame for their own suffering. Pay no attention to those who would twist the beautiful power of Cosmic Ordering by wording the Law of Attraction incorrectly.

Clearly, the things that you focus on most, in conjunction with true emotional desire, will manifest in your life. You will learn to train your mind and body to function at energy frequencies that resonate with the Cosmos. Cosmic Ordering ONLY attracts positive things, people and experiences into your life. There is no danger that Cosmic Ordering could bring bad things to you.

Even though you will learn to maintain positive thoughts and feelings, you will still need to counteract the accumulation of negative energy stored in your body. A powerful system is needed to break the negative influence of past situations that cause you to repeat harmful patterns in your present life. The daily manifesting routine will help you to raise your vibrational frequency, making you supremely powerful to manifest your desires.

Negative thoughts and feelings that damage your life have a cause and can be reversed. By learning to think at higher frequencies, you will gain a clear mind, an understanding of your life's mission and a consistent focus on your dream life for sustained periods of time.

Manifesting Vibration

Your mind and body tend to vibrate at a basic bio-magnetic frequency known as your manifesting vibration. The higher frequencies of manifesting vibration easily and instantly draw towards you the thing, persons or experiences you wish to have. Lower vibrations still attract good things for you, but at a much slower rate.

Fear tends to bring down vibrations to lower frequencies. These fears stop you from realising the ideal outcome in relaxed confidence. Higher vibrations are filled with happiness, thankfulness, and a lust for life!

Cosmic Ordering Reworked

The fundamental theory behind Cosmic Ordering states that all you have to do is ask the Cosmos and wait for your request to be fulfilled. Still, thousands try this and often fail. Despite a flood of books on the subject, the excitement died almost as soon as it rose because most people could not find a way to make manifesting work for them

I too was drawn to the mystery of the claims these books made, although I must admit that I have not read any of them. I have acted on feedback from my Cosmic Friends and reviews. I did not understand how the universe would respond with precision in a caring, kind and timely way. However, I did see that there were people succeeding at the method. I began to wonder why it worked for some and not others.

With this in mind, I began gathering evidence to understand how the process worked. After poring over this matter, I suddenly realised that the universe was not granting wishes. It was presenting opportunities. It was then up to the requestor to notice and act upon those opportunities. If this is true, then the entire concept of Cosmic Ordering needed to be reworked.

Not only that, but this reasoning explained more clearly and logically how Cosmic Ordering truly functioned. I had found a solid basis for logic that would allow me to create a method to Cosmic Ordering that could be done by anyone.

Understanding this fact will help you to see that you are not seeking the love and caring of the universe. You are looking within yourself, training your mind to recognise opportunities when they arise. Think about someone at home asking you to retrieve something you have never seen before. Until they describe it too you, you flounder about the room looking aimlessly, even though the object is right in front of your eyes. Once you know you are looking for something, let us say 'red', it appears instantly before you.

Consider the multitude of opportunities presented. And since the universe is huge and immensely complex, the opportunities can be presented in any manner of ways, but we must train our minds to know what to look for. We need to teach ourselves to look for that 'red'.

The Cosmos is like a vast, powerful river of ideas, people and opportunities. This river is always flowing by you. Learn to spot the opportunities and pluck the realities from the river.

By applying a simple process to the way you communicate with the Cosmos, you can make your Cosmic Order and then be ready and able to spot the opportunities. To clarify how this works, I will go back to the classical concept of Cosmic Ordering.

Cosmic Ordering Basics

In Cosmic Ordering, we place a request and send it out into the Cosmos. We believe whole-heartedly that the universe has infinite power and energy to transform our thoughts into reality. We then wait for the Cosmos to make a decision on our request and then accept whatever it offers.

Cosmic Ordering Principles

While researching this, I realised waiting for the universe to decide if it will grant your wish is problematic. The universe is indifferent emotionally. It presents opportunities and solutions in a passive way, not as a finger-pointing god that says 'yes' or 'no'.

Looking at it this way, we see why so many failed at Cosmic Ordering. Traditional concepts of this technique left everything up to the universe, omitting the most important part of the process. YOU! By leaving out your role in all this, traditional Cosmic Ordering leaves too much to chance. However, the entire reason people use Cosmic Ordering is to ensure their lives are not subject just to random luck. We want power over our lives.

There is nothing wrong with leaving your future to chance, but if you want to lead an exceptional life, you will want to understand these principles. Personally, I want to lead an exceptional, positive, successful life. If you feel the same way, you will want to understand how the combination of your conscious and subconscious minds, work together to play the active role needed to achieve reliable results.

I do not believe in 'magic'. I believe Cosmic Ordering works for a much simpler reason.

The Real Cosmic Ordering Power Principles

Many claim to have created a new way ahead for Cosmic Ordering, but my own Cosmic Ordering Power Principles take Cosmic Ordering a step further. In using this technique, you first make a request. You focus intently on the request and imagine many potential ways it might come about. This sets in place a 'trigger' in your subconscious that will be activated when the right solution presents itself. Passively, the universe will show us a multitude of possible solutions. Your subconscious will recognise the opportunity and urge you towards action.

This method is an improvement over traditional Cosmic Ordering for many reasons. It is simpler, more sensible, and it

117

relies on specifics. The method can be tested and refined and is easily taught in one set of guidelines that work for everyone. The method also explains why Cosmic Ordering has not worked for some people.

Some people have a natural propensity for seeing solutions when they arise. We often hear of people who can think of 'creative solutions'. These people are not actually creating the solution. They are recognising a potential reality and making it come about. Still, anyone can gain more skill with practice because it is no different than any other acquired talent.

You will learn how to use these principles to learn how you can set triggers to help you recognise solutions. Those with a natural talent for it may not need training. However, I believe a little guidance will be helpful to anyone, even those who have placed successful Cosmic Orders in the past because it will help even experienced practitioners hone their skills. Cosmic Ordering principles often mean the difference between Cosmic Ordering being only mildly effective or working so strongly it seems to be on supplements.

Until now, no one could provide an adequate explanation for why Cosmic Ordering worked, much less why it worked for only some people. By showing you the precise mechanisms at work in Cosmic Ordering, you will learn exactly how it works and how you can use it daily to instil immediate positive changes that will last a lifetime.

Positive Thinking Power

Positive thought has the strength to cause diametric shifts in the energy around you to cause good things to happen to you. This is the theory of the power of positive thinking. A great many people have faith in the power of positive thought. There are also many who see it as babyish New Age pop psychology. What has always fascinated me is that they are both correct!

Positive thinking is essentially a system of beliefs. Whether you believe it can work or you think it is a load of baloney, you are right. For those who do not believe in positive thought, there is a catch 22. How can you challenge your doubts if you are unable to believe in positive thought to try it out? Those who are willing to give it a try need not worry that they will be shut out from the benefits of positive thought. They only need to start small.

Once you begin to see positive change, the power of positive thinking will grow in your life like Jack's magic beanstalk. You may believe positive thinking is rubbish now, but when you give it a chance, you will be amazed at the power it holds for you.

I think of it as less of a theory and more of an infection disease! Have you ever noticed how fear is catching or how anger can spread through a crowd, causing a riot? Positive emotions spread just as well. One smile leads to another and one kind word is passed on the next person. Fortunately, good feelings spread much faster than negative ones. Notice how tension can be broken in an instant with a funny joke. When someone laughs, all negativity scatters. If you get a nasty email, unless someone else is there to break the tension, the negativity will sit with you for hours until a positive influence comes along.

By now there are at least strands of belief in your mind that positive thought really works. This is all you need to get started. The next step is to undo the knots of doubt from you mind. I will show you how to take that negativity and mulch it down to pulp, helping you reap the harvest of the loom of life's possibilities.

You are in Control
In starting out, the first thing you should realise is that you are in control of time, it does not control you. Slow down and be in the present moment. All possible futures spring from here, so it is important to stay focussed on the here and now. Being ever-present is the key in the art of manifesting. You may notice that your mind tries to spring forward in worrying about what might happen next, or get caught up in the past mulling over past

119

wrongs. These thoughts only distract you from the unlimited source of power only available in this moment.

All of the Cosmos is contained in this moment. It is like the seed of a plant with the potential for a full grown tree contained within. When you allow your mind to dwell on the past or future, you miss out on the source of all things, connected to everyone and everything. Your mind is more powerful than you know, giving you a powerful tool to create your life as you would have it. When you free your mind from distractions of yesterday and tomorrow, you give the essential core of your power to manifest room to shine through.

Connect to the Universe

Connecting your mind with the Cosmos requires that you accept the presence of the higher spiritual power residing in you. This power is easily accessible to you. You only need to open your mind to receive the ever-present intelligent source that is swirling around and within you.

Become familiar with the direct conscious link you have with this sacred source of creative power. Set aside time every day to sit or lie quietly where you can explore and strengthen this link. When you feel this connection, it is time to ask the Cosmos to bring your desires into reality. When you do it with sincerity, the results will amaze you. Through your daily practice, your relationship with the Infinite will become stronger. You will associate your desires less with your mind and more with your heart.

No Doubt

Patience truly is a virtue. Because you have all the time in the world, be infinitely patient! You will find an understanding deep within you that lets you release your anxiety, fears and doubts. You will realise that you have the choice to maintain the faith and conviction needed to bring your desires to fruition. Discover a deeper knowing inside you that can help you let go of anxiety, disbelief and doubt.

Cosmic Ordering Principles

The universe is a supporting force. When you affirm your wants, it will always be by your side, helping you to achieve your goals. Learn to let go of control and allow the divined intelligence to help you. Everything you have and everything you are was given to you by the universe.

If you begin to doubt, be on the lookout for the sources of your doubt. Are you falling into old patterns? If so, gently redirect your thoughts to a relaxing knowledge that all things come in good time. Connect with the universe through trust in its power and it will instantly grant your wishes. The universe is infinitely patient and your infinite patience will resonate with the Cosmos to bring about the spark that ignites the creative process. Trusting is about surrendering to the universe and letting go of your ego.

Magical Manifesting Mankind

Wherever you go, take a moment to touch base with the knowledge that you are the seed of that potential tree, no matter what your current circumstance. Those with faith can attain anything. Use meditation to connect with the part of your mind that has faith in the universe. Talk with those doubting parts of your mind and communicate your magical power to synchronise with the universe and change your life. If scepticism persists, release that part of your mind. Refuse to let it dominate your thinking and let your divine light shine! The world is a place full of miracles. Everywhere you look is evidence of the universe's mysterious powers. This same magic resides in you and as you develop your connection with the universe, you will see that magic in all things.

Direct Positive Thoughts

Show the universe that you are committed to making your dreams become reality. Do this by allowing your mind to direct only positive thoughts in the direction of your desires.

Connect with the desired outcome in a positive and open way. This means asking openly for what you want but without obsessive attachment. Your positive thoughts tell the universe that these desires are more than just important to you; they are sacred. Think of the difference between a child asking nicely for a cookie or demanding it with a fit!

Asking properly gives superior results. Picture your greatest desires happening in your life, without clinging. Visualise your dreams and assume the picture you create is real! Give sacred honour and respect to your desires, since they are gifts from the higher power within you.

7

Manifesting Zappers

Indifference to your dreams
Too often, we have vague dreams that we fail to feed with love. Indifference to your dreams is the result of a sloth-like attitude, where enthusiasm is only mild and fleeting on occasions when we are entertained. We fall into the easy comfort of daily routines, never truly living, believing that this is all our lives can be. In actuality, the possibilities in this existence are as endless as the infinite universe. When we see all of the tiny miracles created by the universe every day, we fall in love again with the world and with our dreams. To escape this trap, we must give up the comforts of false security and inaction.

Have you ever noticed that those who do what they love for a living seem to be more successful? When we focus on loving what we do and doing what we love, our lives are transformed from the illusions of the mundane into the colourful reality of a richer, fuller life. Each day is a gift, worthy of remembrance. You can overcome this barrier by becoming an active participant in your life rather than a spectator. Do something, ANYTHING, towards achieving your life's dream and you will be moving in the right direction.

Fear
Fear holds you back. It is akin to keeping one foot on the brake while you try to accelerate with the other. Nothing blocks your connection with the manifesting force more than fear. Our fears are nothing more than traces of the negative thoughts and judgements we place upon ourselves. They are based on illusions from the material world. These beliefs were placed by

123

you and can be freed only by you. Let go of your fears and all of your desires will become attracted to you in a way that feels miraculous.

Wild Chattering Mind

When allowed to roam unchecked, the mind is weak and easily distracted. You must practice vigilance in observing your mind's thoughts by keeping focus on your breath. Over time, you will gain control of your mind's wandering and develop the ability to stay focused on your goals. Do not allow your mind to become an untamed jungle, filled with hungry wild tigers, where your only priority is to survive. You can tame your mind easily when you cut down the untamed jungle with your sharp focus.

Self-Esteem

Self-esteem is a relatively new concept in human thinking. The term refers to the idea that we take pride and respect ourselves. This phrase began to be used widely in society during the '60s and '70s, used as a generic catch-all to address difficulties in parenting.

Parents were eschewed for failing to build confidence in their children, accused of creating misery in the adult lives of their children. This new thinking encouraged parents to build and cultivate happy, confident children.

While this sounds good on the surface, as it did to many parents then, the practice overstepped its limits, resulting in children will such high self esteem that they became selfish and irresponsible. Because their parents always put their children's needs ahead of their own, these children grew to be adults that expected the entire world to put them first.

Still, there are other extremes to self-esteem. We are often taught that high self-opinion means vanity and selfishness. This seems counterintuitive to the idea that we should put ourselves ahead of others. So what is self-love? Is it the way to an inflated ego or a happy life? Many feel conflicted when they praise themselves, feeling guilty for an imagined vanity and have difficulty truly loving themselves.

These conflicts make self-esteem a matter of balance. Striking the right combination of humility and self-esteem, modesty and greed, takes practice. You may need to work hard to accept yourself as worthy and deserving, while still remembering that the world does not revolve around you. Think of it this way: You are a miraculous, divine and sacred being of light and so is everyone else. Your divinity does not make you better or more deserving than anyone else, but it does make you a powerful, important force in the universe.

Drive out Negativity
If you are struggling with negativity or doubts about Cosmic Ordering working for you, then it may be best to start small. It is one thing to assert and believe, 'When I wake up tomorrow, I will wake up the first time the alarm goes off instead of hitting snooze five times and feel sleepy all day.' It takes a bit more faith and strength of will to believe it when you say, 'I will awake tomorrow living an independently wealthy life with a mansion on a hill.' (Unless you are already very wealthy, in which case you might aim to get a small island!)

When you are starting from scratch with positive thinking, you may need to tear down the old and build anew. This means rooting out and disposing of the old negative thoughts and replacing them with more positive ones. This is often a gradual process as the patterns of negativity can build up over a lifetime, becoming deeply engrained in your psyche. When you notice your positive thought creates a positive outcome, you will be braver and more confident. You will see that positive thoughts are not a sign of weakness, but a proof of strength. The belief that good things only happen to other people will begin to fade, being replaced with an understanding that the Universe bends to your will.

Consider what might be keeping you from trusting in the universe. Even positive thinkers sometimes do not wish to relinquish control in their lives to mere thoughts. It is likely that your disbelief is sowing seeds of negativity that are like weeds in a garden.

The best way to be rid of them is to tear them out by the roots. In the following section, you will learn about common stumbling blocks to positive thinking, and how to overcome these obstacles to bring about a healthier outlook on life.

Feel the Pain

Despair, hopelessness and depression can make it exceedingly difficult to think positive thoughts. But the more aware you become of how you are sometimes on the rise from your depression, the more enlightened you will become. Every positive moment presents an opportunity for living your potential.

Each challenge is an opportunity for growth.

If you are going to wallow, why should you do it for long periods of time? If you have not reached the point where you can resolve these feelings, then you can limit them. When you are in despair, set a timer for five minutes and embrace your unhappiness.

Really feel it and hold it. Then move on when the timer rings. This idea is much like emptying the trash. You empty your pedal bin of unwanted elements, wash your hands and move on.

Reaffirm Positive Thought

Clearly, great achievers think differently that the majority. Notice how those who succeeded in any field, whether it is finance, sports, politics or otherwise, did not achieve their goals through negativity.

For this reason, it is vital that you immerse yourself in positive thought, surrounded by like-minded people. Share your positive thoughts with these people. Also share your positive thoughts with yourself by writing down your goals and posting them in a place where you will see them every day.

126

Manifesting Zappers

Power Imagery to Overcome Negativity

The following exercise will help you learn to create and use images, the language we use to communicate with the Cosmos. Words, the substance of your thoughts, are helpful but the true power lies in the combination of images and words together. Creating a power image is the process of visualising yourself in a position of power. Try to think of a time when you felt you were last in a power image position.

Imagine that place in your mind where you feel both empowered and strong. Maybe you remember a time when you held a position of strength in a conversation. This is not power over someone else, but a strength of will inside you.

Journaling is a powerful way of refocusing your mind. Write your power scene with a clear description showing that you live in a position of power in this moment. If you are writing about something that occurred in the past, describe it in the present tense. Feel the sense of power as you write. A first draft can help you gain confidence in the process. Tell the story as it was, then rewrite it for the present. Refer to only your feelings, not those of others who were there. Include your thoughts, perceptions and emotions.

As with any work of art, more can always be added. Develop your 'Power Picture as a work in progress that you can always add to. Whenever you feel that sense of inner strength and power, add to your power picture. By writing about these experiences when they occur, you are opening yourself to further explore your personal power with a deeper understanding and belief in your self. This will help you to understand how you enter your power position and how you lose sight of it. Keep your power picture alive and growing, not static.

Empty Yourself

When writing about your power position, be sure to include all of your feelings, both physical and emotional. Engage all of your senses. Remember smells, sounds, and other physical sensations. Write about the energy, the feelings of your power position to capture the strength of your personal power in words. Show how the power came from within you, not from any external source. While the help that others give should be acknowledged, do it in a way that shows you are grateful for the help, but the power was within you and emitted from you.

Leave your power picture in a place where you will see it often. Perhaps you will keep it in your top desk drawer.

Live in your place of power by referring back to it often. If you find yourself falling into a position of weakness, set a timer and allow yourself the feeling for a few minutes, then shut it off. Be sure to re-read your power position when you are done feeling those negative feelings and find your way back to where you want to be.

Take time to reflect on small changes as you notice them. These are like a trail of breadcrumbs that you follow towards success. Notice incremental changes in your way of responding to life. Reflect on how and why these changes took place. As you practice this habit, you will be able to notice these changes more readily and see that you are always changing, always moving toward your goals. Being aware of your present consciousness shows that your consciousness is always lifting.

Remember that your positive power position picture is your present condition. The past is dead and gone. The present is all. The future is only the present waiting to occur. The past cannot provide hope. Hope resides in the present.

Claim your power by framing your power picture and naming it. Use images to create the picture and words to name it, giving it the creative power that words and images have when used together.

There are numerous Cosmic Ordering zappers, of which it would be difficult to cover them all herein. One of the main ones, self-limiting beliefs, I cover later on in this book.

8

Unlock Affirmation Power

Power of Positive Thinking

Before success becomes a reality, it begins as a state of mind. Your experience is determined by your thoughts. Life is what you make of it. Your true greatness resides in the knowing of an honest purpose, based on a fair assessment of your self worth. To understand why this is so, consider that you act upon your beliefs. Actions are initiated by belief. You will not take action in favour of an idea you do not believe in. Your ideals and actions based on those ideals are held in place by your faith and belief.

When you take action based on your beliefs, you create a subsequent reality. Any action you take creates some consequence. Each action meets with an equal reaction. Whether you start talking to someone next to you in line at the store, take a class to learn a new skill or just open the refrigerator for a snack, the action results in a tangible reaction. The conversation may lead to a new friendship. Your new skill may turn into a new job or hobby. Opening the refrigerator results in finding a snack to curb your hunger.

When we were young, we had dreams and expectations. We imagine things, we keep thinking about what we want to be, what we want to do, what makes us proud and happy and what we will become.

We grew up, and things seemed like having their own way. We accept our success or failures and we move on. The rapid change, the need to do the urgent things, the works, the pressures and the failures, all kill part of our visions.

Things have changed, but they cannot really take away the

129

dreams. We still have to dream on, to visualise our desires, our wants, our vision of our future, even when we are considered too old for such things.

Colonel Sanders started his business when he was sixty, and started the whole successful KFC business. The main thing is not the age - whether being too old, or too young, but it is the desire to dream on, and the courage to realise it.

Vivid visualisation, taking it to sleep, thinking constantly about it, talking about it, planning it, adding all the spices to our dreams will make us a bit closer to the realisation of our dreams.

Entrepreneurship starts with a dream, a simple wish of tiny restaurant operation, or a huge business of real-estate development, or a modest training centre for English education, or just any other self-employed money earning fun.

The ability to dream on is one of the fine qualities of the human race that other species do not possess. So dream on, and put a deadline: make it a giant dream, a tiny one, an old everlasting one, a newfound one, a hobby related one, a change of life one, a religious one, a stupid one, a stroke-of-genius one, or just whatever, just continue to dream on. Then, just go and do it!

Self Belief

The actions resulting in reactions are a universal law and create your personal paradigm. The variable in the equation rests within your inner strength and level of belief. Weak beliefs make you less likely to take the action need to result in your desired reality. If you do not act on your beliefs, you cannot initiate the events that will manifest the reality in your life.

Many have difficulty understanding this concept, making it harder to implement. It is the human condition to repeat old mistakes and resist change, even though we know in our hearts that the only constant in life is change. You may recognise the saying that insanity is defined by the expectation that the same action could somehow produce different results.

Unlock Affirmation Power

Successful, happy people have mastered change. They accept and embrace it. These people have no fear in examining prior failures and determining what changes may create a better outcome. This is NOT the same as repeating mistakes. Such people do not wallow in comfort zones. They know that change requires courage. They have no fear from occasional set backs. They simply dust themselves off and keep going, without doubting the end result or altering their vision of success.

The first step in forming your personal paradigm is creating a clear and precise picture of success.

You must have the ability to see and visualise the end result. The goal must be a singular achievement that you gave great passion for.

When you understand this truth, you can start to shape your reality by taking daily steps towards creating your picture of success. This is not a simple or easy task. If it were, more people would be successful. It takes work, courage and faith. You must have the fortitude to persist in your beliefs, putting aside all negative encounters.

See setbacks as learning experiences that teach you more about how you will attain success. Failure is a strength building opportunity, not a result. You cannot fail if you refuse to give up.

You need not worry about what actions you will take. Once you have a clear and fixed picture of your goal in mind, the actions you take towards that goal will occur naturally. It is inevitable.

All action is initiated by your beliefs and your actions create the reaction of a new reality for you. You will effortlessly begin to see new opportunities and solutions. You will connect with people who will propel you towards success.

Achievement is no big secret. It is available to all at all times. Success results from your certainty in your own power. Your power lies within your beliefs to create and manifest your personal paradigm. So what is your paradigm? What are your beliefs?

131

Cosmic Ordering: You Can be Successful

The Power of Inner Knowing

Humans only use about 2 percent of their brains in active consciousness. This means that 98 percent of your power lies in your non-conscious mind. Your inner beliefs have direct access to the infinite universal powers giving them the strength to produce results.

You may have heard of the terms higher self, wisdom or other terms for this. The point is that the universe created you and all other things. As your creator, this power is on your side and wants you to succeed. When you harness this power to create your life's desires, it becomes easy and effortless. Your inner knowing connects you to the universal power, which simply responds to your desires. Unless you communicate your desires to your inner knowing, it will take on all your beliefs, even the negative ones.

Each time you have a thought or imagine yourself in a situation, you inner knowledge takes on those thoughts and responds in kind. Think of the times each day that you form a mental picture of what you do not want? Perhaps you worried about what might result from a problem and pictured that result in your mind. Your inner knowing receives this image, plus your thoughts and emotions that direct you away from this outcome. These contradictory messages cause much confusion resulting in poor results.

When you direct your thoughts consistently towards the same purpose, your inner knowing clearly understands what it is you want, allowing your action to create the proper result. For this reason, training your mind to focus clearly on your intentions creates results. These consistent messages produce a clear understanding in your non-conscious mind of what it is you really desire. The mind then begins harnessing your connection with the infinite to create your desires.

Instruct Your Inner Knowing

I have already told you a great deal that will help you to manifest your desires, but what I am about to tell you will

132

speed up your results exponentially! You can instruct your inner self on which messages to accept and which ones to reject. For example, you can tell your inner knowing to listen up to whichever statements you start with the words, 'I am' or 'Inner Knowing' and to listen intently until you finish with 'Thank You'. Tell your inner self that all your other thoughts, pictures and images can be ignored. You can tell your inner knowing what to listen to and what not to listen to. This helps you to counteract the negative effects of the unhelpful thought patterns you may occasionally slip into.

Take action by signalling your inner knowing. Tell this part of your mind what signal to act upon and what signal ends the transmission. Communicating with your inner self to take action on only those items you specifically instruct revs the engine of your destiny, giving you speedy results!

This signal is akin to opening the limitless power of the Cosmos to manifest your desires.

A word of caution here: You must have a clear understanding of your life's purpose. Your inner knowing will only respond to requests that fit your purpose. Whether your purpose was created consciously or not, you must be clear on what your purpose is to effectively use your non-conscious mind. If your signals conflict with your life's purpose, the results will be temporary at best.

Your purpose is formed from a combination of you and your inner knowing. Most people create their life's purpose without being consciously aware they have done so. You may need to form a new purpose before you can harness the power of your non-conscious mind.

Your inner knowing has veto power. You should understand that communicating with your inner self is a two-way process. When you communicate your new life's purpose to your inner knowing, watch for subtle signals to see if your inner self approves. You may even ask for a sign so large, it could never be missed. You can ask for feedback on the idea. Does your inner self have ideas to make the purpose work for you both? Perhaps your inner self has some vital information that you must understand before it will accept your life's purpose. You may learn the purpose you selected is wholly unsuited to you and you must try something else. Your inner self is never going to let getting rich be your life's purpose. However, if your purpose naturally results in making money, you are likely to get as much as you want.

Affirmation Power

As you may know, affirmations are positive statements that you read or say to yourself. This simple but powerful technique can be used to help you reach your goals. When practicing affirmations, repeating the same positive statements each day, you will achieve 'affirmation imprinting', which is a way of creating an indelible mark on your subconscious. When this happens, your subconscious mind sees the affirmations as physical realities in your life.

The perceived differences between the world you see and the way your subconscious is being told the world is now will create a tension that stimulates the production of new ideas and solutions. The subconscious mind will seek to match the world you see with the world it understands. While it will feel as though positive changes are appearing magically, it is really just your subconscious mind finding ways to match your current reality with the ideal reality you impress upon it. To use this principle most effectively, you should word your affirmations in a specific manner.

The Power of Affirmation Imprinting

Traditional affirmation statements are personal. Therefore, you use the terms 'I' and 'My'. A proper affirmation could be worded such as follows: 'I am confident when speaking in front of a large audience', not, 'You are confident'.

An Alternative View

When it comes to phrasing affirmations, there are two schools of thought in how to direct an affirmation. Some prefer to direct the affirmation as if it were at another person, 'You enjoy healthy food'. However, I much prefer and have found success with directing the affirmation at myself, 'I enjoy eating healthy food.'

The traditional positive affirmation has its detractors; some prefer to use a method that has to do with using a different voice. For example, instead of saying, 'Every day, in every positive beneficial area of my life, I am increasing my effectiveness, productivity and efficiency by one per cent', you can say, 'Every day, in every positive beneficial area of your life, you are increasing your effectiveness, productivity and efficiency by one percent', or, 'Every day, in every positive beneficial area of his (or put your name here) life, he is increasing his effectiveness, productivity and efficiency by one percent'.

By altering the voice you use in this way, it is thought you feed the part of your mind that cares about outside opinions. We all have a part of us that craves approval and praise to confirm we are on the right track with our personal beliefs. This can fulfil the needs of that part of us. Whether saying 'you', which feels like a direction to your subconscious mind, or saying 'he/she', which feels like outside opinion, you are still feeding the needs of the part of you that cares what other people think. It is worth trying different ways to work with affirmations, and here you can decide for yourself which method you prefer.

Use Positive Statements

The statements must be positive. State your affirmations in a way that supports positive outcomes. Rather than, 'I don't eat junk food,' say, 'I eat healthy meals each day'.

Negative affirmations are ineffective because your subconscious mind sees your affirmations as images. You cannot create an image of NOT doing something. The subconscious only sees the 'eat junk food' part of the statement

135

and reinforces the behaviour. This is why you must see the positive image of eating healthy foods instead.

Your affirmations must also remain in the present tense. While it may seem logical to state your affirmations in the future as in, 'I will eat healthy meals every day,' this sort of statement creates no tension between the current world and the world as you want it to be. This does not create an action that the subconscious mind can take to match up the two worlds.

Also consider that when you say you will do something, it only serves to confirm you are not taking that action now. This matches the image your subconscious holds, leaving it no motivation to change. By simply altering your affirmation to a present tense statement, you create the necessary tension to motivate action by your subconscious. This is crucial information for you to consider when writing affirmations. Now we are ready to put this knowledge to work by performing some exercises in powerful affirmations.

Behavioural Changes

Affirmation Imprinting should be done with a plan. During the planning stage, you want to choose no more than three behaviours you would like to see change. When beginners try to make too many changes, it reduces the chance of any one item becoming successfully imprinted on your subconscious mind. Ideally, you should choose just one behaviour, especially if this is your first time working with this technique. When you begin seeing the positive effects of the affirmations, then it is time to begin another affirmation.

Next, take ten index cards, size 3.5 x 5 inch. Using the guidelines I set out for you, properly write your affirmation in large, bold writing. Place these ten cards around your home or office where you will see them always. Put one by your bed, another on the refrigerator, one in the bathroom and another in your car (you get the idea). Keeping one on your physical person is also helpful, so consider putting one in your pocket or wallet.

Unlock Affirmation Power

When you go to bed at night and when you awake in the morning, repeat your affirmation out loud twenty times. You may feel a slight sense of fear or apprehension when you do this. It is not uncommon to think, 'What if it doesn't work?' Push these fears and doubts aside and just do it. Put enthusiasm into your voice and smile when you read your affirmations. This positive energy will help you create a strong impression on your subconscious.

Do this again each time you see any one of your index cards. Remember to smile and state your affirmations with enthusiasm and faith.

You will know when imprinting occurs because positive changes will appear in your life as if by magic. When this happens, you can then start with new affirmations and continue on. This may seem like a child's game it is so simple, but it has worked for countless people who had the will and discipline to practice this simple method regularly.

Inspirational Affirmations

In some form or another, positive affirmations are included in every self-help personal development plan, and with good reason. These affirmations really work. They are small inspirational notes to yourself that direct the actions of your life. They help you stay focused on your desires so that you are always working towards your goals.

Affirmation Structure

People first starting with positive affirmations almost always make the same mistake. They try statements such as, 'Every day, in every way, I am getting better and better'. Or maybe, 'I am getting thinner every day'. Some might try, 'I am a thin and beautiful person'.

So what's the problem with these statements? They are positive and refer to you personally. So what's wrong here? The problem is that these statements are too vague and abstract. The examples outlined above have no specific value with which to give them power. Consider, 'Every day, in every way, I am getting better and better'. Getting better at what exactly? Delaying your own progress? The affirmation, 'I am getting thinner every day' is too vague as well. Thinner how? Are your bones getting smaller? Your brain? 'Getting thinner' suggests you are not thin now, only reaffirming your lack of thinness. Effective affirmations have specific and tangible properties. Instead, make a statement with a specific value such as, 'Every day, in every positive valuable area of my life, I am raising my success, output and competence by one fold'. Don't worry that this is small. When multiplied daily, it becomes ten fold, twenty fold and so on.

Be True to Your Self

It is important to recognise that straying too far from the truth is lying. Lying to yourself is not a good thing. It's called denial. If you are morbidly overweight and you affirm, 'I am thin and healthy,' you are making a grossly inaccurate statement. It holds no action, no explanation for how why you are becoming thin and healthy. What exactly are you doing about it?

Action Statements

Action is an important ingredient in positive affirmations. No great achievement was ever made without action. Even 'going with the flow' requires action of some sort, because that in itself is an action. Stopping at visualisation is like aiming at a target and never firing the trigger. Never going beyond positive affirmations is the same way. Not only must your affirmations be specific, personal and truthful, they must also contain action. Include an action statement that shows you are taking action, not just wait for something to happen. You can do this by altering your statement to say, 'Every day, in every way, I am taking proactive steps towards achieving my ideal, healthy weight in a motivated and effective manner'.

This is different from 'I am at my ideal weight' or 'I am

getting thinner every day'. They do not address actions on your part, rather they show passive becoming or being. The more detailed statement tells your mind that it is your actions that will achieve the goal, not that you only want to wait for it to happen.

The Sharp Inner Voice

The small but sharp voice in your head that questions you in your statements when you say, 'I am getting better every day,' chirps in with, 'Yeah, right'. You present the affirmation, 'I am opening myself to wealth and abundance around me' and the sharp inner voice replies with 'What are you doing about it?'

When not addressed properly, these attacks can limit the effectiveness of your positive affirmations. To prevent this, you need to make your affirmations 'Sharp Inner Voice-Proof'. There are times you will notice the sharp voice comes at you with a pre-emptive attack. You may notice a thought like, 'I'm no good, I'll never amount to anything.' or 'Who am I kidding? I fail at everything I try.'

This sharp voice does have a good and useful purpose in your life. It is when we allow the voice to become nasty and hurtful that we run into trouble. That voice has saved you from falling for many scams. It has prevented you from unproductive daydreaming. But you must keep the voice in check if you want your positive affirmations to work.

Recognise the voice for the friend it is; maybe not your BEST friend, but a friend no less. Do not be afraid of your inner voice, but see it as someone within your control, such as a child or pet. Listen to what your inner voice has to say about your affirmations. Write them down and then consider re-writing your affirmations to disprove the voice's statement. You can do this by turning your positive affirmations into questions.

One example of this would be turning the affirmation, 'I am at my ideal weight' into 'Why is it important that I must be at my ideal weight?' or 'How can I achieve my ideal weight?'

You may also try, 'What must I do to achieve my ideal weight?' or 'What would it be like, feel like, when I have achieved my ideal weight?'

These questions direct your attention away from potential blocks. They assume you will reach your goal and ask instead what proactive steps are needed to achieve it. These questions work like swords, sharp and pointed, helping you defend your goals from sharp voice attacks.

But creating a properly formatted affirmation is only the first step in the journey.

The Focus of Your Attention

Consistent focus is vital to realising your dreams, questions become a valuable tool in manifesting your desires. The items that receive our attention and focus on a consistent basis gain energy from our thoughts.

Questions are also constructive, leading the mind towards an outcome. They redirect our focus from the problem at hand to the proactive solution we wish to find. Instead of attacking the statement, the 'sharp inner voice' will attack the problem with something that starts like, 'Well, why don't you try...'

The answer to the question does not need to materialise immediately. Your subconscious will dwell on the question until it finds an answer, as long as you pose the question clearly.

To use the analogy of the sword again, a precisely worded question will cut through the problem, opening a path to your spiritual core where the answer is waiting. Look at those first affirmations again and compare them with the missing links we have discussed. Without these vital elements, your affirmations are attacked, stripped or diluted by that sharp inner voice.

In summary, the five missing links from the traditional form of affirmations are specificity, truth, action orientation, inner sharp voice-proof and stated in 1st, 2nd and 3rd person voices simultaneously.

For first-person affirmations only, transform the statement

140

into a question using the words, 'Why', 'How', or 'What If'. 'Why' forms the reason motivating you to accomplish your goal. 'How' focuses you on the action needed. 'What if' puts your focus on the benefits you may reap from achieving your goal.

When you have prepared the three versions of your affirmation, you can repeat them throughout the day by writing them down and keeping them with you. It is best to practice your affirmations in a relaxed and alert state.

Positive affirmations really do work. They will change your life for good by helping you to manifest your desires. In time, you will learn how to create and supercharge your affirmations. You will see how every thought and every word that comes from you is an affirmation. All of your inner thoughts and perceptions are also affirmations. Every action you take affirms your subconscious belief system, helping to shape your current life experience.

Most of us still carry with us some beliefs that we acquired during childhood that are no longer helpful to us. In fact, some of these beliefs may be dysfunctional and harmful. Even though many 'inner truths' are no longer valid or based on inaccurate perceptions, we can examine our feelings to discover the true source of these beliefs so that we can discard them if necessary.

The subconscious mind tends to run on autopilot at times, responding to particular situations with behaviour patters learned early in life. A child who is frightened by a spider at a young age may grow into a woman who has an irrational fear of these insects. In the past, this mechanism helped to ensure our survival by allowing us to respond quickly to danger. We could never jump out of the path of a speeding vehicle if we had to stop and logically reason out every move. Learned responses and reflexes let us respond to danger without thinking about it first. But beliefs that have laid the foundation for other 'inner truths' can be problematic. If the basic premise of our belief system is based on inaccurate perceptions, then all

141

beliefs built on top if it becomes skewed as well.

Positive affirmations can be used as brief positive statements meant to target a particular set of subconscious beliefs, to confront and weaken the negative beliefs and instil positive self-nurturing beliefs instead. It is like 'brainwashing' except that you are in control of which beliefs you wash away. The format of the statements is of great importance.

Never forget that everything you say, think and do is an affirmation. By making your affirmations positive, you can stay focussed on your goals and pay attention to the words and thoughts to keep your affirmations creating your desired future.

How You know Your Affirmations are Working
When you choose to emit only positive affirmations and hold them as true, your subconscious is forced to react in either avoidance or reappraisal. The wider the gap between the positive affirmation and the inner truth as your subconscious understands it, the more likely you will encounter resistance. Your subconscious finds it simpler to maintain its perceived inner truth or avoid change. It will use whatever methods it has available to avoid the challenge. When you state your positive affirmations that are very different from your core belief, notice the strong negative reaction that bubbles up from your centre. Conversely, when you experience an immediate sense of happiness and well-being, your subconscious is resonating with the affirmation because it agrees with the affirmation. When you begin to have this joyful feeling, you will know for certain your affirmations are working!

Do not fret when you feel resistance to your positive affirmations. This is only a temporary condition that you will slowly chip away at with your positive affirmations. You can hasten this process through a few techniques that I will share with you. These techniques will energise your affirmations and strengthen their effectiveness exponentially.

When you finally overcome resistance, your subconscious mind will take another look at the core beliefs and patterns you have been focused on. You may see a swift and fundamental change when this happens. Your inner self will replace the old belief system with a new positive one that can transform your life. If the core belief was deep and supporting other beliefs, all the beliefs built upon that core belief will fall away. Each of the ideas attached to the fundamental core belief will be re-examined in a new light. You may go through a long period of introspection as you sort out all of these concepts.

Sometimes, we need professional help to aid us in examining our core beliefs, especially if there has been serious resistance or trauma in your life. Examining your beliefs is a journey that will help you let go of the past, but the process can be painful and difficult. It is best (and easier!) to have a support system available to help you work through the difficult feelings that will arise.

Positive affirmations will reprogram your mind, replacing negative beliefs with positive ones. They will change the way you think, feel and act, making positive change come easily and naturally to your inner self. These changes will begin showing in your external life as well when you begin to act and react to situations in a new way.

Fast Affirmations versus Slow Affirmations
Some affirmations work from the first day. You will find great joy in stating them. These affirmations will be very effective, causing quick changes because of the positive energy you put behind them. Other affirmations will conflict strongly with your core beliefs, resulting in a negative reaction from your inner self, almost as if the affirmation feels like a 'big fat lie'. When you feel this type of resistance, the affirmation may take longer to work. No one can say how long it may take to resolve the conflict. It depends on several factors including the issue at hand, the depth of the conflicting belief and your personal level of determination. This is the most important factor because it is your determination that creates your inner strength and ability to change.

143

Cosmic Ordering: You Can be Successful

Your readiness to change can also effect how long your affirmations take to realise. Some changes happen instantly, like a light bulb going off in your head. As soon as you can embrace the change you desire wholeheartedly, then the change will happen. For this reason, the question is not how long positive affirmations take, but how long until you will be ready for the changes. This can only be determined by you.

It does not matter what part of your life you wish to change, or what circumstance of birth you are subject to. Affirmations serve to do more than just make you feel good about yourself. You can use affirmations to make real change in your life. By altering your thought patterns and reprogramming your mind as you wish to have it, you will replace sabotaging beliefs with constructive understanding. This gives you the power to write your own story in life!

Everyone uses Affirmations

Believe it or not, everyone does use affirmations, but because 90 percent of the average person's thoughts are negative, the positive beliefs barely get a fighting chance. Negative thoughts diminish our positive ones and sometimes can even overpower them, because we find bad news easier to believe. The negative thoughts arise from and add fuel to our negative inner beliefs. We often have negative thoughts just to validate our negative perception of our selves. When being bombarded by negative thoughts most of the time, people rarely have the strength or determination to break the cycle. They become trapped in their own negative beliefs. The saddest part of this situation is that those negative beliefs are usually false or based on bad information.

You can cut down the weeds of negative thought in your life through positive affirmations. They are more than just repeated statements or thoughts. It is a way of immersing yourself in positive energy, making the choice to be happy instead of frustrated. The more consistently you use and embrace positive affirmations, the more quickly they will

144

change your life.

Designing an Affirmation

Start now by thinking about the areas in life that you would like to change. What improvements do you want? What benefits would you reap? Take the time to dwell on this thoroughly. Write down the most important things you wish to accomplish in a list.

As you review each item on the list, write out some positive statements for each item. These should be made in the present tense. Remember to focus on what you do want by examining the benefits. As an example, if you wanted to have a fulfilling job, you should write something like, 'I have a wonderful job that fulfils me on many levels'.

Writing your own affirmations targets the things that you want in your life and is an excellent way to create swift and lasting change. Sitting down and putting time into designing affirmations for any given situation you have is an ideal way to get the right affirmations for you.

Reflective Affirmations

Your own reflection is one of the most powerful tools at your disposal. Stating your affirmations while looking in the mirror can create more conviction in your affirmations. Look yourself in the eye while you state your affirmations. Show yourself that you really believe it. When you use the mirror to state your affirmations, you magnify the power of the messages you send yourself. If ever you want a truthful answer to a question, look yourself in the eyes and ask away.

Verbalise Passionately

Use passion in your voice when verbalising your affirmations. The enthusiasm and joy in your voice will be very convincing to the parts of your mind that question the affirmation. Also, joy and enthusiasm resonate at higher frequencies, gaining power as they match to frequency of the Cosmos.

Cosmic Ordering: You Can be Successful

Sing Affirmations Out

Singing can help to reinforce affirmations in the most beautiful way. The mind is open and joyful when you are singing. Sing with joy and a fun loving spirit to make your affirmations a reality!

Penned Affirmations

Writing is another powerful tool in positive affirmations. By writing them down, you commit them to memory and make them more real. By leaving written notes to yourself where you will view them often, you reinforce the positive messages you are sending to yourself. You can engrain the message even further by writing your affirmation down on paper 10 or 20 times.

Delivering Affirmations Subliminally

Subliminal affirmations are those that are delivered in a way that bypasses the conscious mind, delving directly into the subconscious mind. You can find tapes and CDs with such affirmations. However, these affirmations are generalised and do not offer any support. This leaves you waiting for things to happen without taking action yourself.

Paraliminal Affirmations

When I produce affirmations in audio format I use what are called 'paraliminals'. These are affirmations delivered separately to each ear, but at the same time. Sounds a little illogical but they are proven to work far better than subliminally. I no longer use subliminals.

Affirmation Bath

An effective alternative is known as an 'affirmation bath'. You can rarely find this technique on your own because it requires other positive thinking, like-minded people to participate. You will typically find affirmation baths in workshops where several people sit around the person receiving the bath and make positive statements about the bather.

This is a truly amazing experience, with multiple voices sending nurturing and loving messages. The multiple voices from all directions become too much information for the mind to process, but the subconscious picks up on all of it.

I use this technique in group work in some of the workshops I hold. For anyone interested in seeking out further information on 'Cosmic Ordering Experiences' on offer then you can find details on this web site:

www.cosmicorderingexperience.com

I make no apologies for mentioning this or using these few lines to plug this, as many have asked me about these one and two day workshops over the time.

Words of Great Wisdom

The Native American Code of Ethics

1. Rise with the sun. The Great Spirit will listen, if you only speak.

2. Be tolerant of those who are lost on their path. Ignorance, conceit, anger, jealousy and greed stem from a lost soul. Ask that they will find guidance.

3. Search for yourself, by yourself. Do not allow others to make your path for you. It is your road and yours alone. Others may walk it with you, but no one can walk it for you.

4. Treat the guests in your home with much consideration. Serve them the best food, give them the best bed and treat them with respect and honour.

5. Do not take what is not yours whether from a person, a community, the wilderness or from a culture. If it was not earned or given, it is not yours.

6. Respect all things that are placed upon this earth - whether it be people or plant.

7. Honour other people's thoughts, wishes and words. Never interrupt another or mock or rudely mimic them. Allow each person the right to personal expression.

8. Never speak of others in a bad way. The negative energy that you put out into the universe will multiply when it returns to you.

9. All persons make mistakes. And all mistakes can be forgiven.

10. Bad thoughts cause illness of the mind, body and spirit. Practice optimism.

11. Nature is not FOR us, it is a PART of us. They are part of your worldly family.

12. Children are the seeds of our future. Plant love in their hearts and water them with wisdom and life's lessons. When they are grown, give them space to grow.

13. Avoid hurting the hearts of others. The poison of your pain will return to you.

14. Be truthful at all times. Honesty is the test of ones will within this universe.

15. Keep yourself balanced. Your Mental self, Spiritual self, Emotional self, and Physical self - all need to be strong, pure and healthy. Work out the body to strengthen the mind. Grow rich in spirit to cure emotional ails.

16. Make conscious decisions as to who you will be and how you will react. Be responsible for your own actions.

17. Respect the privacy and personal space of others. Do not touch the personal property of others - especially sacred and religious objects. This is forbidden.

18. Be true to yourself first. You cannot nurture and help others if you cannot nurture and help yourself first.

19. Respect others religious beliefs. Do not force your belief on others.

20. Share your good fortune with others. Participate in charity.

9

Cosmic Ordering Virtuality

Your mind and body are intimately connected. There is such a thing as synchronicity between your conscious and unconscious minds. The spiritual, mental, physical and emotional aspects of our lives are closely interrelated. This means that keeping a healthy mind and attitude is aided by keeping a healthy body. This makes exercise another important practice in the attainment of your goals.

Do you wonder how it is that past generations maintained healthy bodies even though they rarely went to gyms or dieted? Look at our current generation of overweight citizens in Western society. Despite major advances in nutrition and physical science, they are fatter and less fit. The fact is our bodies' desire exercise, just as they need food. It is a medical fact that people who are physically active are more stable emotionally. They are also far more alert and healthy.

Along with these advances in nutritional and physical science, we have come a long way in developing new, efficient machines to do our work for us. We expend less physical energy in our everyday tasks. Other generations did not have cars, dish washers, clothes washers and the like. They walked everywhere and did all of their housework by hand. Contrast this with your own daily life. Is there anything you do by hand when there is a machine available to do it for you? How often do you actually break a sweat? If you perish the thought of doing manual labour, at least take time to exercise everyday. Choose something you enjoy so that you will stick to it.

There are so many ways to fit exercise into your routine. You can climb the stairs instead of using the escalator. Park far away from the market and walk from the car. Whatever you do, fit it in so that it coordinates easily with your life. While you are on this journey to find your new self, exercise will help hasten you toward your destination. Exercise is part of loving yourself enough to take good care of your body.

Experience it before You get it

Between our thoughts and the realities they become, there is a space where we can give them a test run. Like virtual reality, we can have the experiences that our dreams will manifest before we actually place a Cosmic Order so that we can be sure this is what we truly want.

In actual fact, machines are already being developed and built that actually serve this purpose. Within a few years they will be well established and in regular use.

Researchers in Britain have designed a virtual 'cocoon', made to provide full virtual sensory input, so that one does not only receive visual and hearing signals, but also touch, taste and smell. This is much like Cosmic Ordering Virtuality ... you can have the experience in the virtual world before you get it in the real world.

These British scientists call their effort, 'Real Virtuality'. Innovators have long worked to recreate reality with computers, offering hopes of an alternate reality for those who seek it. This 'real virtuality' is different because it engages all five senses in a very realistic way.

The 'cocoon' was designed based on studies in cognitive neuroscience regarding how the brain processes sensory input. They can mimic the brain's priority pattern for processing these inputs and deliver just the right amount of detail through engineering. They call this phenomenon the *crossmodal attention affect*.

Consider how it is when you examine a thing closely, perhaps listening to a news piece on the radio. Your focus is not on the items in your visual peripherals, but on the sounds entering your ear. By using this information, researchers are creating a VR system that does not attack all the senses at once, but stimulates one or two senses at a time, the way a person would experience it in the real world.

The idea is to put all this information together in a way that makes you believe you really are tasting chocolate or walking through an orchard listening to the birds sing. This virtual cocoon will change the way we interact in business, giving us low-cost, multi-sensory input no matter where our physical bodies happens to be.

Imagine how this would change commerce. If you could touch the fabric of a dress you see on the internet, or lay on the mattress you are looking to buy, how much more likely would you be to buy the item? The sensory input will give us a higher level of confidence in our purchasing decision, allowing us the same input we would get if we actually bought the item in a store.

Other benefits of such a 'real reality' would include the ability to travel to far away places and experience other environments. You could see leopards in a game park in Africa. Your entire family could all go together even though you are each scattered about the globe. You could go to Albert Hall and choose the best seats for a concert. Designers could gain valuable sensory input on a product design before putting it into production. A doctor can examine a patient from far away, although eventually this will be carried out by a machine. You could learn almost any vocation with hands-on experience.

Your energy flows wherever your attention lies at a given moment. The things you think about expand and like attracts like. You may be familiar with some phrases people use to describe the way thoughts turn into reality. They use words and phrases like: all of a sudden, synchronicity, providence, luck, meant to be, fell into place, destiny, karma, and twist of fate.

Remember, the Law of Attraction stipulates that the energy we send out into the universe joins or attracts to energies of the same frequency, resonance or vibration. This law can deliver

151

what is or is not wanted, depending on the strength of the signal you send. You can use Cosmic Ordering Virtuality to intensify that attraction by tenfold or more.

Right now, I would ask you to get up and close the door. Turn off the television or put on some headphones to block out sounds. Once you have secured some peace and quiet, close your eyes and imagine....

What does FREEDOM mean to you? Is it changing jobs or moving to another location? Get a mental image of what freedom would be. Imagine what JOY feels like. What is your definition of ABUNDANCE? Picture it.

Now that you have imagined what these things would be, close your eyes again and make believe you have it already. On the other side of your closed eyes is the dream home, sports car or great wealth you always wanted. Picture living with your soul mate, in a healthy body. Imagine everything you have ever wanted is waiting there for to see when you open your eyes.

Don't just put the picture in your mind, but include the feelings that having them brings. Feel that you already have it, that you truly deserve it. Now I will ask you a question: How many times in the average day do you focus on what you want, coming to this place of full satisfaction? Compare this with how often you think about negative things, about the things you do not have, like 'I need more money; I am fat; I'm not likeable'? I am telling you now that you cannot expect to ever attract the life you want if you are focusing on the bad more often than the good.

Faith in the good will of the universe is empowering. Consider your personal beliefs. Are they limiting you, keeping you from your desires? Those beliefs are the obstacle to attracting everything you ever wanted. Have faith in the universe and the universal power within you!

The thoughts that you empower with your attention will become your reality. Remember that Cosmic Ordering Virtuality works in both positive and negative directions. The direction comes from you, the power from your thoughts and emotions vibrating in resonance with the power of the universe. Therefore, if your focus in on not having enough of anything, you will get more of the same. Consider your current situations, but this time you KNOW that somehow you will come up with enough money to pay your bills. Even if the money is not available at this very moment, it will be there when you need it. You will attract the circumstances needed to acquire the necessary funds. Either the money itself will turn up, or an idea will come up for how you can create the money.

Your word can be as big as you want it to be, or remain as small as your limiting beliefs make it. It is your thoughts that dictate the size of your world, allow it to grow.

If the Earth
were only a few feet in
diameter, floating a few feet above
a field somewhere, people would come
from everywhere to marvel at it. People would
walk around it marvelling at its big pools of water,
its little pools and the water flowing between the pools.
People would marvel at the very thin layer of gas surrounding
it and the water suspended in the gas. The people would
marvel at all the creatures walking around the surface of the
ball, and at the creatures in the water. The people would declare
it as sacred because it was the only one, and they would protect
it so that it would not hurt. The ball would be the
greatest wonder known, and people would come to
pray to it, to be healed, to gain knowledge, to know
beauty and to wonder how it could be. People
would love it, and defend it with their lives
because they would somehow know that
their lives, their own roundness, could
be nothing without it. If the
Earth were only a few
feet in diameter.

Understanding the frame of mind you need to create your reality is the most difficult part of attracting and manifesting your desires. One must be vigilant in putting energy towards positive things, not negative. When you spend time noticing all of the bad things around you, the difficulty is great. This is where Cosmic Ordering Virtuality can be the most helpful. Only using thoughts to benefit from the Law of Attraction is insufficient for manifesting your desires quickly. It is part of the process, but your emotions must be included.

Now I will show you how to use Cosmic Ordering Virtuality to teach you the way to creating your dream life right now!

Deliberate Creation

When you add emotions to positive thought, you attract your desires faster. When you engage all of the senses in your deliberations, you receive what you ask for. When you have a strong desire, coupled with the expectation that you will get it, then you are ready to receive it. This story that follows shows how valuable all of your senses are, even more valuable than the Seven Wonders of the World.

Junior high school students were studying the Seven Wonders of the World. At the end of the lesson, the students were asked to list what they considered to be the Seven Wonders of the World. Though there was some disagreement, the following received the most votes:

1. Egypt's Great Pyramids
2. The Taj Mahal in India
3. The Grand Canyon in Arizona
4. The Panama Canal
5. The Empire State Building
6. St Peter's Basilica
7. China's Great Wall

While gathering the votes, the teacher noted that one student, a quiet girl, hadn't turned in her paper yet. So she asked the girl if she was having trouble with her list. The quiet girl replied,

Cosmic Ordering Virtuality

'Yes, a little. I couldn't quite make up my mind because there were so many.'

The teacher said, 'Well, tell us what you have, and maybe we can help.'

The girl hesitated, then read, 'I think the Seven Wonders of the World are':

1. To touch...
2. To taste...
3. To see...
4. To hear... (She hesitated a little, and then added...)
5. To feel...
6. To laugh...
7. And to love.

The room was so quiet; you could have heard a pin drop. May this story serve as a gentle reminder to all of us that the things we overlook as simple and ordinary are often the most wonderful - and we don't have to travel anywhere special to experience them. Enjoy your gifts!

You may wonder how Cosmic Ordering Virtuality is any different from the Law of Attraction. Well, the Law of Attraction is akin to a boomerang. Whatever energy you send out comes back to you. However, Cosmic Ordering Virtuality is like the Law of Attraction on steroids! It involves knowingly offering vibrations so that you do not create unintended consequences. Most people, unless aware of these laws, offer negative vibrations unknowingly.

Without Cosmic Ordering Virtuality, you must rely on the element of chance that is in the Law of Attraction. If you happen to witness a heart-warming event, you will be happy and send good energy into the universe, thereby getting it back. If you witness a terrible crime and harbour negative thoughts about it for long enough, you will send out negative energy and receive the same in kind. The Law of Attraction is neither good nor bad. It is pure energy, influenced by your vibrational frequency. Because of this, your must learn to loosen up and take things in your stride.

The Law of Attraction without Cosmic Ordering Virtuality puts you in the role of an observer. You focus on your reality as it is now and the resulting vibration is emitted out into the universe. The Law of Attraction sends more of the same back to you.

If you are in debt, you see this reality all around you with calls from collection agencies and demand for payment notices in the mail. You see that you do not have enough money to pay your bills and send out the corresponding frequency as you observe that reality, low-frequency vibrations of fear, worry and doubt. The Law of Attraction brings that negative, 'I am in debt' vibration right back, causing another cycle of low vibrations and being in debt.

I am not saying the Law of Attraction is a bad thing. It can work in your favour or be harmful. But you must understand how the Law of Attraction and Cosmic Ordering Virtuality affect each other.

When using Cosmic Ordering Virtuality, be sure you find a place of serenity and peace, away from distractions. Begin by focusing on each of your senses: touch, smell, sound, taste, sight and awareness. Yes! Awareness is one of your senses. It is the 'sixth sense' and each of us has it, so start using it. Give each one of your senses a warm up by focusing on the sensory input in your environment.

Feel the sensations in your skin from where you are sitting or lying. Feel the pressure of your body weighing down on the chair or ground beneath you. Really FEEL it! Let those touch sensations be absorbed as your awareness begins to awaken.

Next, engage the sense of smell. Notice the aroma in the room or where you are, whether dusty or floral. Perhaps you can smell the remnants of the evening's cooking in the air. Absorb that aroma fully with your sense of smell. Focus on your breathing to let you notice and attend to each particle of smell in the air. Break down the mix of smells into their

Cosmic Ordering Virtuality

separate components. Notice every smell you can.

Now use your ears. Listen to the sounds of your body and breathing. You may here a fly buzzing at a window or a plane travelling overhead. Listen to the sounds of the building groaning in the wind, or the tick of the heater coming on. Absorb those sound vibrations into your body. Embrace the sounds and become one with them.

Use your sense of taste now. Recognise the taste in your mouth. Open your mouth to breathe in and taste the air. Absorb the tastes in the air, letting it come all the way to the back of your throat. Allow it to permeate your deepest self until you recognise the flavour.

Now pay attention to the objects around you with your eyes. Really see what is there by using your inner vision. See things for what they truly are. See them not only as objects for their usefulness, but also for their connection with the Infinite. See beyond your eyes to view the deep energy vibrating within all things. Absorb all that you see into yourself.

When the five physical senses are engaged, your awareness awakens and responds within your creative core to connect with the universe. Now that your link is clear and true, you can place a Cosmic Order by running the mini-mind movie, engaging all of your sense with the words and images. Hear the sound of your new car's engine, smell the new interior, feel the leather seats with your hands, feel the vibration coming through your legs. Feel the air rushing through the open window. Hear the radio playing. Gather each minute detail and include them in the imagery. Because there are so many details to include, it is helpful to use visualisation ahead of time to do a run through before you place the actual Order.

By joining all of your senses and engaging them actively with your imagination in your Cosmic Order, you are practicing Cosmic Ordering Virtuality.

The story of the Round Tuit. Guard it with your life, as Tuits are hard to come by especially the round ones. This is an indispensable item. It will help you become a more efficient worker.

For years we have heard people say, 'I'll do it as soon as I get a Round Tuit.'

Now that you have one, you can accomplish all those things you put aside until you got a Round Tuit!

10

Quantum Linguistics in the use of Deliberate Creation

Now we are getting to the really heady stuff! Quantum Linguistics refers to the patterns of thought that explore issues from many dimensions. It can be thought of as magical thinking. Quantum Linguistics seeks to examine the nature of linguistics and the ways in which the conscious use of language can eliminate the barriers problems present. You may have heard Plato's story about the people who lived in a cave and saw shadows on the wall. Because they had never lived outside the cave, they believed the shadows were the real world. Plato likens this world to the cave, with the images and events we see only being illusions, shadows of reality. The story illustrates how our world is defined by our interpretations of events.

Quantum Linguistics means to study the way thought patterns evolve and to explore the many dimensions or quadrants of a thought process. Our world of illusions is contemplated and perceived by the way we thread thoughts together, creating our lives in the form of thoughts.

This mode of study takes a deep and penetrating look into the nature of linguistics and how we push back the limitations that problems present, by employing skill and consciousness to the words we use. Quantum Linguistics can be thought of as the natural laws governing the flow of language, just as Quantum Physics governs the motions of physical bodies.

The entire field of quantum theory was only discovered earlier in the previous century. Although ancient cultures have been practicing these theories in spiritual form for centuries, we are only now beginning to understand these concepts on a scientific level.

By using language, we create and de-create our collective world. When you speak, you are not only describing your own reality, you are actually creating new and infinite possibilities through linguistics. We are like conductors of an orchestra, using our language to shape and form the infinite energy. Thought radiates out and the electrons become translated into our perceptions.

Nils Bohr is one of the first scientists to explore quantum theory. He stunned the scientific and philosophical worlds with his conclusions. He and his contemporaries examined quantum mechanics and found that the quantum field is the void from which all things sprang. It is the nothingness that the matter and energy of our world are contained in.

Neuro Linguistic Programming (NLP) is at the heart of Quantum Linguistics. The only difference between NLP and 'magick' is that magickal rituals use symbols, while NLP uses language. Quantum Mechanics replaces mathematical equalities with a matrix of all possibilities. This principle can be applied to language as well. We can study the dynamic outcomes of our reality through studying the ways in which all potential words and spellings come out in our language, creating the world we live in.

The science of Quantum Linguistics suggests that our thought patterns are in motion. When you think, 'What would happen if you did?' there are two positives being presented: would (A), and did (B). Conversely, 'What wouldn't happen if you did?': wouldn't (-A), and did (B). The Non-Mirror reverse of that statement would be 'What wouldn't happen if you didn't?': wouldn't (-A), and didn't (-B). We can use combinations of words to create an infinite number of possible realities.

The pattern of language is often directed by shifting negatives and positives in thought forms. Consider the different meanings in these sentences using essentially the same words: 1) What would happen if it didn't have interesting possibilities? 2) What wouldn't happen if it did have interesting possibilities? 3) What wouldn't happen if it didn't have interesting possibilities?

At this point, I'm sure you are wondering what this has to do with you. I will show you how you can use Quantum Linguistics to create the changes you desire in life.

Pick an action you have been contemplating that runs through your head on a daily basis. If you do not have such a thought, just pick something you have always considered doing that you thought about recently. Now we will explore the possibilities inherent in that thought.

What I am about to show you works WONDERS for those who struggle with worry. If there is something on your mind that has been causing you anxiety, be sure to select that. Now use the sentence structures I showed you and examine the thought. 'What would happen if I did do it?' Notice the feelings of joy and hope that bubble up.

Come up with as many thought results as you can in considering the action or non-action. When you have run out of thoughts, ask, 'What would happen if I didn't do it?' Notice how your focus changes. Where do sensations spring up in your body because of this thought? Again, consider everything that might happen if you didn't do it.

Now phrase the question, 'What wouldn't happen if I did?' Once more, you will see shifts in your consciousness as the possible outcomes run through your mind. You may realise that there are some things you just can't expect from the thing you desire.

By spending plenty of time contemplating each question deeply, you will learn much about yourself and your motivations. You will notice how the different possibilities create different feelings inside your body and mind. The more time you spend on this, the more satisfactory your results will be.

Cosmic Ordering: You Can be Successful

Finally, try 'What wouldn't happen if I didn't do it?' You may feel an enormous expansion when you ask this question. Let your mind dwell on this one as long as you have time for. You may see all the things you will miss out on if you choose inaction. This thought can be a great motivator.

Another way to examine the infinite possibilities is to participate in a light and sound session. This is for those who own or use *Light and Sound* Mind Machines. Choose the question you wish to address before you begin. Perhaps you are already in a session and an issue comes up. Use that pattern. When you have the question to ponder, ask the four questions and see what the results are.

These questions done in conjunction with a light and sound session can have powerful and profound effects. You can try playing with the light variables while asking the questions to see what happens with your thoughts and emotions. Some users have reported that a frequency in the Alpha to Gamma range creates quicker responses. Try the questions at slower frequencies as well to see how you respond. I have found some of my best answers using Delta or Theta frequencies in my sessions. I suspect this is because the low frequencies minimise the intrusions of the conscious mind into the thought process.

My experience has been that no exact frequencies affect any two people in the same way. Each person gets different results. However, the general brainwave states have provided fairly consistent results across a spectrum of users.

You can also experiment with closed-eyed and open-eyed glasses. As you might expect, you will tend to find deeper answers to your questions when using the closed-eyed glasses. Perhaps the glasses reduce distractions from the outside world. Open-eyed glasses are still useful in other ways. Both glasses appear to have equal value in the linguistic process, but can produce differing results.

There is no limit to how much fun you can have in playing with the sets of questions. By imagining these different outcomes, you allow your unconscious mind to frolic in the fields of possibility. These questions uncover potential solutions that may have evaded your conscious mind until you asked them. These possibilities raise your level of awareness and help you find solutions to all of your so called problems.

Language guides us through our 'social reality'. It is the limitations and extensions of language that condition our way of thinking about social problems and processes. Mankind does not live wholly in an objective realm, nor does he inhabit merely a world of social activity. We are at the mercy of the language our society uses.

It would be a mistake to think that you can adjust your reality without using language. Language is not just the incidental means of thinking about and solving problems of communication or thought. The fact is that our experience of reality is largely built up unconsciously by the language patterns of a particular society.

Each language is so different from the others that no two languages can represent the same social reality. By extension, we can deduce that each society lives in a wholly different and distinct world. They are not merely residents of the same world with funny-sounding names. This contradicts many of the things we were taught as children. The truth is that people are NOT the same all over.

Consider a poem. How one comes to understand its meaning requires not only an understanding of the individual meanings of each word, but the reader must also understand the significance of the words in relation to one another before he can truly understand the meaning. He must understand the feelings and attitudes of the whole community to understand the suggestions and undertones contained in the subtext of the language.

When you realise that words are actually the given social patterns of a society, you see that even very simple acts of perception are skewed or altered by language. A good example is to examine the NLP term, 'The map is not the territory'. This concept means that your perception of reality may not be in line with the way reality actually is. To put it another way, there is no reality other than the one you perceive.

What you may call 'Out there' is only the view of the world from your specific beliefs, inner landscape, social standing and prejudices. This is more likely to be similar to the landscape of many around you than to be similar to those from different cultures. This means that like quantum mechanics states, the reality is dependent upon the observer.

In quantum physics, we are shown that matter sometimes behaves as a particle and other times as an energy wave. This duality depends on how the matter is observed. We decide which reality we see. Is the matter a thought or a physical reality? Physicists have also shown that the same atom (not two similar atoms, but a single atom) can be seen in more than one location at a single point in time. This means that location is not an absolute. An atom can be in two places at once.

In the same way that beauty is subject to the judgement of the observer, reality appears to behave the same way. By extension, our assumptions about reality may also be questioned as well. Now let me explain how linguistics fit into this puzzle.

Think of the great Martin Luther King and his inspiring phrase, 'I have a dream', and see the ideal example of the ways that language affects and permeates the quantum movements in global awareness. When those words of inspiration emitted from King, all people who heard it experienced that dream right along with him. The signal was picked up and amplified by all who listened. The people experienced this dream as if it were their own and felt a connection with a common cause. There was no more 'we', but a single, high-frequency 'I'. This message of hope holds as much power now as it did when it was uttered all those years ago. That is how strong language is.

Not only is the content of the message important, but also the format. The Obama USA campaign for president understood this when they chose their slogan: 'Change? Yes we can'! Here is another four word phrase filled with positive energy. It is a message that instantly instils hope for all. It creates a feeling of global unity and awareness as it was intended to!

It may be that we close our minds because we look for too much certainty in the life around us. As a way of coping with our fears, we look to KNOW. But this kind of knowing is not useful to us if we are to evolve as beings. Requiring such certainty narrows our perspective and limits the possibilities that we might perceive.

By understanding linguistics and how these patterns can be used to open our minds, we will discover new ways of thinking and solutions that never occurred to us before. This new open mindset reconfigures our brains to make them more resourceful and more useful.

Imagine a world where there is no end to the possibilities that lie before you. Instead of a world with good and bad, where we pick out the good and cling to it, how much better would it be to discover all those possibilities available to use before someone else decides our fate for us?

A blind boy sat on the steps of a building with a hat by his feet. He held up a sign which said: 'I am blind, please help.'

There were only a few coins in the hat. A man was walking by. He took a few coins from his pocket and dropped them into the hat. He then took the sign, turned it around, and wrote some words. He put the sign back so that everyone who walked by would see the new words.

Soon the hat began to fill up. A lot more people were giving money to the blind boy. That afternoon the man who had changed the sign came to see how things were. The boy recognised his footsteps and asked, 'Were u the one who changed my sign this morning? What did u write?'

The man said, 'I only wrote the truth. I said what u said but in a different way.'

What he had written was: 'Today is a beautiful day and I cannot see it.'

165

Cosmic Ordering: You Can be Successful

Do you think the first sign and the second sign were saying the something? Of course, both signs told people the boy was blind. But the first sign simply said the boy was blind. The second sign told people they were so lucky that they were not blind. Should we be surprised that the second sign was more effective?

Moral of the story:

Be creative.
Be innovative.
Face your past without regret.
Be thankful for what you have.
Think differently and positively.
Handle your present with confidence.
Invite the people towards good with wisdom.
Live life with no excuse and love with no regrets.
When life gives you a 100 reasons to cry, show life that you have 1000 reasons to smile.
Don't believe your doubts and doubt your beliefs.
Life is a mystery to solve not a problem to resolve.
Life is wonderful if you know how to live.
Prepare for the future without fear.
Keep the faith and drop the fear.
Each day is as special as you want it to be.........MAKE IT GREAT.

11

Universal Laws

The Law of Allowing

The Law of Allowing represents the principle of taking the least action necessary to bring about a result. You can apply this law to bring the freedom you seek. You can be yourself in your personal relationships and have the freedom to steer your career in any direction you desire. You can create your life in whatever form suits you. This law applies in two ways: there is allowing others to be as they are and allowing the universe to bring us that which we desire.

Consider the ways in which you look at others and the ways they behave. No two people are exactly alike, though they may share traits in common. Each one of us is unique and even twins who have the same DNA have some differences between them. The Law of Allowing means learning to accept, not only tolerate, the differences in others: 'I am that which I am. While I am that which I am, I allow others to be that which they are.'

If you are using the word 'should' in reference to others, you have some work to do before you can apply the Law of Allowing. If you have specific ideas on how another person should think, feel or act, you are not aligned with this principle. Your Perfect Pictures of how others should be can lead to suffering. It can damage your life and your relationships. It is the antithesis of allowing. The 'should' mentality is often based in a habit of judging other people.

Judgment is an emotion that vibrates at low frequencies. The Law of Attraction means that you will attract more low-energy people and situations into your life if you continue to follow this pattern. The need to control others, to make them conform to your vision, often springs from your own negative feelings about yourself. If you do not find a way to release these judgements, you will never have true freedom. Judgement is bondage. When world leaders engage in this sort of behaviour, wars start.

Even behaviours that go against basic politeness can be accepted and embraced. Imagine yourself at the dinner table, watching someone talking with food in his mouth. If you think he 'should' not behave that way, you may be disgusted and irritated with the behaviour.

You have a burning desire to make him stop, but you do not want to look bad in berating him. Now, instead of just accepting and embracing this dining companion's way of eating, you allow negative feelings to eat away at your mood, stealing your freedom.

Just like magnetism and gravity, the Law of Allowing is a fundamental law governing the universe. The law is eternal and all encompassing. It is absolute and applies in all situations. It does not matter if you accept the existence of such laws, because they will influence your life anyway.

The negative emotions that you allow to reside within you are stopping you from receiving the gifts you wish to receive from the universe.

The negative emotions are holding a space where you want only positive emotions to be. When you release your resistance to all things around you, you release resistance to receiving. Let go of judgements and you will be ready to allow abundance, freedom, happiness and all things you desire to enter your life.

Now consider what you have learned about the Essential Universal Laws. Do you see now how they work in unison to create reality? It is a perfect system for allowing all possibilities. It does not limit reality to only one way of being. It allows for all creatures to find happiness, regardless of the circumstances of their birth, as long as they can allow it to happen.

Universal Laws

The Law of Sufficiency and Abundance

There is nothing you need from the external world to reach your dreams. Everything you need is right inside of you. Many of us have developed a false sense of reality, believing the world to have limited resources. To truth is that we live in a universe of abundance, where there are no limits.

Every good thing you want to have or experience is available in unlimited supply. The idea of 'not enough' is an illusion. There is enough of everything in abundance for all. As a society, we have come to accept a lie as truth, the lie of scarcity and limitation.

I am here to tell you the TRUTH that abundance is within you. The limitations you view in the external world are constructs of your own beliefs. The life you were given was provided so that you could enjoy it in any way you choose. Do not cheat yourself by buying into the idea of scarcity, or that someone else's attainments somehow limit what is available to you. You are a being of pure universal energy, represented in physical form. Abundance and well-being are the fundamental building blocks of our universe and of you.

When you base your beliefs on the idea of limitations, you hamper the ability to create your desires effortlessly. The 'lacking' mentality controls your life, keeping you in a negative state of longing and encouraging a sense of competition with others that only serves to limit the possibilities available to you.

It is common for people to feel what they have or what they do is not enough. Don't believe that lie. Now that you know about the Law of Attraction, you should understand that if you believe you do not have enough, that is just what you will get. If you believe you cannot do enough, you are right. If you feel you have too little, you will continue to have too little.

Now you must learn to accept and utilise the TRUTH. You are enough, in fact, you are more than enough. You are limitlessly abundant! Right now, in this moment, you are perfect. You cannot be (right now) anything other than what

169

you are. You are whole, complete and exactly as you are meant to be. If you fail to accept this TRUTH, you will never have enough, nor will you live the full and free life that you deserve.

For a moment, I want you to consider your desires. At what point will you believe that you have finally found the ideal relationship? Will you be satisfied when you have a million in the bank? Will you be happy when you lose 10 pounds? What will tell you that you finally have enough? What will it take for you to feel satisfied? When will it be enough?

By always looking outside of yourself, at the situation surrounding you, seeking it to be more than what it is right now, you fail to appreciate and value what you have been given already. Chasing after external things or events will never satisfy you. There is always something more to do or achieve.

However, when you accept your current circumstance as perfect, as being only that which it can be, you begin to feel the peace of satisfaction. Clearly, nothing could be missing, or you would not be here now. You had enough food to sustain your life. You had enough funds to acquire the things you own. Take a moment to recognise this and be grateful for what you have now, and allow yourself the excitement of the bounty to come, when you will manifest all that you desire. This is how you will find true joy and satisfaction.

Consider the possibilities that will be open to you when you align your thinking with abundance. What if you believe you are enough, that you are worthy? Everything you need is here now inside of you. You have the capacity and ability to create all the wealth you could desire. Everything you need to attract the right job or mate is there waiting to be utilised.

Apply this law right now by being satisfied with now. Do not wait for satisfaction to come from some external source. It will never arrive. Instead, begin here and now. Accept the abundance that is already in your life. Set goals and see yourself already there. Resolve to succeed no matter what. Abundance creation occurs when we become satisfied with the now and excited about the possibilities of the future. This makes it vital that you understand all of the laws, no just the Law of Attraction.

The Law of Pure Potentiality

Pure Potentiality means that our true essence is pure consciousness. All things come from a Source that is pure consciousness and pure potential, looking for expression in form. When you recognise your inner self as a Spirit of pure potentiality, you align yourself with the power that manifests all energy as matter. All things are possible with unlimited potential for creativity.

You know from the Law of Sufficiency and Abundance that there are no limits in the universe. The universe itself and all things in it are unlimited. Limits are artificially imposed by our negative emotions like fear, doubt, and insecurity. When you allow yourself to believe in limits, your ego feels fear and looks for ways to free you from fear, such as money, power or prestige. However, these attainments hold limited satisfaction. If you have great wealth and it is suddenly gone, suddenly you are imprisoned by your poverty.

But when you feel love and faith towards yourself, understanding that you are a part of and made of the same stuff as the limitless universe, all things will be given to you when they are needed, with no limits. When you understand this and align yourself with pure potentiality, you have no fears and can be truly free.

Learn to know yourself and all that is inside you, since the entire universe resides there. Understand that you are the Source and the Source is you. Your understanding gives you access to pure potentiality. This is why meditation is so useful. By knowing yourself fully and just allowing yourself to be, you solidify your understanding of and connection to Source and the pure potential of your life.

You have been connected to pure potentiality in your life, whether you recognise it or not. Any time you have communed with nature, seeing the innate intelligence of every living thing,

171

you were connected to pure potentiality. When you watched a sunset, or absorbed the scent of a flower deep into your soul, you were connected to all things.

Know only love and banish fear. Understand that you have no limits, that you are Pure Potentiality. Nothing is impossible because all things are possible. Align yourself with the Law of Pure Potentiality. You will feel centred and at peace.

Read the following out aloud inside of your head, feel the power of the words as they surge through your mind, allow them to reach your subconscious mind:

I am very powerful!
Whatever I set my mind on having, I will have.
Whatever I decide to be, I will be.
The evidence is all around me.
The power of my will has brought me precisely to where I am right now.
I have made the choices. I have held the thoughts.
I have taken the actions to create my current reality.
And I have the power to change it into whatever I want it to be.
With the choices I make, I am constantly fulfilling the vision I have for my life.
If that does not seem to be the case -
then I am deceiving myself about what I really want.
Because what I really, truly want, I will get!
What I truly wanted in the past, I already have.
If I want to build a billion-dollar business, I will take the actions necessary to do it.
If I want to sit comfortably watching TV night after night -
I will take the actions necessary for that.
Don't be disappointed in my results -
they're just the outward manifestation of my priorities.
I will be sure of what I truly want,
because I am sure to get it!

172

Universal Laws

Be Still for a Minute
Yield to abundance by letting go of all struggles. Let all of your fears, worries and doubts fall under the category of lost causes. You may notice that the direction and purpose of your personal battles is fading, yet you continue to fight. When you let go of those negative feelings, it is like rescuing yourself from quicksand by simply being still and allowing yourself to float. The sense of relief you feel will bring true joy.

Just as you struggle with your fears, struggling in manifesting is a self-defeating behaviour. Do not put too much attachment on your desires. Put them out of your conscious mind.

For this moment, step aside and let the stress flow on its own. You do not need to maintain active involvement in it. It will still be there when you get back. Let go of the 'not having' without regret. 'Not having' is only an illusion of the present moment. In truth, there is no loss, no mistakes, and no problems. All things are perfect. Now you can step back into the flow of your concerns with a clear mind that will work to find solutions, not regrets. Now you will feel more peace, joy and satisfaction.

Struggles Strengthen You
Struggles were not intended to harm or upset you. They are there to strengthen you and put you closer in resonance with the universe. When you put away fears, you embrace struggle, making it no longer difficult to bear. Have no expectations and you will have no fears. When you cling to expectations, you allow fear of failure to create tension and stress. Let go of fears about what will happen. However things turn out, it will be the right result for you. Let go of caring about what happens and you will finally be free of fear.

Stop Waiting
Concentration is the greatest source of your inner power. By focusing all your attention, like a steam engine closing all

valves, you generate all your mental power toward the ends you desire. Centre your mind on just one purpose at a time, rather than spreading yourself thin. A steam engine cannot run when all of its valves are open. Build up power in your mind by concentrating your focus on a single goal to direct all your energy to one purpose. The reason some people succeed in manifesting and others don't lies in differences in concentration.

Concentration lets you secure anything you desire. All wishes will be granted, dependent on your level of concentration. By applying focus to what you want and concentrating all your power to it, you will manifest it. The most successful manifestors are those with the strongest focus. The intensity and duration of your concentration is key to all persistence, diligence, endurance and determination.

We convince ourselves that life will be better after we get married, have a baby, then another. Then we are frustrated that the kids aren't old enough and we'll be more content when they are. After that we're frustrated that we have teenagers to deal with. We will certainly be happy when they are out of that stage. We tell ourselves that our life will be complete when our spouse gets his or her act together, when we get a nicer car, are able to go on a nice vacation, when we retire.

The truth is, there's no better time to be happy than right now.

Your life will always be filled with challenges. It is best to admit this to yourself and decide to be happy anyway. One of my favourite quotes comes from Alfred D Souza. He said, 'For a long time it had seemed to me that life was about to begin - real life. But there was always some obstacle in the way, something to be gotten through first, some unfinished business, time still to be served, a debt to be paid. Then life would begin. At last it dawned on me that these obstacles were my life.'

This perspective can help you to see that there is no way to happiness. Happiness is the way. So, treasure every moment that you have.

Universal Laws

Stop waiting until you finish school, until you go back to school, until you lose ten pounds, until you gain ten pounds, until you have kids, until your kids leave the house, until you start work, until you retire, until you get married, until you get divorced, until Friday night, until Sunday morning, until you get a new car or home, until your car or home is paid off, until spring, until summer, until autumn, until winter, until you are off welfare, until the first or fifteenth, until your song comes on, until you've had a drink, until you've sobered up, until you die, until you are born again to decide that there is no better time than right now to be happy.

Perceive Manifestation

When a ship approaches land, there are certain signs that appear before the sailors actually see land. In the same way, you may perceive signs of manifesting working in your life before the dream becomes real. The signs show us that the reality is on its way, that it has already been given. All we need to do is allow ourselves to receive with patience. Usually, our desires unfold within the gradual flow of time.

Do not mistake the signs for a watered-down version of the manifestation itself or you will be disappointed. When we communicate our desires clearly, the universe knows just how to answer. Accept the initial sign as a reason to expect your desires to become realised.

Your Desire Perspective

It is easy for many people to equate desire with yearning, but these are two different things. When you focus on what you want with the idea of 'not having', you are not creating the positive energy needed to create. If you see desire as something you have only partially, something you have wanted for a long time, you are again seeing it from a 'lacking' perspective.

This can condition your mind to equate desire with not having. But this is really just a state of resistance to desire, not desire itself.

175

Cosmic Ordering: You Can be Successful

You can easily manifest anything when you have no fears of not receiving. Overcome this fear by detaching from the 'wanting'. Allow yourself to accept things as they are now.

Find Peace within Yourself

Letting go is about finding peace within yourself as you are now. It is about accepting that you may never get what you want. If you can be okay with your life as it is now and understand that your desires may never be fulfilled, your fear vanishes.

This is not the same thing as resigning yourself to failure. I'm not saying you should give up, I am saying you should accept what IS. Coming to terms with your life and your current situation simply means being okay with yourself. Love yourself for who you are now. Just as you love a child for the way he is now, not withholding your affection until he is at his full potential, you should love yourself as you are now. As with a child, you will still be open to giving yourself what you want, you will allow yourself to hope.

Manifest your Desires Right Now

The closer you come to full acceptance of yourself, the more quickly you will receive the gifts from the universe that you desire. Manifesting your desires has little to do with chance or luck. You do not stumble upon happiness, you make it happen. Anyone can create ANYTHING they desire.

Your desires do no remain unfulfilled because of any chance of circumstance, birth or education. You are the only thing that stands between life as you live it now and the life you desire to have. This is good news because it means that nothing outside of you can stand between you and your dreams!

The Law of Detachment

The Law of Detachment can be difficult to relay. It states that you must relinquish all attachment to anything it is you wish to

176

attain. This does not mean you are squelching your desire. It means that you no longer rely on luck or chance to bring your desires to fulfilment. Letting go of attachment is letting go of fear. It is about trusting the universe and yourself. When you detach yourself from the outcome, you show that you trust that the Universe will fulfil the desires that are best suited for you.

Understand that the Cosmos provides what you need, which is not always what you want. When you come to this understanding, you will learn to do whatever is needed and move on. The end will take care of itself. You will see that everything arrives exactly when it should. When you trust the universe to supply all things in perfect time, you get out of your own way and allow your desires to reach you more quickly. Striving and straining are signs of fear and insecurity. These emotions create barriers that block the efficient flow of energy from the Universe to you. Learn to trust and you will have direct access to the limitless opportunities available in the ever-present.

Detachment is synonymous with allowing. When you focus your intentions but detach from the outcome, your desires will become reality. The Law of Deliberate Creation, the power of intention, and the Law of Detachment work in harmony to manifest your dreams. Detaching from goals and desires let you be flexible, trusting that the Universe will give you just what you need when you need it. In trusting, you open yourself up to potential vibrational matches that the universe provides, that you had not even thought of as a solution to your problem. Detachment lets you remain open and accepting of whatever the Universe brings, which can be even better than anything you imagined.

Universal Law of Three-fold
When the power of energy is used in magick, it is returned to the sender three times stronger than when it was sent. This is the Three-Fold Law.

To understand this better, consider the cause and effect

177

principles in a spell. For example, when you aim to help another by sending out positive energy to solve an issue, and the problem is resolved, you immediately feel good about yourself. This influences your thoughts and by extension your state of consciousness. Positive emotions are stirred and the body is physically stimulated to release hormones into your blood stream.

The combined result is a mind and body harmony that lifts your spirit. So with one small act of kindness, you have received the energy you sent back three-fold: in mind, body and spirit. Take a moment to reflect on what the result would be had you sent negative energy!

Mankind's Law of Polarity

The Law of Polarity addresses the illusion of duality. The law states, 'Unity is plural at a minimum of two.' The opposing poles of polarity are actually just two extremes of a single thing. Positive and negative are not two distinct things but one thing. Energy is just energy. Consider fire, an element that can be destructive or creative. Whether it is negative (burning) or positive (life saving) it is still only fire. Temperature is another example where it can be cold or hot, but each is only temperature. Furthermore, cold and hot can have different meanings to different people. All things are like this. All things are relative.

You may be wondering what hot and cold have to do with abundance creating. Understanding that two things are actually only sides of one thing, helps you to understand that whether something is good or bad depends on your perception of it. You can alter your perception to recognise something that you regard as bad to something good. Now that element of your reality is a positive force in your life. You replace the low-frequency energy with high-frequency energy.

Another way of looking at the Law of Polarity is to consider the two sides of existence, the physical and the metaphysical. The physical side of reality encompasses those things we see, touch and feel. The metaphysical relates to feelings and energy. To create your desires, you must integrate both sides of reality, both action in the physical world and energy in the metaphysical. When these two sides are included, you are combining the physical and metaphysical to create the reality. Both extremes of reality must be included to create a whole. You must have both action and energy for things to manifest.

These Universal Laws cannot work alone. They work together as parts of a perfect system. Just as Time and Space work together, these elements are parts of one whole. Nothing can occur in space without the passage of time to allow movement or change. Without matter, time becomes meaningless because there is nothing to change. These things work together in unison and have no value without the other.

This story shows exactly how Universal Laws work. A man in the Old West was being tried for stealing a horse.

You need to remember that stealing a horse in the Old West was a very grave and serious offence. A person could be hanged if found guilty of such a deed.

It so happened that the man whose horse had been stolen had always made it a point to get the best of any person with whom he had any dealings. He had never tried to do anything good for anyone other than himself. Consequently, the man whose horse had been stolen didn't have a single friend in the entire town. The case was tried and presented to the jury.

The evidence against the accused man was pretty strong. After about thirty minutes of deliberation, the jury returned to the court chambers.

'Gentlemen of the jury, have you reached a verdict?' the judge asked.

The chairman of the jury stood up, 'Yes we have, your honour,' he replied.

'What is your verdict?' inquired the judge.

There were a few moments of silence and then the chairman spoke, 'We find the defendant not guilty if he will return the horse.'

After the judge had silenced the laughter in the courtroom, he admonished the jury, 'I cannot accept that verdict. You will have to retire until you reach another verdict.'

The jury went back into their room to deliberate toward another verdict. No member of the jury had any particular liking for the man whose horse had been stolen. At one time or another he had gotten the best of each of them. About an hour passed before the jury could reach another verdict. They re-entered the courtroom. They took their place in the jury box and the courtroom grew silent.

'Gentlemen of the jury,' began the judge, 'have you reached a verdict?'

The chairman of the jury stood up, 'Yes we have, your honour,' he replied.

'What is your verdict?' asked the judge.

The courtroom was totally silent. You could have heard a pin drop. Everyone eagerly awaited the verdict. The chairman read the decision reached by the twelve good men, tried and true.

'We find the defendant *not* guilty, and he can *keep* the horse!'

The courtroom burst into laughter!

Moral of the story: If you spend your life trying to take advantage of others, never caring about them in any way except what you can get from them or what they can do for you, you will end up a loser, like the man who lost his horse.

If you desire a friend, then be a friend. If you desire for other people to help you, then help other people. If you desire justice at the hands of others, then practice justice toward them.

12

Mastering Universal Laws

What does it mean to become a Master? A Master is one with skill or proficiency in a particular field or practice. A Master is always learning, at the forefront of his field. He discovers new ways of looking at things through experiment. A Master understands that a truly wise man is smart enough to know that he has more to learn. A Master is practicing his craft at all times, honing and sharpening his abilities.

Mastering the Universal Laws is not like becoming a Master craftsman. You do not need to spend years in apprenticeship servitude before you are ready to call yourself a Master. Once you fully understand the Universal Laws and then apply them consistently in your life, you will be a Master. When these behaviours become habit, you are well on your way to mastering the Universal Laws.

Now that you have chosen to be a Master, begin applying the laws in your life right now. You can create a system that will help you determine if you are applying the laws successfully. By creating a plan of specific actions and exercises and combining them with a plan for implementation, you will ensure your success. Without a plan for implementation, you may have some success, but you will not be a Master. It will be too easy to set aside your exercises for the day or put them off until later, falling into a habit of non-action that will result in a static life.

Defeat Self-defeating Patterns
Making excuses is one of a host of self-defeating behaviours and mental patterns that can block your success. Such mental

habits build up over a lifetime. They are often no one's fault, just a habit that one falls into.

These negative patterns represent negative beliefs that may turn into self-fulfilling prophecies. Maybe they only put you in a state of limbo, floating in mediocrity. They can also be dangerous, trapping you in self-doubt and misery. These negative patterns harm your confidence and sense of achievement. Until you change these habits and beliefs permanently, you will be unable to move forward in your life, whether that is towards advancement in your career or in your financial affairs.

This story that follows exemplifies exactly what I mean about changing self-destructive patterns, but there is a moral to the story!

There once was a little boy who had a bad temper. His father gave him a bag of nails and told him that every time he lost his temper, he must hammer a nail into the back of the fence.

The first day the boy had driven 37 nails into the fence. Over the next few weeks, as he learned to control his anger, the number of nails hammered daily gradually dwindled down. He discovered it was easier to hold his temper than to drive those nails into the fence.

Finally the day came when the boy didn't lose his temper at all. He told his father about it and the father suggested that the boy now pull out one nail for each day that he was able to hold his temper. The days passed and the young boy was finally able to tell his father that all the nails were gone.

The father took his son by the hand and led him to the fence. He said, 'You have done well, my son, but look at the holes in the fence. The fence will never be the same. When you say things in anger, they leave a scar just like this one. You can put a knife in a man and draw it out. It won't matter how many times you say "I'm sorry," the wound is still there.'

The little boy then understood how powerful his words were. He looked up at his father and said, 'I hope you can forgive me father for the holes I put in you.'

'Of course I can,' said the father.

We often limit ourselves from the success that awaits us by our negative beliefs, but these can be flushed away. You are who you make yourself to be. Everything that happens in your life is of your own creation. When things are going poorly and you feel locked behind the gate that leads to your desires, understand that you were the one who locked the gate. By doing some inner work, you can unlock the gate and eliminate the obstacles in your path.

You do not need to be a 'born leader' to become one. Charisma can be acquired, even if you are an introvert. There is no special degree you need or programme you must follow. You need not spend years of trial and error to learn and move forward.

The Power to Change Things

Your success means nothing to others. It only matters to you. On the journey to fulfilment, when things become difficult, it is easy to forget that you chose this path. Do not forget that it is your power that created this path and your power can change it.

Whenever your reality conflicts with your desires, you should remember that it is only because you have not made the two elements harmonise. Use words to change your situation rather than complaining about it. Complaining accomplishes nothing and sends out negative energy. Remember that the way you live your life is by choice. You are free to choose the life you want. It is stunning how few people recognise their own power to choose in life. You need not float like a leaf on a pond. Soar like an eagle instead.

Place your attention on the part of your life that conflicts with your desired reality. Do not avoid the problem or try to ignore it. Take responsibility for your own life. Your dissatisfaction is either your choice or your fault. Either you choose to be dissatisfied with a life that can be fulfilling, or you choose a life that is not satisfying. Spend time

183

concentrating on the solution, not the problem. Either you need to change your situation, or you need to change your attitude about the situation.

It is likely that you already know what changes are needed to achieve your goals. Whatever it is you seek, you can have it, but you must ask for it. You must decide to take what is rightfully yours. If you are not succeeding, you must either change the situation or learn a new skill that will allow you to do so.

The universe is all around you, encouraging you to succeed. The universe wants you to find happiness. Do not fear taking those obvious steps needed towards success.

The Empowering Beliefs are the Greatest Energy

Were you to open a window into the minds of great achievers, you would find strong similarities between these people. They all have a common belief that life is what you make of it. While actions may speak louder than words, they are not more powerful. Your thoughts are truly the most powerful source of energy in your life. Your brain controls so much more than the movement of your muscles.

Consider the famous quote, 'I think, therefore I am.' By now, this phrase should mean much more to you than the simple explanation that life must exist for thought to exist. It is much more than that. This statement says that *you exist because you think*. The great minds you have read about in history, Einstein, Jefferson, Mozart, Da Vinci, were no smarter or more creative than you, but they knew how to use their minds to create the life they desired, to think the right way. This is the only thing that differs between mediocrity and greatness in human beings.

You may find this an awkward concept, to 'think the right way'. How could there be a wrong way to think? Well, if you are working towards a specific goal, then there definitely is a wrong way to think. If you have no goals in life, then by all means, think however you please. A mind occupied by negative thoughts is thinking the wrong way. The energy from those thoughts is sending a strong vibration to the universe.

Open Your Mind

Now that you have placed your Cosmic Order and reinforced it with the techniques I have explained, what is next? You should look for signs of your dreams taking form around you.

You will not always receive exactly what you asked for. Sometimes you may only get part of what you want, or you will learn that you need to do more work before you will get your desires. You may receive an opportunity to achieve your desires rather than the thing itself. The co-creative process is an ever evolving thing that requires you to proceed with heightened awareness, allowing you to recognise opportunities when the Cosmos sends them your way.

You can liken manifesting with baking a cake. You provide the Cosmos with all the ingredients it needs. The Cosmos mixes it all up and sets it cooking in the great hot oven of the universe. While you will not see the cake rising, you may smell the sweet aroma of chocolate when it nears completion. This smell will tell you your desires are on their way. This is using your perception. The Cosmos may give you just a slice of the cake when its done to be sure you like it. And if so, you will get more and more, until you feel sated.

Opening your awareness to the signs of manifestation is an important part of the co-creating process. Open your mind to opportunities that arise and take action when appropriate. In time, your sixth sense will also help you see the right action for you to take towards achieving your desires. Your intuition recognises the reality around you on another level and can bring you vital information about signs coming to you from the Cosmos.

Fine Tune Your Awareness

Meditating regularly will help you fine-tune your awareness and strengthen your intuitive skills. While you are working on those skills, you can also gain insight by paying close attention to your feelings. By focusing on the energy signature inherent in the circumstances around you, you will make better, more informed decisions.

In order to take advantage of intuitive knowledge, you should focus on the energy underlying the decisions you contemplate by noticing how they make you feel. Does it feel good? Try to remember a time when you guessed wrong about something. Does this feel anything like that did? At that time, was your ego in control, or your eternal self? Now think of a time when you guessed correctly. If the energy feels more like a correct guess, you may be on the right track. Trust your instincts and act on them.

Innovative entrepreneurs admit that they sometimes use intuition, even in large important business decisions that can change the lives of millions. They talk about knowing in their 'guts' that a choice was correct. While it will take practice to sharpen your instincts, keeping open awareness of your feelings will make you much less likely to miss an opportunity when the universe presents it.

13

Unlocking the
Power Deep Within

Belief!

Cosmic Ordering will not function without your personal belief
that you can create abundance in your life. The fuel that fires
the creative process is belief. Anything is possible when you
believe.

The modern world is overrun with doubters and
disbelievers who fail to commit themselves fully to faith. Then
there are some who fail to hold solidly to their beliefs by
running from inspiration to inspiration. They never stick to one
idea and change their belief system with every new fad that
appears in their field of perception. This insecurity, doubt and
fickleness keep people from forming their desires and living
the greatest life they can.

Consider a team of soccer players vying for the world cup.
Do you think they have even the slightest chance if they do not
believe they can win? If they doubt, there is a strong chance
they will lose. They must have the faith to motivate them
forward. No one would exert so much energy towards a goal if
he or she expected to fail.

Think of the great minds of the past century, or the
successful people you know now. These adventurers,
entrepreneurs and explorers attained their full potential and
reached high levels of success because they believed they
could. Of course they also had hard work, determination and
constancy, but it all began with a basic belief that they could
(and deserved to) achieve.

Cosmic Ordering: You Can be Successful

Do you think there is anything or any special knowledge that only the rich and famous can have? If this is the case, it is only because they hired coaches, hypnotherapists and counsellors to help them. Successful people hire professionals who can teach them to master the power deep within them. These professionals train athletes, CEOs and celebrities to use the power of their minds in visualising their goals more clearly. This really works! By activating your power of attraction, you can draw good things to you like a magnet! The life resources, social connections and circumstances you need to realise your desires will all be attracted to you.

Now I will share with you a visualisation method that you have not been told about. The technique uses both hypnosis and visualisation to create an extremely powerful combination. It will make turning on the Power of Attraction as easy as turning on a light switch. Once you gain some experience with this technique, you will be astounded at its simplicity.

I will show you the great secrets of your mind and the way reality works to help you secure everything you want. This process, although based on scientific principle, feels like magick. You can finally experience the realisation of all your desires, success, wealth, love and happiness.

Time is Your Slave

Time is not simply a straight line carrying the physical universe towards a single destination; it is much more complex than that. There are infinite various time streams existing in conjunction with each other and the physical universe can follow any one of these paths. In the realm of the spirit, we can see many potential versions of the physical universe but we can see only one version of time. In the physical world, we see many potential futures, but only one version of space.

Choice is the splitter that creates all probable futures. When you contemplate an action, the time stream is split, creating two or more time streams awaiting your choice. Your emotions connect you with the probabilities ahead. The stronger a probability, the more intense the emotions pulling us towards it. If you are pulled towards the future you desire, it is ideal. However, when the future that you gravitate towards is not to your liking, you must use your force of will to choose the preferable probable future.

By focusing energy intentionally on the probable future you desire, you give it energy, making it stronger and pulling you towards it with more force. By Law of Attraction, the present physical reality is pulled in the direction of the probability you choose as it gains strength. For this reason, you need to manifest deliberately to be the conscious creator of your destiny. You must make some difficult choices, learning how to interpret inconsistent signs and differing circumstances.

This story typifies the same situation but with differing circumstances.

Hot sun. Salty air. Rhythmic waves.

A little boy is on his knees scooping and packing the sand with plastic shovels into a bright blue bucket. Then he upends the bucket on the surface and lifts it. And, to the delight of the little architect, a castle tower is created.

All afternoon he will work. Spooning out the moat. Packing the walls. Bottle tops will be sentries. Popsicle sticks will be bridges. A sandcastle will be built.

Big city. Busy streets. Rumbling traffic.

A man is in his office. At his desk he shuffles papers into stacks and delegates assignments. He cradles the phone on his shoulder and punches the keyboard with his fingers. Numbers are juggled and contracts are signed and much to the delight of the man, a profit is made.

All his life he will work. Formulating the plans. Forecasting the future. Annuities will be sentries. Capital gains will be bridges. An empire will be built.

Two builders of two castles. They have much in common. They shape granules into grandeurs. They see nothing and make something. They are diligent and determined. And for both the tide will rise and the end will come.

189

Yet that is where the similarities cease. For the boy sees the end while the man ignores it. Watch the boy as the dusk approaches.

As the waves near, the wise child jumps to his feet and begins to clap. There is no sorrow. No fear. No regret. He knew this would happen. He is not surprised. And when the great breaker crashes into his castle and his masterpiece is sucked into the sea, he smiles. He smiles, picks up his tools, takes his father's hand, and goes home.

The grownup, however, is not so wise. As the wave of years collapses on his castle he is terrified. He hovers over the sandy monument to protect it. He blocks the waves from the walls he has made. Salt-water soaked and shivering, he snarls at the incoming tide.

'It's my castle,' he defies.

The ocean need not respond. Both know to whom the sand belongs...

I don't know much about sandcastles. But children do. Watch them and learn. Go ahead and build, but build with a child's heart. When the sun sets and the tides take - applaud. Salute the process of life and go home.

Create your Desired Outcome with Magick

When you make changes to your reality through the force of your will, you are using magick. You intend to create a desired outcome and it happens. Practitioners of magick are able to sense and direct energy with a connection to the divine. Every thought, action and spoken word you create is a magickal influence on reality. The only difference between you and a magician is that the magician is conscious of his creations. When your creations align with your higher divine self, they will be most effective.

A spell is nothing more than a combination of intent, will, visualisation and a light meditative state. The manifestation emerges from deep parts of your consciousness and the light meditative state gives you direct access to those regions. By creating a quick visualisation, you move into the realm of alternate possibility and create the desired reality, then leave quickly before your presence interferes. This is how you use Intention to create and use allowing to let go. When you believe your intentions are possible, hold them firmly in mind, and they happen.

The following story shows you what I mean.

Two men, both seriously ill, occupied the same hospital room. One man was allowed to sit up in his bed for an hour each afternoon to help drain the fluid from his lungs. His bed was next to the room's only window.

The other man had to spend all his time flat on his back. The men talked for hours on end. They spoke of their wives and families, their homes, their jobs, their involvement in the military service, where they had been on vacation.

And every afternoon when the man in the bed by the window could sit up, he would pass the time by describing to his roommate all the things he could see outside the window. The man in the other bed began to live for those one-hour periods where his world would be broadened and enlivened by all the activity and colour of the world outside.

The window overlooked a park with a lovely lake. Ducks and swans played on the water while children sailed their model boats. Young lovers walked arm in arm amidst flowers of every colour of the rainbow. Grand old trees graced the landscape, and a fine view of the city skyline could be seen in the distance.

As the man by the window described all this in exquisite detail, the man on the other side of the room would close his eyes and imagine the picturesque scene.

One warm afternoon the man by the window described a parade passing by. Although the other man couldn't hear the band - he could see it in his mind's eye as the gentleman by the window portrayed it with descriptive words. Days and weeks passed.

One morning, the day nurse arrived to bring water for their

191

baths only to find the lifeless body of the man by the window, who had died peacefully in his sleep. She was saddened and called the hospital attendants to take the body away. As soon as it seemed appropriate, the other man asked if he could be moved next to the window. The nurse was happy to make the switch, and after making sure he was comfortable, she left him alone.

Slowly, painfully, inch by inch, he propped himself up on one elbow to take his first look at the world outside. Finally, he would have the joy of seeing it for himself.

He strained to slowly turn to look out the window beside the bed. It faced a blank wall! The man asked the nurse what could have compelled his deceased roommate who had described such wonderful things outside this window. The nurse responded that the man was blind and could not even see the wall.

She said, 'Perhaps he just wanted to encourage you.'

Stop Allowing the Disapproval

Happiness in life requires that you have the freedom and intelligence to do what you wish. To find strength, you must learn to stop allowing the disapproval of others to penetrating into your inner beliefs. If all your opponent has to use against you is his disapproval, he is poorly armed. Each success will give you more confidence against these forces who would seek to control you. You will be able to approach life with a sense of personal strength and workability.

Life itself is a conflict between any manner of opposing forces. Strength conflicts with weakness, intelligence with stupidity. Avoid creating idols by looking up to others so much that you fail to create greatness in yourself. While the success of others should be an inspiration to you, your focus should remain on creating your own success in life.

All that you want and all that you aspire to attain is driven by the force of belief. To use Cosmic Ordering successfully, you must believe not only in the technique, but more importantly, in yourself!

If you have difficulty believing in yourself and your abundance creation capabilities, you need to take care of some inner housekeeping first. Failure to believe in yourself fully is often because of old bad habits, negative thought patterns and life events that have resulted in a low sense of self worth. Many people place too much weight on past mistakes and become convinced that they do not have the ability to succeed. The criticisms of others can also bring down your sense of worth, reinforcing this negative belief. It is important to understand that failure is a part of the learning process. Failures are better termed 'strengtheners' because they teach you what you need to know in order to move forward towards your goals.

Build your self-esteem and faith in yourself by digging deep to find the root causes of your feelings and rip them out. NLP is one excellent technique for challenging your negative beliefs productively. When you master self-belief, you will have the ability to manifest the ideal life. Your powers will increase tenfold and you will begin to manifest all you need.

Know *No* Limits

Every extraordinary person you look at has overcome seemingly impossible hurdles to reach their goals. Each one has a dramatic story to tell. They were faced with obstacles or lacked certain necessities to achieve their goals. Still, they succeeded anyway, as though those interferences did not exist. This is how a person lives without limitations.

An obstacle is only a limitation when you allow yourself to see it as one. Limitations do not exist as such. They are dynamic and can be changed or altered, however you need them in order to achieve your goals. Your perception creates your reality, so whatever you believe something to be, that is what you make it. Therefore, if you refuse to categorise a situation as limiting, then it will not impose any limits upon you. When you have an unstoppable mindset, nothing can get in your way. Once you understand that limitations do not exist, you will be irresistible to others.

You may notice that other people react to the same proposal differently, depending on who it is coming from. This often has little to do with politics or fickleness. It is because people welcome into their lives things that they believe will complete them. If you feel you are lacking, that feeling transmits to others who will pick up on it and subconsciously decide they do not want what you have to offer. In this way, you are creating your own limitations, which again, do not exist. They are illusions that you create with your own mind. When you recognise you have no limitations, others see that as well and welcome you into their sphere of influence.

Just as you seek freedom, other people do as well. They are drawn to freedom and positive energy like moths to a flame. Just being around a person with no perception of limits is a liberating experience, making you feel like you too can do anything you desire. When you let go of the idea of limitations, you will be amazed to see how people bend so easily to your will. Your lack of inhibition will help others to drop resistance and be more accepting of you and what you have to offer.

While it is true that money cannot buy happiness, it is wrong to think that happiness and the goal of wealth are incongruent. It is natural to allow your happiness to be aligned with whatever it is that is important to you. To think that you should stop material things from altering your feelings is equally incorrect. This kind of thinking is the reason many remain stagnant, never able to realise their full potential. All things have energy, so it is logical to understand that the energy of money will affect our feelings.

Without feeling, meaning caring about acquiring wealth, you will not have the motivation need to move forward towards your goal. To deny that feeling robs you of the impetus to take actions towards what you want. By denying your feelings of desire for wealth, you will stagnate. Motivations spring from feelings of pain or of pleasure. Each feeling serves a purpose

194

and is useful in its own way. Rather than denying the feeling, use it to compel your actions towards attainment.

Manifesting Abundance Essentials

Giving just to receive is a futile effort. Do not fall into this temptation. Your reasons for giving can be based on the good feelings you wish to receive, but to give with the expectation of financial reward is insincere. Giving should always be totally altruistic and heartfelt. Only with sincerity can you connect openly with the Universe. Giving with a lack of sincerity blocks the energy channels for abundance creation.

Do not forget to give gratitude every day. Give thanks for all you have and all the situations in your life that give you joy. Practice random kindness everywhere you go. Give anonymously to strangers and spread the abundance that is already present in your life, if you could just perceive it.

Trust in the Universe. Have total faith in your power to manifest abundance not only in your life but in the lives of others. Be willing to give that which you need, for it will be provided to you again by the Universe.

Live Life to the Max

The planet is inconceivably abundant. It gives us all that we need, not just for our day to day survival, but for comfort and health. The universe's generosity never ends. When we give something back, there will always be enough of what we need and want. Notice the multitude of variety on Earth, the wide range of plants, flowers and herbs covering its surface. Not only do these living representations of the Cosmos provide beauty, they clean the air we breathe, allowing us to remain healthy. They offer us sustenance for food and healing. Think of trees and all the uses we enjoy from them. They make medicines, furniture, our homes, paper, charcoal, etc. Not a day goes by that your life is not enhanced by an article that began as a tree. Nature's diversity provides abundance every day. To benefit from this abundance, we must partner with nature and the universe. Your curiosity, wisdom, imagination and ingenuity work with nature's abundance to form the abundance in your life. We learn to manage our natural resources on a global scale, which brings even greater abundance to both nature and ourselves. Partnering with nature is your way of co-creating in your daily life.

Being a co-creator means you must begin working with the Cosmos to significantly change the energy that influences your life. You may find the issues are greater, deeper emotionally than the mundane or frivolous things you have been Ordering. But take heart because Cosmic Ordering these great things is no more difficult or different than manifesting small everyday things.

The same techniques and energy that will manifest a new pair of shoes will also help you find the perfect mate in life. Issues connected to relationships, happiness, health and wealth take up a great deal of our consciousness. However, asking for abundance in these areas is simple. The only challenge is changing your negative thoughts, words and actions that you have grown during your lifetime. You can do this with belief and commitment.

14

Formula for Rapid Abundance Creation: Finance, Career & Love

Many of us can feel frustrated thinking our Orders for career, wealth or love are not being fulfilled. But signs that wealth is on the way are often overlooked. Close your eyes for a moment and remember how good happiness feels. Remember the times when wonderful things arrived, such as a birthday present or an unasked for raise in pay. Maybe there was some good news, or an especially romantic evening. Let all the fond memories flood your consciousness, without worrying about the details too much. Just remember the feeling and essence of happiness. Picture yourself laughing and celebrating your great luck. Now open your eyes and try the following affirmation.

'My intuition tells me that great things are coming to me! A truly wonderful event is about to happen within 24-hours!' Affirm it often and expect great things. Wait for a small sign that your fortunes are turning. You may find some money in the street or get a compliment from your boss. You may hear some good news from a friend that will make you see that good things can happen to you too. This practice will help you become more in-tune with your sixth sense.

Your intuition is not like some magickal switch that you turn on when you need it. The switch is always on, like background noise, or a radio playing softly in the living room. You catch a word or two of something that interests you and you switch your focus to hear it better. You choose which bits to listen to and which to let remain in the background.

Sometimes, you only catch a little snippet of a report on the radio and you know something bad happened to someone you love, but you don't know what happened exactly. Maybe you hear a little bit of good news from the weather report and you don't know if it will be sunny or cloudy, but you know the weather will be warm and mild.

There are times when your sixth sense feels like it is at full volume, giving you incredible detail into events to come. Some experience earthquake warnings or hear from someone on the other side. Sadly, it sometimes tells you that someone you love died before you even get a phone call to tell you so.

Do not become hung up, thinking that every hunch must lead to a windfall. Wealth comes in varying forms and some hunches have no relation to money until they are acted upon. I have a friend who found himself thinking of someone that he had not talked to in years. He felt compelled to call the old friend. Even without the phone number, the hunch became stronger. After a few days, he was in the mood for a certain restaurant and when he went there, he ran into a mutual friend who just so happened to know the long lost friend's phone number. Finally, he called his old friend and it turned out there was an opening at his friend's company that would be a huge step forward with his career. He was perfect for the job. All this came because thoughts of his friend popped into his head. This was not chance or luck. It was intuition, ESP, sixth sense, whatever you want to call it.

Soulful Wealth

On the subatomic level, all things are energy. We are all made of the same stuff and we are all linked to one another. The universe is an enormous ocean of energy that vibrates at various frequencies, presenting our senses with the illusion that all things are separate. We imagine we are separate from each other and all other things, including wealth, because of the way our senses decode energy. Our senses break down the vibrations into different categories that we call 'things'. These 'things' only exist because we observe them. Otherwise, they are all simply energy waves.

Your success is dependent upon where you put your focus. When left unchecked, our attention is scattered in daily life. We jump from getting the kids to school, to the bills, to work and every other small thing involved in our home life. This scattered mind is in the beta mind state, ideal for multi-tasking, no so good for connecting to the Infinite. When we set aside the part of the mind that decodes and interprets reality as separate things, we can fantasise more readily and have positive and constructive visualisations that allow us to believe our visualisations are the reality.

Our beliefs are the most powerful energy in our lives. They either allow or prevent certain experiences for us. Physical circumstances are only illusions made by our minds. A truly wealthy person is not that way because he has money. Instead, wealthy people have money because they are already wealthy inside! Consider the following two personalities.

The first person became a millionaire while still in his early twenties. But, because of many poor judgements, he lost all his money. Within a year, he had it all back. This happened because he lost his money, not his wealth. Money is only one of many symbols that represent wealth. The millionaire may have lost his money, but it was only a symbol representing the reality of true wealth in his life. He attracts more wealth to him magnetically through no striving or trying. He cannot help gaining money because he is truly wealthy and symbols of wealth will abound in his life. There are thousands of people like this out there and the only thing stopping you from being one of them is that you have not made the decision to be one of them.

Now consider another person who was raised in a home with constant talk of how there is not enough money. He never considers how his attitudes about money affect his life. This person wins millions in the lottery, and then loses it all in a year. His energy simply cannot maintain the attraction to wealth because he is not internally wealthy. There are also many people like this in the world whose lives are actually made worse after attaining wealth and losing it all.

Wealth is only a decision away. If you are not experiencing wealth, you should understand that it is all around you waiting for you to notice it. Poverty and lack are just illusions we create and by shifting your consciousness to wealth, you will see that wealth abounds in your life already. The more you notice wealth in your life, the more will be granted. Your thoughts, words and actions will all resonate with wealth, creating your experience. Your beliefs change your reality when you stop letting reality change your beliefs.

There is a story I would like to share with you about a son and his father, they were walking in the mountains. Suddenly, his son falls, hurts himself and screams; AAAhhhhhhhhhhh!'

To his surprise, he hears the voice repeating, somewhere in the mountain: 'AAAhhhhhhhhhhh!'

Curious, he yells: 'Who are you?'

He receives the answer: 'Who are you?'

Angered at the response, he screams: 'Coward!'

He receives the answer: 'Coward!'

He looks to his father and asks: 'What's going on?'

The father smiles and says: 'My son, pay attention.' And then he screams to the mountain: 'I admire you!'

The voice answers: 'I admire you!'

Again the man screams: 'You are a champion!'

The voice answers: 'You are a champion!'

The boy is surprised, but does not understand. Then the father explains: 'People call this ECHO, but really this is LIFE. It gives you back everything you say or do. Our life is simply a reflection of our actions. If you want more love in the world, create more love in your heart. If you want more competence in your team, improve your competence. This relationship applies to everything, in all aspects of life. Life will give you back everything you have given to it.'

Formula for Rapid Abundance Creation

Visioning versus Visualising

So many ask about what is different about visualising when compared with visioning. Visualising is a process by which the conscious mind reasons. Visioning is spiritual and governed by intuition. You can train your mind to receive flashes of inspiration. You can learn to work out 'divine pictures'. When we learn to say, 'I desire only that which Cosmos desires for me,' the inner self takes on an entirely new set of blueprints.

Planning

It is improbable that you will become rich overnight, but you can formulate a plan to encourage the development of wealth in your life. See the big picture and you will understand that even small changes work towards your end goal. Just by saving a little here and there or cutting small expenses, you are taking advantage of opportunities the universe has presented you. Do not forget to be thankful for these gifts.

Create a plan that forges a clear trail to your goal and stay with it. Create new saving and spending habits until you get some breathing room with your finances. Thank the Cosmos for your new found freedom. Do not insult the Cosmos by throwing this gift away and going back to your old habits.

Winning...Luck or Intention?

An enormous number of people by lottery tickets each week or enter other competitions for money. These people pray and hope to win. The truly 'lucky' ones walk away with the jackpot. It happens every day all over the world in cultures that give precedence to material things and monetary gain. How do you become one of these winners?

We will begin by thinking a little about the word 'luck'. It is defined as a force that brings either good fortune or bad. If luck is a force, then it must have energy. Anything with energy can be changed and we can influence energy with our thoughts. Therefore, we can deduce that we should be able to increase our likelihood of winning by manifesting good fortune. While there are other forces also acting on fortune, we can increase our influence over fortune. But first, we must feel lucky and believe we can win.

Do you think of yourself as a lucky person? If not, your energy is only reinforcing the belief. If you do feel lucky and tune into the feeling of luck, your potential for good fortune is much greater and more attainable.

Many winners have unknowingly practised Cosmic Ordering. They had fun just entering the competition for sport or pleasure.

In imagining what they would do with the money in a positive way, they influenced the outcome. Others simply buy their ticket and let go of any attachment to the outcome. Whether they win or lose means nothing to them.

When these people do win, they are labelled as lucky. They are singled out as one who beat the odds. This cliché suggests they won through their own will, not pure chance. Your energy plays a part in the outcome of any event. You can do so as well by remembering some important points.

Do not forget that money is only a material representation of energy. It is a means for trading to acquire necessities and you only need enough to pay for your needs.

If you want to earn large sums, you need to be prepared to work for it. That means long hours and often a lot of stress. Take a moment to consider what you will give to the world in exchange for financial abundance.

Avoid energy blockages and self-limiting thoughts to allow the free flow of energy in and out of your life. Develop a healthy relationship with money so that you see it as neither God nor devil. Avoid dwelling on lack and look for signs of abundance all around you.

Offer something of value to the world and you co-create abundance in your life. When you do what you love, it becomes a passion, not a job. This makes money flow easier. Trust that the universe will always provide the opportunities you need when you need them.

Formula for Rapid Abundance Creation

Financial Abundance Creation

When placing Cosmic Orders, there are seven steps you can follow to make your Order more effective. First, be clear in what it is you want. Be as specific as you can and include details as to how much money it is you want.

Second, put your focus on your desires. Write down your Cosmic Orders to reinforce what you desire. Make affirmations that thank the Cosmos for the financial abundance in your life.

Third, use the techniques that work best for you to affirm your goals. Check to see if you have emotional attachments or changes that need to be made in your attitudes towards money.

Fourth, keep your positive intentions strong. Believe in financial abundance, but detach from the need to attain it.

Fifth, open your channels of awareness. Be open to receive both your desires and signs that financial abundance is on its way.

Sixth, believe! You are financially abundant and more is on its way.

Finally, remember to give back. Make an anonymous donation. Share in the financial abundance, knowing that once you are spiritually wealthy, the flow of money will always continue.

Abundance in Finances

One day a father and his rich family took his young son on a trip to the country with the firm purpose to show him how poor people can be. They spent a day and a night in the farm of a very poor family. When they got back from their trip the father asked his son, 'How was the trip?'

'Very good, Dad!'

'Did you see how poor people can be?' the father asked.

'Yeah!'

'And what did you learn?'

The son answered, 'I saw that we have a dog at home, and they have four. We have a pool that reaches to the middle of the garden, they have a creek that has no end. We have imported lamps in the garden, they have the stars. Our patio reaches to the front yard, they have a whole horizon.'

When the little boy was finishing, his father was speechless. His son added, 'Thanks, Dad, for showing me how poor we are!'

Isn't it true that it all depends on the way you look at things? If you have love, friends, family, health, good humour and a positive attitude toward life, you've got everything!

You can't buy any of these things. You can have all the material possessions you can imagine, provisions for the future, etc, but if you are poor of spirit, you have nothing!

It is common for people to seek abundance by winning the lottery or getting a high-paying job. If you find yourself wishing for these things, you would do well to examine why. What is it you truly seek? Is it security or freedom? The answer may surprise you!

When it comes to money, many people, especially women, associate wealth with security and stability in an effort to make up for their own lack of such feelings. Others may see money as a means of escape, giving them freedom and self-esteem. This view of the benefits of wealth is most common in men. It is important to understand that money is only a tool. It is something you exchange for products or services that you desire. Were you to find yourself alone on a deserted island, all the riches you possess would mean nothing. The best use you would find for those paper notes is to fuel your fire at night. Money would offer you no security or freedom. It would not provide food or shelter. Obviously, none of us are living on a deserted island, but it can feel as though you are all alone when you try to attain the necessities of life with little money.

Some are obsessed with money. It is all that drives their actions. They pursue it constantly and each gathering of wealth is meaningless because they only seek to get more. In some cases, they fail to acquire the money they seek and become desperate, resorting to underhanded means. This makes some people view money as a bad thing. It can be viewed as a trap, keeping you from doing what you desire because there is not enough of it. Understand that money is only a concept. It is neither good nor bad. You make it good or bad based on your perception of it. You should not see money as bad any more than you view any other tool, such as a hammer, as bad.

Money, like all other matter, is also energy. It comes in and out of your life with the natural flow of change. If your focus is always on money, it will become a trap, controlling your life. When you focus only on your lack of money, you become struck in a constant struggle. Your obsession with excess will put you in a state of endless striving for more; no matter what the cost to your health or emotional well-being.

The amount of money you have depends entirely on your perspective. Whether you see yourself as lacking or having wealth is governed by your attitude. Look around you, not just in your country of origin, but the entire world. Your current level of finance would constitute great wealth in a third-world country. In fact you are very wealthy right now when compared on a global scale. If you continue to focus on lack, you will strive and struggle, never attaining enough, making you a slave to money. Separate yourself from the need to always acquire more wealth and you will see that money no longer has a hold over you. Exactly what you need will appear easily and automatically, just as easily as breathing comes to you.

It really should be easy. Unfortunately for most, it is not so simple. Releasing the obsession from money is perceived as a danger. They feel that if they change focus, they will not have the motivation needed to make more money. People who see their lack of money as a lack of financial security and freedom worry incessantly about not having enough. Every price increase is seen as a personal attack, resulting in angry feelings. Every time an expense crops up, they worry about how to cope. They wish and yearn for better paying jobs and see themselves as unlucky. The obsession controls every aspect of their lives, creating tension in everyday life and in relationships. In fact, concerns about money are so prevalent, they are the most common cause of divorce in otherwise happily married couples. All this stress impacts your health and well-being. The obsession only attracts more lack, creating insecurity and fear in an endless cycle of the pursuit of money.

Breaking the negative habit of obsessing about money is not easy for many. The materialistic mores of our society equates wealth with quality of life. Money is a basic necessity in that it secures the necessities in life, so that we can live in comfort, support a family and enjoy your free time. The topic of money is bombarded at us through news and other sources, often shown in a negative light. Creating financial abundance is a struggle for more people than any other desire, even love. Still, the basic principles underlying wealth creation are the same as fulfilling any other desire. To overcome your obsession with money, you need to begin thinking positively about abundance.

True financial abundance lies within YOU and your being a co-creator. You must send positive thoughts to the Cosmos while taking action towards enriching your life financially. The universe supports doers. The universe expects you to use your skills, passions, experience and qualifications, or your ability to secure these qualities. By using these qualities, you are of service to everyone around you and the universe gives you opportunities to create financial abundance in the process. It is an exchange of energy, as money flows in and out. Hoarding money prevents the free and easy flow. You must give freely of yourself in your actions to create the reality you seek. Every step brings you nearer to your goals, having a snow-ball type effect where the Cosmos opens up more and more opportunities as you take advantage of those presented to you.

Recognising money as only a physical manifestation of energy allows you to detach. What matters is that you have enough to live a fulfilling life. 'Enough' for one person could be an overflow of abundance for another. You should understand what your true needs are. Know what 'enough' means to you. Know what your expenses are, including what you need to set a side for that dream vacation. Acknowledge with grateful acceptance that which you already have; the abundance of food on your table, the joy your children bring, and the kind neighbours you share your weekends with. Do not take abundance for granted by focussing on lack.

Pay attention to what you can give that others need or value. This is where your abundance will spring from. Use your skills and experience to give something of value to others around you or society as a whole. The universe requires this of you as a co-creator. The universe gives you its all, so be sure you are doing the same to allow the free flow of energy and wealth in your life.

A woman came out of her house and saw three old men with long white beards sitting in her front yard. She did not recognise them. She said, 'I don't think I know you, but you must be hungry. Please come in and have something to eat.'

'Is the man of the house home?' they asked.

'No', she said. 'He's out.'

'Then we cannot come in', they replied.

In the evening when her husband came home, she told him what had happened. 'Go tell them I am home and invite them in,' he said.

The woman went out and invited the men in. 'We do not go into a house together,' they replied.

'Why is that?' she wanted to know.

One of the old men explained: 'His name is Wealth,' he said pointing to one of his friends, and said pointing to another one, 'He is Success, and I am Love.' Then he added, 'Now go in and discuss with your husband which one of us you want in your home.'

The woman went in and told her husband what was said. Her husband was overjoyed. 'How nice!' he said. 'Since that is the case, let us invite Wealth. Let him come and fill our home with wealth!'

His wife disagreed. 'My dear, why don't we invite

Success?'

Their daughter-in-law was listening from the other corner of the house. She jumped in with her own suggestion: 'Would it not be better to invite Love? Our home will then be filled with love!'

'Let us heed our daughter-in-law's advice,' said the husband to his wife. 'Go out and invite Love to be our guest.'

The woman went out and asked the three old men, 'Which one of you is Love? Please come in and be our guest.'

Love got up and started walking toward the house. The other two also got up and followed him.

Surprised, the lady asked Wealth and Success: 'I only invited Love, why are you coming in?' The old men replied together: 'If you had invited Wealth or Success, the other two of us would've stayed out, but since you invited Love, wherever He goes, we go with him. Wherever there is Love, there is also Wealth and Success!'

Whatever religion you are, if indeed any, you have probably heard the Christian phrase, 'It is easier for a camel to go through the eye of a needle, than for a rich man to enter into heaven.' It is equally true that you can pass through a needle's eye more easily than to make wealth suddenly appear at your door. Your Cosmic Orders should not focus on suddenly winning the lottery or having some philanthropist come to your rescue. You must give of yourself to receive.

Let me explain this to you by telling you about an email communication I sent to a Cosmic Friend in response to a complaint that an Order for money was not fulfilled. I believe it will help you understand more about Cosmic Ordering and the attainment of wealth.

The email I received told me little, other than that there was some sort of block with her Cosmic Order, no doubt a wish for instant wealth from a lottery or similar source. She said she had repeatedly wished for her Order to be filled and she simply could not understand why to Cosmos was not responding. Sadly, her communication made it apparent she was feeling desperate and frustrated.

Right away I saw several reasons her Order remained unfilled. She wanted to win great wealth to cure what ails her, but she never asked for a means to how this would be manifested. Cosmic Ordering is not tantamount to some magickal wizard that says, 'Poof, you are rich!'

Cash is a commodity. It is much better to ask for the means to have cash, rather than asking for cash itself. It is highly improbably that money will land at your door unexpectedly, but it could come through increased income, selling goods, winning something, or any one of a number of methods. Asking for the means to earn was the way to make her desires for wealth more attainable.

Money is not god or devil, but merely a form of energy that makes us more of who we already are. Greed begets greed and love begets love.

Although I did not know her circumstances fully, I knew enough about Cosmic Ordering to know that she either had a deep-seated lack of faith in the Cosmos, blocking her Order, or she had some deep trouble in her current business life.

Another matter with her communication was that she had said she wished for her Orders to be fulfilled regularly. Placing an Order once is sufficient. Ideally she should have placed strategic reminders about the home.

Finally, her emotional state was of great concern. I feared my Cosmic Friend would fall into becoming so disillusioned that she would surrender to the idea that she lacked money and give up trying. Some people fall into this pattern and begin thinking that poverty is some sort of challenge by fire. They think poverty will cleanse them and make them into another Dalai Lama. They wear their hearts on their sleeves, professing how they cleansed their souls. Well, I told my friend to say 'X+@#! That!'

I explained that she has a birthright to live in wealth, health and happiness however she wanted it. I cautioned her against digging a hole that would only deepen over time. After a while,

I explained, that hole would feel like a safe familiar place. This biggest problem with being stuck in a hole is that you cannot see the light. I'm certain you have heard the phrase, 'When you find yourself in a hole, the first thing to do is stop digging!' I recommended she cleanse her chakras before engaging in any further Cosmic Ordering.

I asked my friend to take heart and avoid feeling sorry for herself. I wanted her to understand that wasting money only puts her temporarily out of money, but wasting her time was wasting her life.

I explained to her that the she can manifest ANY GOAL OR DESIRE. She just happened at that particular time in her life to be focused on creating wealth. I pointed out the apparent inner turmoil within her. I agreed that the concerns people faced about their jobs and the economy were understandable, but she needed to simply turn off that influence. I told her to turn a deaf ear to the gloom and doom. Even when the economy is booming we hear such talk. I told her to make a choice, right now; to improve her life and that it would happen.

I tried to communicate to my Friend that Cosmic Ordering is not something to be done willy-nilly. She could not place an Order and think, 'that's it!' then go back to Cosmic Ordering when in a time of need.

I advised her to think about what would happen if she placed a different Order each day. Eventually, the process would become as easy as falling off a log. How would she ever be able to focus in a time of stress and need if she had not trained her mind? I reminded her that making money a god in her life would make it plague her like the devil.

Working out Affirmations

If you have ever felt frustrated like my Cosmic Friend, it could be helpful for you to practice this exercise that I use to work out blockages in my affirmations. It helps you to get at the root of your feelings, to reword your affirmations and make them more powerful.

Formula for Rapid Abundance Creation

Close your eyes and imagine a large whiteboard or blackboard in front of you. On the board's left side, you will see your positive affirmations about wealth. If any negative thoughts or doubts arise, do not squelch them. Put them on the right side of your imagined board. Next, review your negative thoughts and think about how you may turn them into positives. Here is an example exercise that I performed.

On the left I saw my positive belief, 'I deserve wealth and I attract it now'. On the right I saw my negative beliefs, 'Spiritual people should not want money, but I want to be rich, so does that mean I am not spiritual? I am so confused, but I really like this affirmation, so I'll keep saying it until it feels right'

So under those two items, I pictured on the left my affirmation again, 'I deserve wealth and I attract it now.' This time it felt better. So on the right, I put down my feelings, 'Okay, I'm beginning to feel better. I know that spiritual people deserve wealth just like anyone else. And if I don't have money worries, I will be free to spend more time helping others.'

Next, I moved on to another affirmation, 'Happiness and the sales of my book are soaring!' On the right, I imagined the negative affirmation, 'I'm not sure about this affirmation. The word "soaring" makes me feel out of control. Maybe that's the problem there. I'm afraid I will lose control somehow if my book becomes a bestseller. It's like I would go soaring away. Let me word it another way.'

Then I went back to the left side of my board and imagined a new affirmation, 'It is safe for my book to be a bestseller. I am a best-selling author.' Then on the right, I imagined the words, 'Yes, this is right. Let me try more affirmations.'

I continued to the left side of my board and wrote, 'I deserve nice things.' On the right I pictured the words, 'My mam always said that the best things in life come for free. Does that mean I can't have nice things that cost money? That seems wrong. Deep down I know my mam was not trying to tell me that there are no nice things that cost money.'

211

Cosmic Ordering: You Can be Successful

On the left side of my board I saw, 'I deserve nice things. I remain open to the channels of wealth, including through the selling of my book. I desire, deserve and attract wealth right now!' On the right side, I then pictured, "I know this is a correct affirmation that will work. Perhaps I should add an element of safety since it seems important to me.'

Then on the left side of my board I saw, 'I deserve nice things. I remain open to the channels of wealth, including through the selling of my book. It is safe to succeed as a writer and I am succeeding. I desire, deserve and attract wealth right now!'

This practice demonstrates how many issues can come bubbling up that have been preventing the fulfilment of your desires. This is a fun and powerful process that you can try in the morning to ensure your affirmations are working for you. After a few days of this practice, you will have a better sense of your real desires and the resistance attached to your affirmations.

Jobs and Money

Let go of money. It will not bring you happiness. The best it can bring you is the thrill of winning, but this only satisfies your ego for a moment. This temporary thrill is not true happiness. When you give fuel to the need for money with your emotions, you block its abundance. You create more lack if you perceive lack. Let go of money and focus instead on what you truly need, wealth!

Finding an Abundant Career

Look at your current career. Is this what you were born to do? You are blocking the path to abundance if you are not engaged in a profession that you love. Look at your career path and see if you can steer it closer to your dreams. This will help you manifest the path to opportunities that will let you put the passion in your work that will bring opportunities for abundance.

Formula for Rapid Abundance Creation

Perceptions on Limitations

Sometimes we are influenced by other people in our career choices. In school, our teachers, parents and career advisers all have opinions about what is best for us. Although well-intentioned, these people often push us towards careers focussing on the cash earning potential rather than the emotional rewards.

While it's true, you can do anything you want in life, some professions are clearly better for you than others. You may have particular talents or passions for certain subjects that can be used to create a truly rewarding work life. Our perceptions about limitations often stop us from chasing after the career that is meant for us. We think thoughts like, 'I don't have a college degree,' or 'I don't know how to do that,' or 'It does not pay enough.' There may be limitations in circumstances at one point in time that make it difficult for you to follow the right path, but those limitations can be removed. It is never too late to find the job that is right for you. Finding your life's work will connect you more directly with the Cosmos so you can create abundance.

The Right Career Path

When seeking the right career for you, take some time to think about your interests. What do you spend most of your free time on? Where do your passions lie? Consider any special talents you may have or personal qualities that would fit well to a particular career. In what kind of situations are you most happy? Are there business ideas you have thought of pursuing? Maybe you already know what your dream job is, but do not know how to acquire it.

Consider available opportunities. You may want to ask the universe for guidance to help you find the right path. When you send this Cosmic Order, be sure to align closely with your intuition and watch for signs that will lead the way. Open your awareness to the Cosmos' messages.

Your intuition will guide you towards the right

opportunities. Often, those who are unhappy in their jobs already know what they would rather be doing. However, self-doubt or sheer laziness blocks them from making the changes necessary to find their life's work. Excuses like low pay or the need for university classes are common. People often settle for the safe job with a weekly salary while moaning about the rat race and creating negative energy all around them.

If you are not living the life you want, it is no one's fault but your own. You must stop putting negative energy behind your thoughts, words and actions. Instead, be crystal clear on what it is you do want, not what you do not want. Think of it as a radio station that is not tuned properly. The static interferes with the music. When you fail to tune into the positive, you are not receiving the strong Cosmic signal you need for an abundant life.

When you gain clarity of purpose in your career choice, begin clearing out those old negative thoughts that were holding you back. Focus only on what you want, not on what others around you want. Do not let your inner critic tell you that you cannot do it. Eradicate that old way of thinking and retort with, 'Oh yes I can!' When you remove these negative influences, the path to abundance will become easier to see. Then you only need to follow it!

Map Your Path

Be ready for instantaneous change. It could happen this way, or it may happen more slowly. Just be open to the changes that are going to happen in your life.

In mapping your path, consider any education or skills you may need to acquire. Will you need to perfect your craft? Consider what knowledge you may need to proceed. Also examine your emotional landscape. What emotional obstacles lie in wait? If you lack confidence or have emotional conflicts to resolve, these need to be attended to right away.

Be ready to give up something for your reality to materialise. You will need to do some hard work to co-create the reality you want. Stay flexible and let go of all negative dialogue, doubt and fear.

Be Assertive!

Sitting around just waiting for the Cosmos to deliver the perfect career will not get you anywhere. You must be assertive and proactive to co-create your life. The Cosmos will provide abundance opportunities, but it is up to you to take action.

Guidance for a Successful Career

Remove emotional blockages that have prevented you from taking action towards the perfect career in the past. Change whatever is needed inside of you. Notice what makes you feel really alive and find a career that allows you to do it every day. Pay attention only to your own feelings; do not be influenced by others.

Stay alert for signs that will guide you towards the right career path. Look for opportunities everywhere you go. Trust your instincts and trust yourself to know that if it feels right, it is right. Surround yourself with your passions to attract more of them into your life.

Enthusiasm can carry you farther than you think. Your love for what you do shows and attracts more opportunities for your. Follow the career that makes you happy. Know that it is never too late to change.

Cosmic Ordering Blueprint for Career Success

In your Cosmic Orders for an abundant career, make sure you are crystal clear about what you want. Focus on it and state your wishes in detail. See yourself in your career and write down the Orders to reinforce them. Affirm to your self, 'I am in a fulfilling career.' Remember this is all about what you want and what works best for you. Use whichever techniques work best.

Do not forget to take a close look at your emotional

215

landscape and make changes where necessary. Use all the tools available to you to gain confidence and self-esteem. Keep your intentions strong and positive by avoiding procrastination and always working towards your goal.

Keep awareness channels open and look for signs that will show you that you have found the right path. Do what you were born to do and the universe will provide ample opportunities for success. Assert yourself and take advantage of these opportunities.

Creative Power of Thought

Your creative powers to act are initiated through thought. When you think in a certain way, you will attract riches, but you cannot rely on your thoughts alone.

You must also focus on personal action. This is the biggest obstacle on which some otherwise scientific thinkers stumble. They fail to follow thoughts with personal action.

Humans have not yet evolved to the state where we can create directly from the formless substance, assuming such a feat were possible. We must rely on natural processes or the work of our own hands. Not only must we think, but we must supplement our thoughts with personal action.

Your thoughts can compel wealth to gravitate to you, but it will not arrive without somehow being transferred from its original state. Gold does not fly from the mountain and land at your door.

Instead, the universe will Order the work of men so that someone discovers and mines the gold for you. Business transactions on the far side of the globe will be directed in a way that brings the gold to you. You must then arrange your affairs so that you are able to receive the gold when it comes to you.

While your thoughts will make all things living and non-living work towards your ends, your personal activity must also allow you to receive what you desire at the right time. You will not get it for free and you cannot steal it. You must be giving more value to the world that you recover in monetary gains.

You can use thought in a scientific way by forming a clear and precise image in your mind of what it is you desire, holding strongly to your purpose and understanding with thankfulness and faith that you will get what you want.

You need not try to guide or manage the creative process. You need only to hold fast to your vision, stay with your purpose, and keep your belief and gratitude. Still, you must also act in a particular way, to ensure that you can get what is yours when it arrives. You must be able to meet the things in your visualisation and Order them properly when they arrive. It makes sense that things will come to you by way of others' hands. These people will expect something of equal value in exchange. You can only get what is yours by giving the other person what he has rightful ownership to.

You must combine your thoughts and personal actions. A great number of people, whether consciously or not, engage the creative forces through persistent desire, but never realise the dream because they have not made arrangements to receive. By thinking, your desires are sent to you. By taking action, you receive.

Whatever action you take, you must take it NOW. The past is gone, so you cannot perform action there. It is essential for clarity of purpose and vision that you dismiss all thoughts of the past.

Just as the past is gone, you will not know what your future actions will be until the moment arrives. If your present actions are always focused on the future, you will be distracted by the unknown, responding with a divided mind, making your Order ineffective.

Put all of Your Mind in the Present
Avoid setting in motion abundance creation and then just sitting down to wait for the result. Otherwise, you will never get what you desire. You must act now. Time is an illusion. Now is all there really is. If you want to be ready to receive

your desires, you must start now.

Your action, whatever it may be, will take place in your current work or business. Your action will affect your current environment. You can take no action where you are not, nor can you act where you were before or where you will be. Actions can only take place where you are now. Do not fret about yesterday's work or how well or ill it was done. You can only do today's work, so you should do it well. Worry about tomorrow's work tomorrow. The time you need to do it will be made available to you.

You should not wait for your environment to change before you take action. You instead change your environment by action. Take actions that change the current environment so that you will be in a better environment. Keep hold of your beliefs and purpose while you see yourself in the improved environment with every ounce of your desire, strength and mind.

Do not waste the ever-important NOW on day dreams or castles in the clouds. Hang on to the one crystal clear vision of what you want and take action NOW. Avoid casting about, running from one dream to the next, every time you are inspired by some new thing. Steadiness of purpose requires that you maintain your vision. Do not wait for some remarkable event to propel your actions. Now is the time to act and if you act in a certain way, you will surely find wealth.

If the business you engage in feels wrong, do not wait for another business to come along. Change the business you have. See yourself in the right business and believe that you will find your way into it by acting in the present.

Utilise your current business as a way of acquiring the one you want. Alter your current environment to suit your needs. When you hold a vision of the right business for you with faith and purpose, the Cosmos will move the right business in your direction. Your actions will cause you to move towards the business, making you meet it sooner.

If instead you work for a company and think you need to

get another job to reach your desires, do not simply place and Order and wait. You must instead see yourself in the job you want and take active steps with faith and purpose to get it. When you do this, the job you want will be yours.

Each day is either successful or not. The successful days are the ones when you get what you desire. If you see every day as a failure, you will always be poor. If you see each day as a success, you will surely get rich. Failure means failing to do today something that you could have done towards your goal. The consequences of inaction can be dire.

Even the most seemingly trivial act can create deep and severe consequences. Your mind cannot understand the workings of the universe. You will never understand all the forces working towards the fulfilment of your desires. One simple act can be the link between the thought vibration and the creation of your desire in the real world. Failing to act in some small way can cause lengthy delays in the attainment of your goals.

Failure happens when you take on too many tasks and perform them inefficiently or not doing enough in an efficient way. If you avoid inefficient acts and perform enough efficient acts, you will gain wealth. When you learn to become efficient, you will see how the attainment of riches is an exact science, just like mathematics.

This means that you must focus your attention on making each act successful in and of itself. Certainly you can do one small act well. Each act will be a success because you have all the power of the Universe working along side you. You cannot fail. To make every act efficient, you need only to put all of your power into it.

Actions are either weak or strong. When each action is strong, you are acting in the particular way needed to make you rich. Each act will be strong and efficient when you hold on to the full power of your faith and purpose. This is where those who use only thought to manifest will fail. To use the power of mind on the one hand and act without the power of mind in place is inefficient. The acts themselves are not successful. However, if your use all power in every act, even commonplace actions, every action will be successful. Because each success opens the door to another, your progress will be amplified, speeding you towards your goals and desires more rapidly.

During work hours, you can simply refer back to your mental picture in order to stimulate the faith and purpose needed to make your actions efficient. Think of your picture in leisure time as well so until just the thought of your image brings forth all the faith and purpose you need.

In Western society today, it has become impossible to live a complete life without riches. You cannot reach your greatest potential while your time is being taken up by the pursuit of money to pay bills or buy food. The things man needs to develop his soul and talent also cost money. Life is so complex now that even the average person must have a lot of money just to survive, much less live a complete life.

Wanting to be rich is not wrong. Everyone desires to be rich because it is the way to a more abundant and happy life experience. Wanting to live a full life is a praiseworthy goal. We live for the body, mind and soul. We should not place more weight or reverence on any one of these. None of these can live independently of the others and none can thrive if the others do not also thrive.

Concentrate Energy - Focus

We know that the universe is comprised only of energy vibrations that differ in frequency or rate of vibration. The universe, as you now know, works by the principle of vibration. All things vibrate and the vibration is energy.

When you focus, you concentrate your attention and energy to one point. Your attention is made of psychic energy. This energy is alive and aware. Wherever you place your focus, you provide life energy for something to exist. The more you focus on something, the more alive it becomes. Lessen your focus and actions, and you reduce the sustaining living thoughts needed to keep your dream alive. Fail to pay attention, and the thing fades out of existence over time. The more focus you give to something, the stronger the attraction and the more intense the vibrations, the faster the thing will manifest.

Think about the word *appreciate* for a moment. Literally, it means to increase the value of something. When you give blessings to the small, the small grows to be large. Failure to focus depreciates value. Put your attention and intention on the positive while detaching from the negative. Do not forget that all things are made of a conscious, living energy. Your focus magnifies that energy. Whatever you focus on will expand. When great numbers of people focus on something, it is magnified to an even greater degree. This is why popular items tend to flourish. Marketers and promoters understand this. Fortune often follows fame. As an idea or thing becomes shunned, it fades away quickly.

The universe attracts through creating and creates through attracting. What you focus on is pulled to you or pulls forces to form the quantum field that will manifest it for you. Your attention causes the wave function to collapse into particles, solidifying the array of infinite possibilities into a tangible experience.

The Law of Attraction shows us how thoughts hold creative power. Imagine that you started some dance classes to learn some particular style of dance like ballet or salsa. If you feel in your heart and have a certainty that you already are a great dancer, you will succeed.

In terms of NLP, this may be referred to as modelling or neurological conditioning. You condition your emotional and mental states to follow successful patterns. Add to this the connection between your mind and spirit, the way your inner landscape forms your outer landscape. You will find that you can master the skills as though the information was with you from birth. The truth is that your circumstances arise from your feelings. You control your feelings with your thoughts. Search

221

within to find how it will feel to have, do or be what you want. This will create the thing in your life. The energy in your emotion will gravitate you to your desires and your desires to you.

To receive your desires, you must be in the appropriate mental state. If you have money, but feel it is not enough, you will have even less. If you fail to appreciate a great friendship, the friendship will fall apart. If you believe that relationships are fleeting, then your romance will deteriorate and the relationship will come to an end.

However, if you believe that each thing in your life is a gift from the Cosmos, you can never lose it. If you believe it is yours by right, you will nurture and protect it. Your mindset will encourage money, friends or romance to stay in your life. Think of a relationship with a friend that stops and starts over time, but remains. We all have relationships like this that endure, even when they occasionally fall away for a time. It is because you both believe in your friendship that it returns time and again.

Even when all other forces are at work to keep something together, your thoughts and beliefs can create a damaging force that makes it fall apart. You will never lose on the outside that which you have not lost on the inside. Things may be taken from you, but if they still exist inside you, they will always return. Anything you lose on the inside cannot stay with you on the outside. You can hold on as tightly as you like, it will still slip through your hands.

If you have a belief that you are ugly, it will not matter what you wear or how much make up you apply. Whatever you do, you will never truly be beautiful. Your expressions and reactions will communicate your ugliness to others. Your efforts will only show your neediness and inner feelings of lack.

Take a look around you and see that the truly beautiful recognise their own beauty. The truly wealthy know that they are rich. To be truly beautiful, it must exist on the interior and on the exterior. Your inner beauty is found in your self-image. What do you see when you look in the mirror? Do you see what is really there? You see what you believe yourself to be. To have, you must be. If you want confidence, you must become confident. If you want understanding, you must be understanding yourself. If you want to be admired, you should make yourself admirable. The things you have are only an expression of yourself, they do not define you. Your inner landscape defines who and what you are. What you have reflects your beliefs, in the manifestation of your thoughts. Whether the manifestation is still pending or not should not change your inner definition. You change reality. Do not let it change you.

Whatever you build within yourself will come to pass outside yourself as well. Change your inner self and see your outer world change. The energy you emit will attract and create your results. When you change the energy frequency, you change the result. Consciousness defines Being. Having means carrying vibrational resonance with the frequency of the energy in that thing you seek.

What You Seek, You Attract

It is easy to forget the simple truth inherent in all things. People chase after forms without recognising the essence of the forms.

Be what it is you seek to attract. If you want the perfect love, be perfect love. Many desire the perfect partner, wanting that person to enter our lives and stay forever. Still we fail to acknowledge that we must take the actions necessary to be the perfect partner before we will attract the same into our lives. Work on yourself first, and you will prevent many painful experiences and prevent the losing precious time and energy.

The things in the reality you experience follow either an internal or external pattern. If you want to include something in your reality, you must first include it in your self. If you want something banished from your experience, you must banish it from yourself. It is good, natural and healthy to have the goal

223

of finding true love but your true love will never arrive if you are not first a true love to yourself.

Abundant Relationships

Emotional connections with others, whether romantic or platonic are vital for human happiness. No matter what your particular idiosyncrasies, you have the power to enrich the relationships in your life. You can find your soul mate, develop a deeply satisfying family life and have supportive, endearing friends.

If you find relationships challenging, you need to do some inner searching. Most often, the problems we see in others are only reflections of problems existing in ourselves. When we address those problems, the negative energy patterns that created the difficulty will dissipate and our relationships will become more abundant.

Power of Emotion

It is not difficult to understand the power in your emotions and words, especially in personal relationships. A difference of opinion can easily escalate into an angry argument. This can happen on an enormous scale when disagreements are between governments, resulting in war.

The average person experiences the power of emotion in the form of negative feelings, broken relationships and the emotional baggage that you drag with you for years.

Letting go of the resentment that results from disagreements can be difficult. The ego produces a feeling of self-righteousness that compels you to continue the fight in your own mind. Letting go of this resentment and self-righteousness will release those negative emotions and give you restored harmony and peace, opening your channel to abundance. Loving unconditionally does not heal the relationship, instead look for respect. Too much emphasis is put on unconditional love. How can love have no conditions? Are you willing to accept an abusive partner? Of course not!

Formula for Rapid Abundance Creation

Letting Go

Relationships can last a lifetime. Others, however, sadly become unhealthy. Whenever there is room for healing, you should try all means at your disposal to save the relationship. However, this cannot happen unless both parties have the same desire to rescue the connection. Deciding if it is time to let go of a relationship can be stressful and painful. The decision is equal to acknowledging you have suffered a loss, whether that means ending the relationship yourself, allowing your partner to end it or both of you deciding it is time to allow the connection to break. It is common to experience a sense of grief and loss when you end a relationship.

When one partner is not ready to move on, conflicts arise. Unhealthy attachments create a needy and conditional relationship. These attachments feed negative emotions of insecurity, low self-esteem, jealousy, possessiveness and fear. Healing must take place on a deep level if both partners are to be released from destructive attachment.

You must deal with your unresolved negative emotions in an unhealthy relationship if you are ever to move on and find abundance in your partnerships and friendships.

Nurturing Relationships

Healthy relationships are formed with mutual respect and loving. Both parties must hold a deep respect for the others personal free will and right to choose. Be mindful of your own beliefs, attitudes, pain and suffering. Do not force these feelings upon others. You each have your own path to follow. Instead, approach the relationship with the intention of nurturing.

Finding ways to heal family relationships or other long-standing friendships presents a challenge, especially if those relationships have created feelings of a lack of abundance within you. Learning to manifest healthier relationships takes time and patience.

You must first be ready to accept that others may not

welcome the changes you make, even when those decisions are putting you on the path to abundance. You must not fall back into old habits when this happens. It will be a true test of your will!

Concentrate on manifesting abundance. Healthy relationships begin with you. You must be ready and able to respect yourself and have reverence for the attitudes and feelings of others. This in turn creates a sense of respect for your feelings from others. Your inner work will show you issues that must be addressed and resolved. When you change your inner landscape for the better, the new energy will attract more positive responses in your relationship experiences.

If those around you have little respect or caring for you, it is because you let them. You may notice that people close to you take you for granted or use you as an emotional punching bag. They may manipulate you, taking advantage of your vulnerabilities. When you inspect your own responses to these behaviours, you will see that you are allowing it to happen.

Consider how you respond when a friend is in turmoil and rattles on incessantly about his or her personal problems. That toxic negative energy affects your own feelings. While it is important to be a good listener, you are not an emotional dumping ground. If you allow yourself to be more than simply a good listener, you are sending a signal of low self-esteem, letting others take advantage of your generosity. You must be assertive to maintain balance.

Toxic Relationships

We have all experienced toxic relationships at some point in time. The negative words, intentions, and thoughts of others have an impact on your energy field, adversely affecting you on all levels. Toxic people can be thought of as energy vampires or abundance saboteurs. These psychic attackers often impact vulnerable people to a more damaging degree.

You need not feel any sense of responsibility for teaching such people to behave better. Negative people send out corresponding negative energy (whether they know it or not) and are subject to the rebound effect. Abundance saboteurs who engage in malicious gossip, bullying, or manipulative behaviours are highly vulnerable to psychic attack themselves. Whatever you send comes back to you tenfold. If you send negative energy to those who influence you negatively, you will manifest that negative energy in your own life.

There are many True Loves

We are all magnets to the same energy we radiate. The universe creates abundance, ensuring there are many possible true loves for you. True love is not embodied in any specific person; rather it is an energy trait that some people will vibrate. When searching for your soul mate, you may have many lessons to learn about yourself before you find what you seek. This can take time. Sometimes in life, we find the perfect partner, but the relationship dissolves a few years later. This only means the relationship was right for you at that time. Change is the only constant, meaning either partner can change at any time, resulting in a natural departure. The key to holding on to a relationship for the long term depends on the work each partner is willing to do to co-create a loving relationship. To find true love, whether it is for the first time, or after many failed relationships, requires that you know precisely what you want out of a relationship and emitting the proper signals to attract that into your life.

You are not likely to find an honest, loving and nurturing relationship until you have found true independence and happiness for yourself. This means you must create a precise definition of such a relationship. While attractiveness and physical chemistry hold strong weight in a good relationship, these things do not create truly loving relationships. Such a relationship requires other qualities that bring happiness on a much deeper level, such as loyalty, understanding, support, and shared goals. Your self-love is a positive energy. The Cosmos provides opportunities for you to give love to your true love.

Become a Relationship Magnet

The first step in finding a great relationship is to dissolve any emotional issues that remain unresolved from your past or present relationships. You must also nurture positive thoughts in connection with your relationships to attract positive people. Part of this means maintaining your self-respect by knowing when to be assertive and say 'no!'

When searching for your soul-mate, be sure you know the qualities you are looking for. Be sure to choose those that match you well and take care in what you wish for! Remember that you are one of a kind and someone with the true love qualities you seek is out there waiting for you. Expect perfect love because that is just what you deserve.

Avoid placing Cosmic Orders to try and change someone in your life. Others need to follow their own destinies. Pushing your own ideas on someone else in an effort to change or control them will result in a negative influence in your own life, even when those changes are well-intentioned. When you encounter problems with a relationship, it is usually a problem within you, being reflected in the realities of the relationship. Take a long look at yourself and see how you can resolve these problems internally. Do not try to control the external world.

Remember to always show gratitude and cherish the relationships you gain and see your healthy relationship thrive. Place your attention on the love and nurturing in your relationship and you will see these qualities remain abundant in your life.

15

Tap into Creative
Mind Power

Many years ago three soldiers, hungry and weary of battle, came upon a small village. The villagers, suffering a meagre harvest and the many years of war, quickly hid what little they had to eat and met the three at the village square, wringing their hands and bemoaning the lack of anything to eat.

The soldiers spoke quietly among themselves and the first soldier then turned to the village elders and said, 'Your tired fields have left you nothing to share, so we will share what little we have: the secret of how to make soup from stones.'

Naturally the villagers were intrigued and soon a fire was put to the town's great kettle as the soldiers dropped in three smooth stones.

'Now this will be a fine soup,' said the second soldier; 'but a pinch of salt and some parsley would make it wonderful!'

Up jumped a villager, crying, 'What luck! I've just remembered where some has been left!' And off she ran, returning with an apron full of parsley and a turnip.

As the kettle boiled on, the memory of the village improved: soon barley, carrots, beef and cream had found their way into the great pot, and a cask of wine was rolled into the square as all sat down to feast.

They ate and danced and sang well into the night, refreshed by the feast and their newfound friends. In the morning the three soldiers awoke to find the entire village standing before them. At their feet lay a satchel of the village's best breads and cheese.

229

'You have given us the greatest of gifts: the secret of how to make soup from stones,' said an elder, 'and we shall never forget.'

The third soldier turned to the crowd, and said, 'There is no secret, but this is certain: it is only by sharing that we may make a feast.' And off the soldiers wandered, down the road.

Nearly everyone wants to be successful, yet there seems to be some big secret out there because not everyone achieves this. How do we achieve real success in life? The definition of success varies from person to person, but there is a way to be certain of your failure or success. If you choose to focus on your desires, you will succeed.

Maintain focus on everything you do. When you become overloaded with ideas, finding it difficult to keep focus on just one, do not throw away those ideas. Instead fit them together like pieces of a puzzle to create one idea or a smaller group of ideas.

It is easy to try to change too much at once when you find the great idea that is our life's purpose. Enthusiasm is good, but too much change at once is likely to slow down your success. Being focussed does not only mean knowing exactly what you want. It also means understanding the direction and path you must travel to achieve it. When you set foot on that path, follow where it leads.

Focus. It is a simple yet powerful secret to success. Stay on the path you have forged by sticking closely to your original idea. Avoid the temptation to change the plan more than necessary. Doing this will let you harvest the benefits success offers and achieve more.

Obstacles Make You stronger

When you take the first steps towards achieving any goal that matters to you, you first look at your current situation, environment, and inner self. You may look around and think, 'How can I ever get there from here?'

This mentality puts you in the place of being a product of

your environment. Instead, your environment should be a reflection and product of you.

Your current situation and the place you want to be are simply two sides of one coin, two extremes of one thing: your life.

When you decide to change your life, it is just like flipping a coin to see the other side. It is not more difficult than that, unless you allow your mind to make it hard. You may see obstacles as old enemies that have plagued you since birth. These problems were always there and you either ignored them or never fully overcame them. Now they return once again to block your path.

Even though these demons have haunted you throughout your life, and you have yet to overcome them, remember their very existence serves to help you. These obstacles make you stronger. The higher the hurdle, the higher you will learn to jump.

Do Something New Daily

This simple tip often gets unjustly set aside: do at least one new thing every day. It does not matter if the thing you choose is related to your goal.

When you try something new, something you have never tried before, you will stumble upon some breakthrough, a new way of thinking that will help you gain more ground towards your goals than you thought you could achieve. When you try something new each day, you are actually putting into practice the law of natural selection. Remember the saying that states if you keep doing what you have always done, you will get more of what you always got?

Unless you try something new each day, you will stagnate. It does not matter if the endeavour is something only slightly different from your current practices or radically different.

One way to get into this practice is to start with a fresh paper and write down a solid plan of action for success. Commit yourself to the plans you make. Create a definition of success so that you can identify exactly what you must accomplish each day, the routine tasks that will ensure you progress towards your goals. Break your goals into small, easily attained targets that you can meet each day.

As you make a commitment to achieve theses smaller actions, remember to log your results. Continue to do this, and modify your plan as you learn more. Evolve your action plan to survive and succeed in the environment as it changes.

Magnify Your Focus

You often find teachers or gurus who talk about success though goal setting and achieving, often charging you a fee, only focus on the parts that deal with your personal actions. Yet your efforts will be more effective if you can help others to also get what they want. It does not matter if your desires and those of others are similar or not.

If you have been focussed only on yourself, living life from a selfish perspective, and you are still successful, great! But you could be even more successful and see it magnified if you choose to focus part of your time, words, actions and energy in benefiting the dreams of others.

Take a few moments to take a self inventory regarding your desires in life. Ask yourself if there is anything missing in your life right now. What is it you feel is missing? Consider what you need or need to do to make your life more complete. Think about goals that you may need to accomplish to move forward with your life as you have defined it.

If you already know your life's purpose, can you say you have successfully progressed in realising the purpose fully? If you are still defining your life's purpose, consider ways in which you might begin to understand your life's purpose more fully.

Now take a look at your past and ask your self something else. Have there been incidents where you were successful because you helped others succeed? Consider how you helped others who came to you looking for help in attaining what they desired. If there were none, maybe you can think of a time in which you failed to get what you wanted because you refused help to someone who truly need your help getting what they wanted. If you have failed to help others, think how you might be able to make amends by helping those people now or in the future.

Also consider if your success in any specific past endeavour was because of some selfish move or trickery by you. What were the negative consequences of those unethical actions?

You may find yourself deeply engaged in these questions with many new questions springing to mind. If so, be sure to get out some paper and write down your answers and ideas so that you can draw conclusions and examine the issue fully.

Manifesting those Desires

The simplest definition of success is: just getting what you want. This may seem over simplified, but most people can agree that a successful person, in whatever arena, is a success because he or she achieved a specific goal that he or she wanted before it was obtained.

Before setting out on this journey, it is important to be realistic. There may be things you want that you know deep in your heart you just will not get. I am not talking about things that are achievable. I am talking about impossibilities. Make a list of the unachievable and get them out of your head. Examples of these types of goals are flying by flapping your arms or making a pink elephant materialise from thin air.

Now it is time to make a list of the achievable goals that you always desired but never tried to get. These are things you know you could do if you tried, yet something has held you back from trying or achieving it, whether this was consciously done or not.

To get what you want in life, you must make a decision to clearly define what you really want and need for happiness. It makes no sense to go after whims and impulses that offer temporary satisfaction when you could be focusing your energy on long-term happiness. You would be better off putting energy towards moving forward in life.

Start by asking some honest and difficult questions about the direction your life is heading and the things that really motivate you in your desires. Think about things that you have been after in life and ask yourself what or who you will become once you have acquired it. How will it change your experience once you have attained it? Why do you really want it? Consider what real reasons underlie your need for this goal. Think about how it might affect those around you if you achieve it. What changes will you see? Is it that you truly want? Also consider what will not change one you achieve it and why you want it.

Getting what you want is easy. It happens all the time, every day, every hour. The hard part is making the decision to clearly define and understand exactly what you need and want. Knowing yourself is the hardest part.

That does not include the physical process of getting what you want, the prevention, evasion, obstacles and other things that can hinder you from achievement, not to mention holding onto your accomplishments once you have achieved them. Some things, even when you work hard for them, simply fall away if you do not take the necessary actions to nurture and sustain them.

Keep at it

This technique must be the easiest goal setting and achieving formula I have ever found. First you must know what goal you wish to achieve. Do not just have a vague knowing, but a real and concrete understanding in your mind. You can write it down on paper if you like. This is not necessary but some people find it helps. Your vision should include specific visual and physical outcomes that show your goal has been achieved in its entirety.

Now create a simple, straightforward action plan that others have used to achieve what you are seeking and launch the attack. Review and modify your plan as you go, always with the 'attack' mentality in place. Modifications should be used whenever you encounter resistance, difficulties or situational changes. Stay on the offensive unless you deeply feel you are spinning your wheels. If you are not making forward progress, simply stop, take a break and re-evaluate the plan of attack.

Repeat this process if necessary to achieve your goals. You cannot fail if you do not give up. Simply keep at it until you win the battle.

Space, Time...

You must first understand that time is an illusion present in the physical world. It is simply a means for processing the energy waves in our universe. In truth, time is not linear. Actions and events do not always happen in sequence as we see them in our physical reality. Instead of events A, B then C, you can manifest event C before event A. While there is still an order in which these things occur in the physical world, on a higher plane, the order can be altered.

Simultaneous time is a state in which all things are occurring at once. Creations occurs in the present where all probably past and futures are changing by our present actions. They continuously interact with each other, meaning a probably future event can influence thoughts and actions occurring in the present.

While you often hear that the past is dead, this is not entirely true. You can alter your perception of the past, which in turn alters the reality of the past. In this way, the past is still alive, because it does influence your perception in the present. By altering the past in your consciousness, you change the connection it holds in the current reality. You can shatter the illusion of time by going back and changing your thoughts. This influences your present and changes your current experiences. Your thoughts of the past influence your thoughts in the now.

235

Cosmic Ordering: You Can be Successful

You can change your past by altering your memory of it. Changing the way you think about events in the past allows you to utilise an alternate timeline that would be more beneficial to your current situation. Reinventing your past recreates your present. The alternate pas you choose will lead to certain events in your alternate present. By manipulating reality with your consciousness, you create synchronicities for the present or near future in the timeline you experience now as the alternate and actual timelines merge.

Changing your perception of the past also influences others' perception of your past. You are not just changing things in your own consciousness, but also in the consciousness of others. The merger of actual and alternate reality in your life creates the same mergers in their reality. We all have negative experiences in our lives, but it is our perception of the experiences that makes them negative. If you instead choose to perceive the event as good, seeing the positive benefits you gained from the experience, the perception of others will also see those benefits.

When you change your perceptions about the past, you are literally altering the past and your memory of the past. Reality exists only in your consciousness. The mind develops associations between your memories. By altering your perception about a past event, you change all other associations that stem from the memory. You can actually create temporal shifts in those elements of the past that others are unaware of. Any medium in which the past is recorded will actually reflect the changes.

The future springs from the present, created by the thoughts of mankind's present. Astrology works to predict the future by analysing the arrangement of the universe, which corresponds with the world of thoughts. In everything, there is a cause and effect. Whatever happens in the now will be followed by orderly results, creating the future.

A common misconception about astrology is that it predicts what will happen in the future by some mystical method. The truth is that the alignment of the stars does not determine our destiny, they only reflect it. This is true for any type of divination method.

The future remains in constant flux as the thoughts of men can be changed. This is why divination methods are not always right. Inaccurate predictions only reflect a timeline that was to occur, but was altered due to a change in thought. The future that was to happen changed, and that timeline was replaced by another.

Your fate is controlled by your thoughts. Changes of thought create changes in fate. When thoughts remain fixed or static, fate remains the same. The universe is simply a manifestation of the universal human mind. This universal mind speaks to use via the universe.

The universal mind has knowledge about the future based on our present thoughts. We receive feedback on the results our thoughts generate through signs. The universal mind can be thought of as a guide and counsel. When you listen to this divine intelligence, you get another chance to change the course of your destiny. Because the future is always in flux, the universe also remains in flux. Your changing thoughts affect the arrangement of all things in the universe. Just as when you change your clothes, you look different in the mirror, changing your thoughts reflects a different future. This also explains how a second psychic reading can produce different results from the first.

Even the features on your face and lines on your hand change when your thoughts change. These changes alter the reading of your fortune. Your inner landscape is reflected in the world around you, in material things. Understanding this can clear up many misunderstandings about the divination process.

The misconceptions people have about astrology and psychic readings can cause problems. If a reading results in a future you find distasteful, you may have negative thoughts about a future you think is destined and unchangeable. Those

237

negative thoughts ensure that negative result and you fulfil your own prophecy.

People who understand the truth rise above the idea of a fixed destiny. They know they can reshape reality any way they desire by tapping into the infinite Source living inside them. The human mind vibrating in harmony with the universal mind has the power and authority in all things.

We are each making our future with our thoughts. If you allow others to control the way you think, you are putting your destiny into someone else's hands. Only you and the Cosmos understand what is best for you, so you must take control of your own mind. You need not look to astrology or psychics to know your future. You can create your own future however you want it to be.

Our Reality is a Mental Construct

Some theorise that the universe is manifested in various ways on differing mental planes of reality. The physical universe is an illusion and is not as physical as it may appear. It is really just another layer in the mental universe. Time and space are not present in the physical universe alone, they exist on other planes of reality as well, but it is experienced in another way on those planes.

Think of the physical universe as a hologram. The world we perceive is only a simulation, much like a computer program. Each level of reality exists within the same program. The laws of physics work simply to control the reactions of particular properties within the physical universe. The universal mind that controls the laws of the physical universe will only suspend those laws by its own discretion.

The popular film, 'The Matrix,' showed the reality of our universe beautifully. Our reality is in fact a mental construct. We live in the matrix. Instead of computers decoding the contents, our minds are decoding energy to create the reality we perceive. The energy and ways in which we perceive it are generated by the universal mind, which is comprise of the collective human consciousness and The Cosmos.

Think about these important questions. Do your five senses operate only as energy receptors to relay electrical signals along the nerve, into the brain to be processed as data? Would we be able to perceive the world we live in were those electrical impulses to be cut off? Is it true that our body is just a life support system, taking oxygen from the air and carrying it to the cells in our bodies for nourishment and repair? Must we have this blood to be able to process energy?

A scientist may study the way a physical system operates so that he can work with it. He must follow the rules of that system if he wants to function within it. But the physical systems we perceive are only simulations that allow us to order our minds and reality on a physical level. The simulation masks true reality for the sake of easier survival in the physical realm.

We are not really seeing through our eyes and the associated nerve system. We absorb energy, sensing things directly through our consciousness. We are not really alive because we take in oxygen to our blood. Our minds absorb energy directly from the universal field. We perceive all energy directly with our consciousness.

Thinking involves the use of your conscious mind and thoughts are substantiated in the subconscious. And the subconscious mind is really a mental field or energy frequency in universal subjectivity. There really is no subjective 'your mind' or 'my mind' as though there were two. There is only One Mind. However, there are subjectivities in the subconscious state of thought.

In thinking, we use a universal creative medium, which is a receptive and malleable substance surrounding and permeating us, surrounding us on all sides. Our thinking is done through and into one common mind, creating dots of thought activity within. We are parts of the universal mind, ordered into individual minds. The universal subconscious medium allows us to think as a universal conscious mind. Your thoughts build a mental atmosphere around you. The only things that enter this atmosphere are those that you allow, whether consciously or unconsciously.

The mind is omnipresent, so there is no other place you can think. No 'out there' exists, there is only here. All things are projections of ourselves, showing on the screen of the external world. Even this process of projection is an experience born of the mind. It is consciousness projected within consciousness.

Internal and external are just illusions because all things are in the one location of mind. This mind is both in all locations and nowhere at the same time. It is only in the now. All things are created by consciousness and nothing exists outside of consciousness.

What you think of as your heart is actually your subconscious mind. When we say that a loved one is always present because he or she is in our hearts, we are using the universal field of subjectivity. While we may see or hear a person with our senses, that is only a means of experiencing the person in physical form. While spirit has to come into form to express itself, once we have experienced each other physically, we understand that there is an unbreakable connection created that transcends special separation. Separation is an illusion. The person's existence remains in universal subconscious that we find in our hearts. This means the person literally is always with us.

Physicality

Time is only a way of reflecting change. Beyond this, time has no existence. The now is all that is real. Time is not really a thing but a measure of our experiences and changes in the field of eternity. Time lets eternity be expressed in definitive terms of human experience. It is needed to allow us to experience within the whole, but it is not a thing of itself. You cannot really measure time. Yesterday is not accessible from now and the present slips continually into the past. You could not point to any particular point in the now before it would be gone to the past. Still, time is a necessary illusion in mankind's experience of the universe.

Space and time are intimately connected. Space is also not a thing of itself. It is only the outline for form. Space is relative, measuring distance within the *absolute*. It is also needed to express the spirit of all in our lives. Without it, we could not process energy into forms and interact with the universe. Do not allow yourself to fall under the confusion created by thinking of time and space as things. They are only relative concepts that allow us to measure and relate to the infinite.

Things residing in time and space are results. They do not create themselves. All are physical forms of the spirit. Form is needed to manifest the spirit. They will come in many shapes and sizes and last for varying periods of time. This system of form is arranged so that the spirit can come into self-expression through self-realisation. The global consciousness is beginning to understand that things are not what they appear and that the matter and form we have relied on so heavily are but transient forms used to express the formless Spirit.

The astral world also contains form, but not in such a definitive way as in the physical world. Still, the physical world is not as concretely definite as it may seem. True reality governs the physical plane and true reality is fluid and changeable. The realities in the physical and metal realms are two parts of one program, running with varying parameters. The physical and astral worlds differ in the manifestation of time. Change is slow on the physical plane, with slower moving energy. On the astral plane, events can take place very quickly.

Only one place is more concrete and definite than the physical plane. This is a place where you cannot alter conditions with your mind. The vibrations are lower and denser than those on earth. Our physical plane, in being susceptible to change, allows us the challenge of realising our desires. Giving up the physical world in order to enter the astral plane as a means to escape the frustration and despair in manifesting on

241

the physical plan would be a loss. We are given the powers of mind needed to fill our realisations as spiritual beings. Physicality allows us to interact with one another in an organised and comfortable way. It allows for change so that we can evolve through our interactions with each other. When you gain the skill of controlling your reality on a physical level, you also gain the skill of controlling your mind to the fullest extent.

One Mind

Understanding how the Holographic Theory of the human mind will allow you to understand how your mind blocks signals it has been conditioned to be uncomfortable with.

To grasp what I mean, we have to go back to 1981 when Dr Roger Sperry won a Nobel Prize in medicine for his 'Split-Brain' theory. His theory essentially concludes that the left brain dominates analytical thought and the right brain is where intuitive thought processes take place. Most people are right-handed, thus most of us do not fully use the more intuitive right brain.

We find that the 10 percent of humans who are left-hand dominant are more creative. They are writers and artists. The thoughts of these people operate on a middle range frequency, approximately 10 cycles per second. The analytical part of the mind operates in the beta range of 14 to 40 cycles per second.

Holographic Theory ties into the way these two portions of the brain work. You are certainly familiar with holograms and how they work. A hologram looks a bit like a photo negative but has swirls and patterns. When white light shines on the image, it takes on a three dimensional appearance. It seems to leap off the page.

These holograms are made with multiple points of reference and image sets of the object that will be made into a hologram. In these images are many viewpoints and perspectives. The light source reveals these different points of reference, causing them to coalesce, forming a three dimensional image. If you cut a hologram in half, you will still have the full picture, but with a small loss of spatial definition, which is not the case with a photographic negative. When you cut the hologram into tiny bits, you still have a picture of the object that is recognisable from any one of the pieces. The level of clarify depends upon the quality of the original hologram.

A leading researcher who believes that the brain likely records information in a similar way is Dr Karl Pribram of Stanford University is. The information gets stored within a family of neurons, not in one certain small group. This explains how the brain can have such an enormous capacity for storage of information. The brain may be storing the information spatially, not in the standard three-dimensional way that current theories surmise.

If this holds true, and if the theories of universal consciousness and the morphogenetic field have it right, then each person's brain acts as a small holographic segment of one total hologram. Your brain is actually part of one mind. It then follows logically that your mind can access the universal mind through the morphogenetic field. You only need to learn how to access it.

Princeton University is among the world's most prestigious universities. It is there that the engineering department set up a division to analyse and study anomalies. The entire scientific community took notice of this. The experiments performed at Princeton have resulted in a new understanding and appreciation for the mind/matter interaction, although sceptics still persist.

The scientists at Princeton looked at more than 800 experiments that were done in strictly controlled conditions. They tested subjection with an electronic random number generator, which is a computer version of flipping a coin. Subjects were encouraged to influence the outcome of otherwise random results. The resulting statistics showed that under some circumstances, subjects could influence the outcome of the 'coin flipping'. This means that consciousness does in fact interact with random physical systems.

Princeton University now runs a *Global Consciousness Project* that monitors the noosphere, or global consciousness. They can see how fluctuations appear in the random generators when global news reaches the masses.

David Hawkins, author of *Power vs. Force*, sets up a system for calibrating human emotions. He lays out levels ranging from 20 to 1000. The worst of these, viewed as negative as death itself, is *shame*. Shame is calibrated at a level of 20 and makes us more likely to become physically ill. The high end of the scale, in the range of 700 - 1000, contains *enlightenment*. This is thought of as the pinnacle of human consciousness evolution.

Just as with low vibratory frequencies, levels below 200 are associated with draining energy and negative integrity. There are many of these, like Guilt (30), Grief (75), Fear (100) and Pride (175). Pride is the turning point where people begin to feel positive, but it only feels good when contrasted to lower level feelings. Pride depends upon external conditions, making it vulnerable and defensive. It can easily revert to a lower level from any external change.

Power begins to show at the 200 level. Courage (200) falls under the zone of accomplishment, determination, exploration, and fortitude. At this level, people begin to emit as much energy as they take from the environment. The lower level emotions drain energy from the surrounding people without sending any energy out.

Other emotions like willingness (310), Acceptance (350) and Love (500) produce even more energy. The 500 level is associated with unconditional and permanent Love. It is non-fluctuating and does not depend on any external factor. It is the level of true happiness, a state of being.

This means that vibrating above the 200 level helps you to co-create your world and raises the consciousness of the whole. This makes you an important force in making the world a better place. Just feeling good helps everyone. Studies show that there is a rising shift in consciousness as the global energy levels rise.

Our emotions determine the vibration levels emitting from our minds. In our connection with the *one mind*, our vibrations levels have an impact on the larger mind. By feeling good with emotions above the 200 level, you are adding power to the world, rather than draining it.

Imagine how the global consciousness would change if a large number of people gathered to vibrate peace and love. Theoretically, it would change the entire world for the better.

Based on this research, we can conclude that even a small number of peace-loving experts, if they could align themselves with the unified field of natural law, would have the power to greatly influence the global consciousness. This type of cohesive conscious field resists external influences.

We can also conclude that if a peace-loving group was big enough, the stress and negative emotion of the entire world could be dissolved. We would not need to put up shields to resist our enemies. Instead there would be no enemy. This would be a way for any nation to defend itself, without weapons, and without killing. Instead of political negotiations, we would use positive emotion to influence social relationships, pulling the plug on the threats of fanaticism, terrorism and war. Each of us influences the other because we are each connected to the other.

Focus on what You Desire
You can raise your level of vibrations in some simple ways. You only need to take responsibility for your own life. Do not give power to others that would change your destiny. When things do not go the way you desire, take a second look at your deep seated beliefs and make changes where needed. Exchange your limiting beliefs for ones that make you feel powerful. Avoid watching the news or reading the newspaper. No amount of dwelling on bad news will help you raise the global consciousness. Listen to music that fuels your positive feelings.

Cosmic Ordering: You Can be Successful

Focus on what it is you want to do in life, not what you want to avoid.

16

Become a Goal Setting Power Machine

Once upon a time, a small bird named Satoo lived in a vast jungle. One hot summer day, a terrible wildfire erupted and the flames devoured many trees and animals living in the jungle. Other birds flew high into the sky and far away to safety, but Satoo couldn't bear to leave her precious jungle home to burn.

Day and night, she flew with all her might back and forth to the river, filling her tiny beak with water to drop on the raging fires. Satoo's rare heart of courage and unshakable determination moved the heavenly gods to shed tears, and a great rain poured down upon the jungle, extinguishing the flames. And so it is that even the smallest actions of a determined spirit can change the world.

Everything is Thought
The universe can be thought of as being comprised of seven states of matter that can be ordered by their densities or rate of vibrational frequency. We are familiar with the first three common states: solid, liquid and gas. The different states of matter each have particular properties with varying rates of motion for the atoms within them.

The fourth state of matter is plasma, or ionised gas. When gas is superheated to the point where its electrons break from the nuclei and join with other nuclei, it creates plasma, which you know as fire. Plasma is highly unstable with molecules repeated breaking away to join other nuclei. This makes it behave in unpredictable and erratic ways. Stars are also made of plasma. It is a powerful and often destructive state.

A beam is another state of matter. It has its own category because particles not in a beam state move in various random directions. However, beam particles, whether they are solid, liquid gas or plasma move together in one direction harmoniously.

Notice how a beam is coherent and well ordered, while the state of matter just below, plasma, is chaotic. This juxtaposition of order and chaos makes an excellent analogy for the idea that the greatest confusion exists just before the point where peace forms. There is great chaos before order arrives. There will be a great war before a great peace.

A beam is also different from other states of matter because it is not dependent on temperature. Without the orderly formation of a beam, particles vibrating with high levels of energy create a friction that translates into heat. However, a beam creates no friction because the particles all move in the same direction and do not collide with the others.

When particles collide, the resulting friction creates heat and a higher vibrational energy. A beam can create heat, but not within or by itself. A beam creates heat when its single-direction particles collide against other matter. When solar photons collide with your skin, you notice the heat from the sun. More intense beams with a greater concentration of particles will create higher amounts of friction, creating more heat when it interacts with other particles. This is why a laser can cause burns. Heat is an energetic vibration created by the friction between one state of matter and another or between two of the same states of matter.

There is also a lower state of matter than the five we have discussed, known as the sixth state of matter, because it was discovered after the first five. It is known as zero state or BEC (Bose-Einstein Condensate). It is denser than a solid and is the most condensed form of all matter. Like a beam, BEC is non-thermal. It emits no heat because its particles are not in motion, leaving no chance for friction to develop.

Become a Goal Setting Power Machine

BEC was introduced to the world by the scientist Bose, who shared his findings with Albert Einstein. Einstein worked with him to publish the work and make it public. The joint effort let the world know about this previously unknown state of matter.

The BEC state comes about when you freeze matter to an extremely low temperature. The temperature must be just a sliver above absolute zero. When in the BEC state, atoms form a wave pattern by overlapping onto each other. This makes the BEC a wave comprised of matter. If it were possible to compress the wave, a singularity would result. If you could condense enough mass into the singularity, you would have a black hole.

Some say that this zero state could eventually lead scientists to develop flat space technology, meaning we could move enormous objects in small spaces through use of a black hole. The problem they are still grappling with is that the critical mass of the black hole would likely compress the matter, shattering and scattering all of its atoms.

The black hole is the source of much mystery. Some believe that were we to actually make a black hole, the universe itself could be torn apart. The truth is that an enormous amount of energy would be needed to compress the BEC to the critical point.

Many think of another form of matter as the seventh state. This is the thought wave, which is the least condensed of all states. These waves are at a higher energy level than beams, moving faster than particles in a beam. Thought waves appear to have no limit to speed, able to be in two places at once. They are both local and non-local.

In essence, all things are one thing. All matter is a manifestation of universal intelligence or thought waves. Thoughts are simply a higher state of matter that can be condensed into any of the other states of matter. In the end, it is the universal mind that is the raw material for all things.

Further, these theorists believe that the universal mind is responsible for the different states of matter. For instance, why is water liquid at room temperature, ice at colder temperatures and gas at higher ones? It is believed that the universal mind exists in the matter and creates a 'memory' of the other states. Matter is mentally programmed with the arrangement of the atoms, and particles in the manners that produce these different states.

The Belief System

You already know that belief is the most important part of abundance creation. For this reason, learning to manage and create the beliefs you want deep in your subconscious mind is a very useful skill. Your beliefs are the most powerful tools you have.

These beliefs are not about religion, they are about you. Your practice of goal setting, affirmations, positive thinking and creative visualisation will come to little without your faith that the method will truly change your life.

Take a moment to consider what you believe about yourself. Both consciously and subconsciously, what do you think about yourself? Do you like yourself? It is likely you have some positive and negative beliefs. Each belief will either propel you towards or block you from your goals.

Next think about whether these beliefs match the way you want to feel about yourself. What self-beliefs do you think are good to have? Which ones do you want to have?

Write your beliefs down on paper in the form of affirming statements like, 'I am always taking the right actions aimed at improving myself daily'. Then choose one of the items on your list. Be sure to choose an affirmation that is easy for you to believe. Avoid outlandish ones.

Check to see that you truly, deeply want this belief in your subconscious mind. Use the 'Why?' *Effective Questions* to be sure this is what you want. Come to the core of your motivations. Ask why you want this belief and how you can believe it. How would it feel if you already had this belief? Do you really want to believe it? If you can answer 'Yes' to these questions, continue on. If not, refine the affirmation until you can agree that you really do want to believe it.

You need to be sure that the belief you choose will fit well with your current system of values. If it contradicts beliefs you already have, there may be a problem. Although you do not need integration with your current beliefs, it is helpful that the beliefs work well together. Remember that it is normal for some beliefs to be true at certain times and not at others.

Use effective questions to install the beliefs you desire. Ask if the belief contradicts other beliefs. Consider if the belief can give you the kind of emotions you need. How does the belief help you move towards or accelerate you towards your goals? Think about anything you may need to risk or sacrifice if you choose to believe in this belief right now. Consider if the belief is proper and appropriate in the context you have applied it to. Ask what implications, positive or negative, will result if you install the belief in your current belief system.

If after asking these questions, you still feel uncomfortable with the belief, just move onto installing it. The clearing phase for belief installation uses the following effective questions.

Do you have any objections, consciously or unconsciously, to this belief? Consider any objections, arguments or conflicts that may be stopping you from installing the belief into your current system. Are there blocks in your mind, undermine the effectiveness of the belief? What are they?

Think about any objections your *sharp inner voice* is coming up with to this belief. Are there any events in your life that can counter the voice's objections? Consider if the voice has a point; if there were times in your life when the belief did not hold true and how often that may have occurred. Think about whether the objection is true at all and how that might be. Is the objection true all of the time? If the objection is true less than half the time, is there another valid statement you should believe in? Think about the likelihood the objection would prove true in real life, not just in theory. If it is true less than 50 percent of the time, or never at all, is it still valid or should it be null and void?

Think about how you can reduce or stop the conflict from causing problems for you in the real world. If an event arises that counters the belief, how will you react? Are there ways you can evade such a conflict?

Once you have completed the clearing phase of questions, move onto the motivational or filling phase. Spend time thinking through each question deeply and really pondering the answers. Add more questions that are similar to those I have suggested. It is useful to ask yourself the same questions repeatedly, possibly with a different wording or approach.

Now that you have cleared your thoughts on the conflicts that may arise to the desired belief, begin filling or motivating yourself. Ask what you would gain if you took on the belief and what you would lose if you did not. How will you feel when you have installed this belief? What will you be like then? Consider what your world will be like and what you will by saying to yourself by taking on the belief. How soon will you be able to truly believe it and how will you know that you have accomplished that?

Consider the ways in which the belief is true and think about the logical reasons, circumstances, life events and facts that prove its truth. Also think about emotional reasons for you to believe it is true. Does the belief simply 'feel' right? Does just believing in it create an excitement or lifting of the spirit in you? How can you recreate conditions in your life that will affect another situation where this belief shows itself to be true, thereby strengthening your belief?

Again, write down your own similar questions the work towards installing the truth of your new belief and motivating you to take on the belief. This method of asking, thinking and answering words whether you put it down on paper or in your mind in a relaxed, quiet, and focused state.

Daily Meta Questions

Daily affirmations and reviewing of motivational quotes are

great ways to reach your goals. You can add to your practice or even replace it with what are known as 'Meta Questions'. These are simple, honest and straightforward questions designed to shift your thinking into a more constructive, efficient and practical pattern.

Meta Questions can be especially helpful if you have a habit of waking in a negative state of mind. If the first thoughts that pop in your mind are of concerns, anxiety or complaints, the method will help you think more clearly. I know this works because I tested it out on those people who admitted they wake up on the wrong side of the bed. This technique has taught me to circumvent the problem by creating a set of effective questions that help correct focus every morning.

You reorient your thinking to the 'big picture' rather than focusing on the small negativities. This quickly puts you back on the right path.

Meta Questions are like super-charged effective questions. Not only do they help shift focus to more constructive thoughts, they also make your questions more efficient and proficient. In other words, the more meta questions you ask, the better you get at asking them.

Begin by asking how you can create better questions for yourself every day. Consider why it is important to think of better questions each day. Ask what it will feel and be like when the quality of your questions keeps improving daily.

Here is a set of questions that I find especially useful. First ask how you can make today's questions better than yesterday. How can you ask even better questions tomorrow than you are asking today?

Now on to the *why*. Why must you ask better questions today than yesterday? Why must they be even better tomorrow than today? Ask what will happen when today's questions are better than yesterday's and tomorrow's questions are better than today's.

You can improve things even more with additional questions. Think about how you can use better questions to improve each facet of your daily life. Why must you do this? What would it be and feel like once you are using these better questions?

Consider how you can use the answers, insights and ideas from your questions to ask even better questions every day. Think about why you must do this and what it will be and feel like when you act on the answers, insights and ideas your every-improving daily questions bring. How will you know if an idea you come up with will be the best possible solution to take action upon your current situation?

There is an endless variety of questions you can ask. By now you should recognise the pattern of 'How', 'Why must', and 'What would it be and feel like.' Followed with 'How will I know?' These effective questions are like compound interest in the bank. Every day the rewards become greater exponentially. And those rewards are much better than any monetary gains you will get at the bank.

You can also take pains to write out your meta questions in a beautiful presentation. Use some software to create them in a beautiful script. Print it out and keep the questions in a highly visible place so you can look at them each day. Spend 10 or 20 minutes in calm contemplation, focussing on your questions. This should be enough to expand your level of power and effectiveness in changing your life for the better.

Life Changing Questions

People like you and I are goal seekers. We are like machines with a single purpose: accomplishment. There is a reason you came to be reading this. There is something you need. There is someone you want to become; something you want to have or do. Quite simply, *you want*.

I call this mode of thinking 'Wishful-ism'. Perhaps you have the urge to become a more confident public speaker. So what are the effective questions that will help you think the right way, make the right decisions, take the right actions and finally achieve your goal?

Become a Goal Setting Power Machine

There are three questions that will get you closer to your goal. They are 'Why must I,' 'How can I,' and, 'What if I'. So with the goal of public speaking in mind, you would ask, 'Why MUST I become a more confident speaker?'. Then ask 'How CAN I become a more confident speaker?' and, 'What IF I AM a more confident speaker?' Let's take a closer look at these questions to understand why they are so effective.

'Why MUST I'. This question is so powerful, actually the MOST powerful question you can ask, because it aims a narrow focus on your PURPOSE. The word MUST says there are no options but to succeed.

When your purpose is powerful, your reasons motivating, the cause great, you find the energy, drive and perseverance to drive through all obstacles and push your way to the goal. Your purpose, or the reason for your desire, powers the goal-seeking machine within you. The stronger and longer-lasting your power source, the more your actions will propel you forward.

The 'How CAN I' is not intended to produce direct solutions in your conscious mind. You need not worry too much about what actions you are required to reach your goal. This question is actually speaking to your inner self, which will work on the problem for you and give you the answers you need.

These words are like the keywords you type into a search box online. Your subconscious is the search engine. You may get matches to your keywords immediately, or your mind may search for months (sometimes years) before the answer is presented, but it will arrive.

When your mind locates the answer, the 'How CAN I' becomes like an algorithm in a computer program, showing you the code or instructions. It will spell out the actions you need to take and lead to the fulfilment of your goals. It will show you the path that leads to your destination.

Now we understand how our goal machine has an energy source and a built-in processor. Let's look at the role played by 'What IF I'. This question is aimed at realising your dream in your mind to help you believe it so you can achieve it.

The question 'What IF I' in essence sends a command to your mind to create a mental picture of the desired goal. Instead of simply creating a visualisation, you are putting yourself in the role of the achiever, with sharp focus and extreme detail. When you ask the question, you instruct your mind to produce the possibilities, details, results and outcomes using your six senses.

This question will help you visualise what you will see when the goal is attained, what you will hear, and what you will feel, smell, taste and understand.

The 'What IF I' creates a three-dimensional model or blueprint in your mind for the desired outcome. It is a set of instructions for your goal-seeking machine so it can do what it has been made to do: create your desires. Now you have it all in place. You have a power source, processor and blueprint for your machine. But without turning it on, it will only sit idle. You must take action and turn the machine on. All the potential in the world goes nowhere without action. The seed does not become the tree if it never sprouts.

More Effective than Goal Setting

Goal setting experts have long relied on a traditional method that may not be as effective as they would lead you to believe. I often wonder if these 'experts' actually practice what they preach. There is a missing link in traditional goal setting, a chasm which is hard to cross if you do not have proper motivation to take the actions necessary to achieving your goal.

The missing link is what is in the mind's eye. 'The Mind's Eye' is your purpose. It is like a vision, an obsession, a passion or a dream. It is grandiose and larger than life. This big picture in the mind's eye is your life's purpose. The drama in these words is intentional. Your life's purpose is more powerful than any other force in your life. A goal is typically a wish for a material object, monetary gain or life situation. Goals are often small and disjointed.

Become a Goal Setting Power Machine

Many times, people go after these small goals without ever considering why they want them. They fail to look at their lives as a whole and see how the path has led them here and where it is going next. Looking at the big picture gives your whole life meaning, creating further drive your purpose.

Take a moment to ask yourself why you want that new BMW. Why do you want to live in a manor house? Why do you want to earn more money? Why do you want to get married? Why? Why? Why? When you ask these questions and keep probing, you will see that motivation behind these goals often comes from a search for happiness, security or freedom. You may simply think, 'I just want them.'

Fair enough. There is nothing wrong with wanting these things. But do you really think the BMW or manor house or big pay cheque or perfect life partner will give you happiness, security or freedom? Will these things make you feel truly alive?

Think to a time when you achieved a goal in the past. When you reached that milestone, what was the next step? Did you think to yourself, 'Well, okay, so now what?'

That happens to a lot of us. Our failure to see the big picture leaves us floundering for the next step in life. By understanding our ultimate, grand purpose in life, we find a meaning that drives us along a continuing path. Your life's purpose is why you were born. You can call it destiny or fate, but whatever you call it, know that it is entirely within your hands to fulfil it.

Your life's purpose is something you can choose, but then again it is not all choice. It is both within and outside of your power to choose. It is the collective total of all the choices you have made since birth, right up until today.

Clearly, you know your life's purpose is within your power because you have made many choices along the way in life. You have asked for this or that, whether or not you got it, building an image or vision of your life, which is your life's purpose; the reason you were born; the thing you must do

257

before you die.

In some ways, however, your life's purpose is beyond your power. The decisions of the past are difficult if not impossible to reverse. In the big picture, all your choices count in one journey through life. Some decisions simply cannot be undone, no matter how much energy or attention you put towards them.

Write your own eulogy. Talk about yourself like you are a historian, or perhaps the funeral director speaking of the dearly departed to the loved ones left behind. Look back and make note of all the great things you achieved. Include your mistakes and failures too, but be sure to write down how you overcame those difficulties. Show how you made a difference in the world, no matter how small or big.

Now that your life has been put into perspective, go ahead with the traditional goal setting methods. Make your smaller goals, but pull your inspiration from your life's purpose. Set goals, and milestones that will help you define and reach your ultimate purpose.

This exercise solidifies your motivations helping you to persist. Even if you have not achieved some of your small goals, you still feel confident because there is a higher purpose you are working towards.

Access Your Creative Time to Change Your Life

We all have certain times of the day when we are most productive. By simply making use of just 120 minutes per day out of the 1,440 minutes available of this productive time, you can overcome procrastination and stagnation as you become a driven productive machine.

When you spend the 120 minutes on your life's purpose, you gain 14 hours of supremely productive time each week. In a month, that's 60 hours. In a year, you gain 50,400 seconds worth of supremely productive time. All that can be used towards your goal, if it is a new business, a great novel, a masterpiece or just a job your boss wants done that can get you promoted.

258

Become a Goal Setting Power Machine

Consider how wealthy you would be if you put a value on that golden time. How much would you gain? If you used, say, 43,800 minutes, being productive, creative, positive, at your most perfect level of achievement, when you can only produce brilliant results, what would be the monetary value of that time?

What would you say 360 super-productive seconds of your time is worth not only to you, but to other people? Set a high value. Whatever you think you are worth, double or triple it. Heck, multiply it by 10, because in those productive seconds, your brain is performing at its peak, synchronised, productive and creative. What ever you create during this time will come back to you 2, 4, 6, 8 or 10 times in value.

Use the 120 minutes to hone your mind and organise your day. Meditate and plan. Spend your time making the rest of your day shine. Invest in yourself and make the remainder of your day, as productive as possible.

You probably spend one third of the day working. It may be a lot to ask for you to be highly productive during all of that time, so let us say we will just make three-quarters of those hours productive. So when you use those 120 minutes to make the other quarter of that time supremely productive, you have now spent one third of the day in productive hours.

Now consider how, after months or years of spending these 120 minutes on making yourself more productive and creative, how much more productive you will become throughout the day. What if your productivity when up exponentially? Now your time is infinitely more productive.

So now about that value you placed on 60 minutes of time, times 10 per hour. Think about how much more powerful and productive your work will be from the investment in your initial 120 minutes.

Okay, so when are those 120 minutes in the day? The first 60 comes as soon as you wake up. This means you will need to get up 120 minutes earlier, wash your face, warm up a little and then spend an 60 minutes planning, thinking, mentally creating

259

or meditating.

Then you will spend your second 60 minutes on mechanical tasks. This is your time of action. Once you have spent 60 minutes planning and meditating, you will want to take action based on your meditations. Get to work and implement your plans. All that thinking and planning has put you into a state where you are raring to go. You will be motivated and driving to accomplish. When you get this drive and fall into your rhythm, you find that the momentum carries you through the rest of the day. You will work and work towards your goals and feel magnetically bound to it. You will not want to stop until it is done. You will BE your work.

Who am I? What am I? Where am I?

Look around you and observe your life. Take a good long look at who you are, making note of what, who and where you are in this moment. Examine what you have and what you have done in all facets of your life.

Now ask yourself some deep questions that may appear simple on the surface. Ask these questions in relation to each of the six dimensions of your life: physical, emotional, spiritual, mental, financial, and social. Who am I? What am I? Where am I? What have I done? What have I achieved? What do I have?

Get a piece of paper and write down these questions. Begin thinking about the answers. If you want, go right ahead and jump on your PC and open the word processor. Type these questions out.

Now breathe for a second. Just relax. This is not some dreary work assignment. This is supposed to be a fun exploration in getting to know yourself; in understanding the complicated, captivating, splendorous creature you are.

Now here's something for you to chew on. If when you ask, 'What have I achieved?' is 'Nothing', be prepared to say what you mean by that. Is it that you think nothing you have achieved is worth remembering? Are you being too modest? Explain it and be specific. Produce some detailed, concrete answers that are backed up by tangible things or situations in your life. Be sure to address the questions with each of the six dimensions discussed.

Now look at your paper and your answers. Think about how you arrived in this place, in this situation, at this present moment. Think about those particular decisions, actions, and choices that brought you to be where you are now. Certainly the things that brought you here were the decisions you made and actions you took. You may think it is coincidence or luck, but even when fortuitous events occur, it is your decision or action to take advantage of it that created your situation. Write down these events, decisions and actions, being as honest with yourself as you can.

When that is done, choose one of those 'decision moments' that you wrote down. Pick one that you think was the most important to the outcome of your life.

Next start with a new sheet of paper and create a headline for that decision. Write down both the headline and a brief description of the results of that decision. Now close your eyes for a bit and remember that decision-making moment. Relive it in minute detail, and ask yourself what your state of mind was when you made that decision. How did it feel the instant before you made the decision? What was happening in your mind that led you to make that particular decision?

You may find that what you were doing then was asking yourself questions, whether in your conscious mind or more deeply, about each option you had available and what to potential outcome would be for each. Whenever you think, analyse or try to come to a decision, you are asking yourself questions. They are vital in finding the right path, whether the conclusions you draw are correct or not. Now you should be able to see how questions have shaped your life.

We can deduce logically that the current life condition you have came about because of the decisions and subsequent actions you took in the past. Those decisions were made based on the clarity and quality of your thinking at the time. We can then logically surmise that *the qualities of the decisions you make are determined by the quality of the questions you ask.*

Understand that if you want to live an effective life, you need to make effective decisions. To make a decision effective, you need your thinking to be effective. To think effectively, you need to ask effective questions. Now do you understand how powerful questions are in shaping your life?

Achieving is an Art Form

Getting what you want in life is an exact science, like mathematics, chemistry or physics. Certain laws govern the process of becoming wealthy. They can be learned by anyone and when they are obeyed, there is a mathematical certainty that riches will result.

Securing property and money is the result of going about things in a particular way. Those who behave in a particular way, whether intentionally or not, get what they want. Those who do not follow these behaviour patterns, no matter how much effort they put into it, remain stagnant.

This is a natural law, just like cause and effect. This means that any person who learns to follow this pattern of behaviour will get what they want without fail.

When two men in the same neighbourhood, engaged in the same business and one fails while the other succeeds, we can see that becoming wealthy is not a matter of environment. While some places may be more favourable to success than others, some environments may be more favourable than others, but the example demonstrates that getting what you want is really the product of the right behaviours.

When we take a careful examination of people who have gotten rich, we learn that they are not really very special. They have no amazing abilities or special talents. Clearly, they did not get where they are because of some special quality in them that gave them an advantage over others. In most cases, they simply became rich because they behaved a certain way.

This brings up the question of whether this way of acting or being is so difficult, that only a few have been able to follow it. This cannot be the case. People with great intelligence and great stupidity get rich; those with great strength and great weakness attain wealth. All kinds of people gain wealth and there is nothing special about any of them. Any one who can read and understand language can get rich.

It does not matter what profession or business you choose. People get rich at any manner of businesses and jobs, while the neighbour next door remains in poverty, engaged in the same business.

It is a valid argument to say you will do better in businesses that you like, that fit well with our personality. Your particular talents and abilities, when well-developed, you will have the most success in a business that benefits from those abilities and talents.

It is equally true that a business that is well-suited to your location will do better. An ice-cream parlour does well near a beach resort. So getting rich does not require that you follow any specific plan of business, but a specific way of thinking and acting. If you have a business and someone in the same area is getting rich at that business while you are not, it is because he is doing things in a certain way and you are not.

The tide of opportunity sets in differing directions and differing times, as benefits the whole to the greatest extent in that point of social evolution. The man or woman who knows how to swim with the tide, not against it, will ride the waves to where opportunity flows.

There is no reason the working class cannot become the master class. The law of wealth applies the same to people from all walks of life. When the working class learns this lesson, they will flourish just as the master class does. As long as the wealth doing things a certain way and continue to do so, they will continue to do well. The workers have the advantage in that they are not held down by the slothfulness that too much wealth unearned can bring.

It is not a lack of wealth that keeps the poor in poverty.

Cosmic Ordering: You Can be Successful

There is enough wealth to go around for all, in fact, there is more than enough. The visible supply of wealth in material things in nearly inexhaustible. The invisible supply of wealth is truly inexhaustible. All things on this planet were made from the original substance, from which all things continue to spring.

Newer shapes and forms are always coming into being, while older ones are fading from existence. All these forms are shaped by the same thing. The supply of formless substance, or original substance, is unlimited. The entire universe is comprised of it and there is still more always in reserve because it is infinite. All spaces, within, between and around the material forms we see around us are permeated and filled by the original substance. It is the raw material that all things were forged from. There is no limit to how much more can be made. Knowing this, you should understand that no one is rich or poor because of nature. Nature has provided more than enough for all.

Because nature renews itself, always growing new, it has an inexhaustible store of riches. That supply can never run out. Original substance is a living substance, imbued with creative energy, constantly creating more. If a supply of any raw material is exhausted, more will be found. When the soil runs out of nutrients, new soil is made. Even if every precious metal was mined from the hills, if man were still to need such things at the state of his evolution then, the original substance would create more. The formless substance knows of our needs and responds to them in kind. The universe will not let us go without.

This law is true of mankind as a whole. The human race is abundantly rich. When we find poor individuals, they are poor because they have not followed the path the universe sets for them. They have not done things in the certain way needed for an individual to become rich.

The formless substance has intelligence and does think. It is living and always tends to create more life. It creates the natural impulses in life in which we seek to stay alive. The urges to expand and push boundaries and form new frontiers all come from this intelligence. The universe is the physical representation of the formless living substance, seeking a means to express itself more fully.

The formless substance is a great living presence that always seeks to create more life and fuller experience. We can see this in the way nature works to advance life and evolve species to make better use of their environments. In these endeavours, all things that administer life are provided in bounty.

You have heard of the cup that overflowed. This is a story of a bucket that is like the cup, only larger, it is an invisible bucket. Everyone has one. It determines how we feel about ourselves, about others, and how we get along with people. Have you ever experienced a series of very favourable things which made you want to be good to people for a week? At that time, your bucket was full.

A bucket can be filled by a lot of things that happen. When a person speaks to you, recognising you as a human being, your bucket is filled a little. Even more if he calls you by name, especially if it is the name you like to be called. If he compliments you on your dress or on a job well done, the level in your bucket goes up still higher. There must be a million ways to raise the level in another's bucket. Writing a friendly letter, remembering something that is special to him, knowing the names of his children, expressing sympathy for his loss, giving him a hand when his work is heavy, taking time for conversation, or, perhaps more important, listing to him.

When one's bucket is full of this emotional support, one can express warmth and friendliness to people. But, remember, this is a theory about a bucket and a dipper. Other people have dippers and they can get their dippers in your bucket. This, too, can be done in a million ways.

Let's say I am at a dinner and inadvertently upset a glass of thick, sticky chocolate milk that spills over the table cloth, on a lady's skirt and then down on to the carpet.

I am embarrassed. 'Bright Eyes' across the table says, 'You upset that glass of chocolate milk.' I made a mistake, I know I did, and then he told me about it! He got his dipper in my bucket! Think of the times a person makes a mistake, feels terrible about it, only to have someone tell him about the known mistake ('red pencil' mentality!).

Buckets are filled and buckets are emptied, emptied many times because people don't really think about what are doing. When a person's bucket is emptied, he is very different than when it is full. You say to a person whose bucket is empty, 'That is a pretty tie you have,' and he may reply in a very irritated, defensive manner.

Although there is a limit to such an analogy, there are people who seem to have holes in their buckets. When a person has a hole in his bucket, he irritates lots of people by trying to get his dipper in their buckets. This is when he really needs somebody to pour it in his bucket because he keeps losing.

The story of our lives is the interplay of the bucket and the dipper. Everyone has both. The unyielding secret of the bucket and the dipper is that when you fill another's bucket it does not take anything out of your own bucket. The level in our own bucket gets higher when we fill another's, and, on the other hand, when we dip into another's bucket we do not fill our own ... we lose a little.

For a variety of reasons, people hesitate filling the bucket of another and consequently do not experience the fun, joy, happiness, fulfilment, and satisfaction connected with making another person happy. Some reasons for this hesitancy are that people think it sounds 'fakey', or the other person will be suspicious of the motive, or it is 'brown-nosing'.

Therefore, let us put aside our dipper and resolve to touch someone's life in order to fill their bucket.

17

Unlocking Secret Knowledge

Are You Reflecting Reality or Creating It?

You may have wondered whether reality is merely a reflection of your beliefs or if your beliefs are actually creating it. You can understand the answer to this question by looking at the differences between the concepts of objective reality and subjective reality. In general, people see reality as an objective situation in which they are trapped. They see the physical laws governing the world around them as absolute. Some examples of these laws are gravity, magnetism and thermodynamics. However, there is another side of reality and even these seemingly concrete physical laws are subject to higher laws of reality.

According to quantum physics, when we look at things on a subatomic scale, we see that all things are really made of a pure energy that is aware, conscious and living. This means that the laws of the physical universe are really governed by a set of conscious mental laws. Therefore, the physical is ultimately ruled by the spiritual.

To say *it is mind over matter* does not express the truth fully. We cannot simply defy gravity by leaping from a building and flying over the city. We must have a potent, justifiable reason for bending the rules. This is why some actions can land you in trouble if both your beliefs and purpose are not aligned properly.

The physical laws are not subject to any single mind. It is a collective consciousness governed by all minds. It is the eternal, endless intelligent awareness of The Cosmos that connects our minds to form a single consciousness. This

267

universal mind determines how physical laws can or cannot be subjugated by an individual mind.

When a person does manage to defy physical laws, it is because he or she has aligned himself or herself in harmony with the purpose and will of the universal mind. This is how miracles come about; where people survive an otherwise certain death; when instantaneous healing occurs.

Objective reality is actually the spiritual law of the universe. It is unchanging, immutable and constant. Whether you believe in this or not is irrelevant. It is there and that is what makes it objective. Your individual beliefs and mind can not subjugate realty to your will unless you are aligned with the universal mind that is above all physical laws.

Spirituality, Truth and Reality
Let us understand this better by taking a look at the components of spirituality, truth and reality. Spirituality can be defined as a 'belief in those facets of reality that are not from or in the material universe'. Spirit is the essence of all reality. A truth is any opinion that conforms to reality.

Objective reality is the present situation that exists, whether anyone known about it or not and whether anyone wants it that way or not. Therefore, truth takes its basis in reality. However, truth is an opinion and objective reality is independent of opinions. When I hear the modern expression, 'my truth' or 'your truth', I really hear, 'my opinion, your opinion'. I say this because the assertion that we each create our own objective reality is a fantasy.

Beliefs Reflect Objective Reality
When your beliefs reflect reality, they are beliefs based in objective reality. They have no power to create or uncreate anything.

In subjective reality, you have more control. This facet of reality is made of your thoughts, opinions and interpretation of experience. This is the inner landscape of your mind. It can be influenced, controlled and shaped by you. This makes subjective reality changeable by way of your belief system.

Now we know that the spiritual law is the highest law and that the world within is of the spirit. The world inside us governs the world outside of us. Your thoughts control your reality. You can maintain control over all facets of reality when you follow the spiritual laws of consciousness. Therefore, we can control subjective reality using the powers of actual objective reality. Subjective reality can change, making it temporal. You choose to belief something else and now you see something else changing reality in an instant or gradually over time.

Beliefs Create Subjective Reality

The beliefs you have that create reality exist in subjective reality. They can form, perpetuate or alter reality.

Some things exist even without your belief. They are out there regardless of your feelings about them. Your belief allows them to come into your personal experience by way of the Law of Attraction. Your disbelief repels these things so they do not appear in your reality. These things are there, existing for others, but not for you.

All of your experiences exist in your world because of your thoughts, either past or present. This paradigm can show you how and why everything that has happened in your life occurred. Consider the things that were already within your inner landscape that caused these words to manifest in your reality, a manifestation of your own thoughts.

The reason I have taken such pains to explain the difference between subjective and objective reality is so that you can choose authentic beliefs that will empower you to form the reality you seek.

Knowledge truly is power. Your greater understanding about your beliefs and the power they hold now puts you in an advantageous position, where all things you desire will be possible for you.

Cosmic Ordering: You Can be Successful

Thoughts versus Beliefs

To truly understand how the mind and reality interact, you need to know how thoughts and beliefs are different. There are literally millions of thoughts running through your mind, but only those thoughts that are tied to emotions, those that are beliefs, have power.

A belief is any thought that is real or true in your mind. You choose which thoughts to believe and which to discard simply with your will. You choose to make a thought into belief by choosing to attach emotion to the thought.

While thoughts can become things, no all thoughts will behave this way. Only those that have a strong emotion attached to them have the power of belief needed to form your desired reality. Your thoughts are first in your conscious mind, and then are absorbed by the subconscious memory, fuelling your creative power both day and night.

This is at the heart of the inner workings of the Law of Attraction. The laws of attraction and repulsion take place entirely in your subconscious mind. Your thoughts can begin in your full awareness, but they must be stored elsewhere to stop from crowding your conscious mind. Once the thought has occurred, it goes on to the subconscious. Consider someone who comes into the world who does not say they are poor, but lives with the unconscious belief that he is poor. As long as that thought remained in the subconscious mind, he would remain in poverty. He may have no understanding of the Law of Attraction, but it would be working just the same.

Your emotions spring from the subconscious mind, where your memories are stored. Your memories and emotions are closely linked and that is why they are kept in the same location of mind. Emotion can be thought of as energy in motion. When more emotion is attached to a thought, the thought is more powerful and effective. Weak thoughts that we care little about have no power. We create things in life based on our subconscious beliefs, not our conscious thinking. That is why consciously wanting is not enough. This is a good thing.

270

Unlocking Secret Knowledge

Can you imagine a world in which every thought that came to mind manifested itself? Our imaginations would become quite dangerous as all of our fears manifested in front of us. We would be terrified of allowing even one negative thought to enter our minds. Just the fear of negative thoughts would create them! We would be afraid to think at all.

Because emotion is moving energy, all activity is emotional. As the seat of emotion, the subconscious mind is the operational facet of the mind. Activities are driven by the subconscious, our creative faculty. The subconscious mind works in harmony with the conscious mind (or will) that directs and instructs our activities. The combination of these two parts of mind involves will and emotion.

Conscious thoughts are weak because they are not enduring; only staying in your conscious mind for a moment. However, when the though dwells in you subconscious and becomes attached to emotion, it intensifies, generation momentum and resonance, continuing perpetually as long as the emotions continue to feed the thought. Your subconscious mind keeps the process going.

Each truth as you believe it is not only conscious as you recall it, but also subconscious and tied to emotion. A belief is merely a thought that has been emotionalised. Very few people can maintain a conscious thought for more than a few seconds. Just notice how long it takes for another thought to enter your mind while you are trying to hold a thought or image in your mind. The impetus comes from the subconscious mind, which is always moving.

For this reason, you must be sure that your subconscious holds attention on your goal. Your conscious mind is simply incapable of doing this. When you instead add emotion to a thought, the frontal lobe, which excels at maintaining focus, is energised and holds onto the required subconscious focus. As a result, you can 'keep your eye on the ball' with your subconscious mind. Your attention never leaves the goal, even as you sleep. Only the negative thoughts that you accept and

271

then emotionalise can manifest in your life.

This is why you should not entertain fears or anxiety. If you simply refuse to allow such thoughts or emotion, they cannot harm you. Of course, this requires that you find a way to mentally overcome fear and anxiety. You do this by moving your thoughts in the opposite direction. When you begin to feel fear, understand that it is the opposite of desire. Therefore, shift your focus immediately to your desires. Become engrossed in the goal, understanding that the subjective is more powerful than the objective. Whatever it is that you fear, the opposite can be found in your desire. Your desire is the solution as it is pure love; you desire it because you love it.

When you feel healthy, the result is health. When you feel wealthy, wealth is the result. You know what frequency of vibration you emit by the way it feels. Feeling is your conscious mind's perception of emotion. Emotions can operate without your conscious awareness until you realise it is there. Thinking and emotion work together, feeding one another. If you maintain thoughts of health and of wealth but do not have the supporting emotion, then your thoughts never gain strength. It is like limping instead of walking.

It could well be that you are thinking the correct words, but not emoting at the proper frequency. Faith is the same as positive anticipation. You know you have faith when you are not certain of the steps needed to get there, but you KNOW without a doubt that you will get there! You expect it fully. Faith is simply an intense knowing. Fear on the other hand is a negative anticipation. The thing you fear does not exist. It has not happened, except in your mind. Remember that thoughts are creative. Anticipate good, concentrate on it and have faith that your subconscious mind will always give the answers you seek. It cannot fail.

Having faith is an action you take and a choice. The mental and physical actions you take create vibration, and therefore feeling. When you behave as though your desire were already real, you act on faith. These actions of faith create a feeling in your subconscious mind, a vibration that emits the signal that your desire is a reality. The subconscious is the intellect of the body. When the physical actions you take are done in faith, the vibration and emotion of your subconscious is also faith.

The visualisations you create in your imagination are your mental images taking action. That image is your belief and faith. It is proof of things unseen and the creative substance of things you continue to hope for. When your mental image is taking action, your physical actions are transformed to take the actions needed for your desires to come about in the real world.

Faith is an emotion as well. The emotion of already having what you seek sends a vibration that attracts that goal into becoming.

Your emotions are seated in your subconscious mind. This is where your emotional heart is. A Cosmic Order is nothing more than an intention. It is your way of communicating to the Cosmos what it is that you want. Were you to block your Orders, you would hamper your intentions beliefs that limit your faith. When you Order, you are in the act of releasing your intentions with the beliefs that free you. The Cosmos hears your Order as long as your beliefs are not blocking the signal.

When you have beliefs that conflict with your desires, then you must also have conflicting emotions. Remember that your beliefs are the combination of thought and emotion. Your faith is what allows you to receive what you desire or pray for. Pay attention to your desires and experience them as real in your mind. Engage in behaviours and physical actions that show your desire is already here.

If your affirmations are not believable to you, your subconscious cannot accept the affirmation to begin working on it. This is why an affirmation stating you already have something that you do not really believe you have or deserve to have cannot work. You must experience your desires already fulfilled. For this reason, you should select and create affirmations that will bring those feelings of accomplishment to life inside you.

Until you have progressed to a point where you can really believe in your ability to manifest, it is best to only use affirmations that you really can believe in. Belief arrives with understanding. You must understand, because only reading these words will not give you the skills you need. The only way for your affirmations to become true when you do not believe them is when your conscious mind has been bypassed and the signal is going directly to your subconscious.

There are forms of paraliminal messaging designed to deliver affirmations so that the subconscious mind can receive and process the information easily. When the message is received and understood by your subconscious, this message sets in and gets moving. Emotions are attached to the thought and that turns it into a belief.

Emotions Communicate with the Cosmos

Your emotions and feelings are the closest match humans can create to the vibrations that the universe can understand. It is how we communicate with all things and is the basis of psycho kinesis. We create the mental state or emotional frequency that synchronises with the object in order to put it in motion. One cannot move objects with only thoughts or words. You cannot command a candle, 'Move across that table!' Instead it is an internal frequency that we create with out thoughts and emotions that causes the object to move.

When we begin to understand the sixth sense, we open our abilities in the paranormal realm. When you learn to perceive your sixth sense, you will also be able to learn to exert it. Energy moves in more than one direction. It goes in and out. Maybe you cannot see the Cosmos, but most people can at least feel its presence, even when they are not aware that this is what they are feelings.

It starts with feelings, then hearing and finally seeing. Typically, these perceptions take place within the mind, but there are those who are affected physically as well. Your imagination resides in the spiritual realm, so what takes place in your imagination is actually real.

The universe exists in sevens. Every seventh wave is the strongest. We have seven days in a week and we see seven colours in a rainbow. There is also a seventh sense, thought perception. Wherever you go, there is an emotional atmosphere, made of the collective thoughts and feelings of the people there. Libraries are excellent places to read because the thought waves of the people there are constantly engaged in reading. The atmosphere become conducive to more of the same energy that is already there, by the Law of Attraction. Remember that feelings are thought forms. To use your sixth sense is to understand by feeling, serving as a link between the five physical senses and the seventh sense of thought perception.

As discussed earlier, feelings and thoughts are symbiotic. No thought exists without emotion. When it appears that one is solitary, it is because the other is detached, in the subconscious mind. Emotions affect your thinking and your thoughts affect your emotions. All things are comprised of energy and your mind is the tool that moves the energy. Emotion is that energy in motion.

In actuality, intuition is a combination of the sixth sense and the seventh sense. You can sense the energy and thought waves of others when you are in their presence. You may draw conclusions based on this perception, noticing how the person is weak or strong, kind or mean, positive or negative. It is equally true that you can project your feelings onto others.

Just as you can process auditory information into visual information by creating a three-dimensional image from the sounds, you can process information from your seventh sense by way of your sixth sense by understanding the meanings behind your feelings. Understanding the feelings perceived by your sixth sense makes your intuition infinitely more powerful. In this way, you use your seventh sense to assist your sixth sense.

Just as the brain reproduces sensory signals from your environment, light rays, sound waves, touch vibrations, smells and tastes, it also reproduces the thought waves found in your surroundings. In the presence of wise people, you are more likely to think wise thoughts. When you gather with fools, you are more likely to behave foolishly yourself. It is just the same with good, evil, strength, and weakness.

In the same way you can evade too much light by looking away, or block someone from hearing what is said by coughing loudly, you can block negative thoughts by overpowering them with positive ones. When you sense something, you perceive it. Your perceptions are thoughts. Therefore, all senses are thoughts.

All is Thought
If emotions are energy in motion, thought is mind in motion. Thoughts are made of vibrations, which are energy. When you sense something, you experience it energy in motion or e-motion. As you touch a glass, your nerve endings send signals to your brain that interprets the feeling based on the energy the glass has. Your mind takes the signal and interprets it as hard and smooth. Where you experience things externally, you are experiencing external emotions. Experiencing them internally makes them internal emotions. A feeling is simply a perception or an emotion that can also run unexperienced consciously as it resides in your subconscious.

All Things are Thinking
As the thought of a form occurs in the universal mind the form takes place. As its thoughts take motion, it creates emotion. All things that you can observe around you are expressions of universal mind's thoughts. This is how all things came into being. The universe we live in is actually comprised of thought, making all things forms of thought. Someday, perhaps, scientists will find a way to manipulate the universal mind's mental programming and create intelligent objects. The

276

intelligence already resides in all things. If we could manipulate it, we could make clothing that unwrinkles itself or a machine that is comprised only of one element that can reshape and form itself into any functioning machine. We can already change the properties of any object by changing the way it thinks.

Seven States of Matter
The seven states of matter, ranging from matter wave to thought wave are all made of the same substance. All things are one thing. Every state of matter is a form of thought wave. All matter is also energy. All energy is part of one whole source of energy. All energy moves; it is kinetic. All things move by vibrating. All energy is awareness. Thoughts are your mind in motion. All things are mind. All things and energy are various manifestations of the same universal mind.

Secret Understanding
Two worlds exist; the internal world and the external. The internal world creates the external. The world inside is mental and spiritual while the external world is material and physical. When you have a clear understanding of both worlds, you have perfect knowledge. The solution is to use the world inside you to rule the world outside. Cause is the inner world, effect is the outer. The inner world always governs the outer. The external is merely a reflection of that which resides within. The conditions in the outer world mirror the inner landscape. These worlds are two, but not separate. They are two different levels of one world.

Our world is cerebral. All things are mind, the universe is cerebral. As it is above, so it is below. As it is within, so it is without. This is the secret understanding, secret knowledge. Secret knowledge is one of the most significant types of knowing you can have, the other being governing knowledge. One gives you consciousness and the other brings you power.

Secret knowledge means understanding the functioning of

the universe and comprehending what is happening. This knowledge is secret because it is not widely known. This knowledge has such power that only those with deep understanding and perceptive abilities can truly appreciate the truth of it. Only those who are consciously aware can see reality for what it truly is.

When you gain such knowledge, you utilise it to govern yourself and then all other things. This is how you use secret knowledge as governing knowledge.

Governing knowledge is the awareness that keeps your psyche running. These are the statement that govern your mind and runs your psyche. It is the governing statements of your mind that establish the things you do, as well as how and why you do them. This is the operational dynamics that maintain control over your thoughts, emotions and behaviours. By governing your mind, it governs your reality.

When you learn to govern yourself, you gain governance over all. When you are able to control yourself you are also able to control others. The only way to control the external is to control the internal. All controlling is self controlling. The maintain control, you must understand and know. All understanding and knowledge is self knowledge.

You have the ability to overcome anything by overcoming it from within. When you overcome that within you, you overcome it on the outside as well.

Handling Cognitive Dissonance

When two thoughts are held and there is a conflict between them, one will go into cognitive dissonance. This can be explained by taking the following example. Picture a man buying a particular car. This person may make the purchase and drive home convinced that it was the best car he could buy. The cognition is that he bought a good car. However, on the drive home, he notices an ad for another car with the same options and features, of comparable quality at a cheaper price. Now he has another conflicting cognition, that the other car

278

may have been the better purchase. This conflict disturbs the balance of cognitions, creating a state in his mind that will try to find a way to balance these two opposing thoughts.

There are many ways this man might resolve the dissonance. Perhaps he could avoid viewing advertisements for other cars. He could also make a decision and decide to keep one of the thoughts and discard the other.

Types of Dissonance
Cognitive dissonance is an element in the decision-making process. Theorists who study this process have categorised two types of cognitive dissonance: *pre-decisional dissonance* and *post-decisional dissonance*.

Pre-decisional dissonance can be thought of in terms of Freud's theories about 'compensation' or what we often call 'over compensation'. In tests, subjects made reward judgements towards men and women. They were then told they had latent sexist attitudes.

In subsequent tests, these subjects gave larger rewards to the females. It is believed that these subjects offered the large reward in a way to mentally balance the accusation of latent sexism. They wanted to prove to themselves that they were not sexist.

Post-decisional dissonance is more widely known. There have been numerous studies that show how people will reinforce decisions they have already made subjectively.

At a race track, gamblers are more likely to believe they have placed a bet on a winner immediately after placing the bet. The theory suggests that the possibility of making an incorrect choice creates dissonance, so people alter their perceptions to make their choices seem more correct or justifiable.

There may be greater post-decisional dissonance, depending on the importance of the situation, how long the subject has to decide and how much or how easily the decision can be reversed.

How to Resolve Cognitive Dissonance

When we are in cognitive dissonance it is natural to seek consonance. This can be accomplished in a number of ways. This process can create discomfort as it requires one to reflect and make judgements about ones thoughts. You will have to admit you made a mistake.

Resolving or reducing cognitive dissonance helps you to feel better. Eliminating contradictions helps you come closer to consonance, where all thoughts agree with one another. Some ways of resolving dissonance require that you bend the truth, which can lead to other wrong decisions. In the long run, taking the harder route of admitting mistakes will actually be the most straightforward course.

Most conflicting cognitions can be resolved by linking the two thoughts with a third thought or piece of information. To return to our car buyer, he may add the information that the car he saw in the advertisement was a first year for that particular model, making it likely to have some bugs that still need to be worked out in the coming years. Now he has a reasoning that allows him to confirm that yes, the advertised car may be a better deal, but the car he bought is more reliable.

18

Unending Possibilities

Placing Cosmic Orders with Loaded Language

Loaded, emotive or high-inference language are all terms to describe ways in which we use language to influence the person listening.

We say the language is 'loaded', as in a loaded gun. Such words and phrases have emotional meanings attached that go beyond the literal meaning and create a strong positive or negative reaction. An example would be the phrase *tax relief* which really means the deductions a person could claim on their taxes to decrease what they owe to the government. Politicians use the word *relief* to imply the measure they enact is taking away a burden.

Emotional appeals can often be seen as contrary to logic. But feelings and logic do not have to be at odds without one another. In addition, actions can be motivated by both logic and reason.

The words you use in a Cosmic Order will separate 'prima facie reasons' from 'considered reasons'. A simple reason, with no logic behind it is a 'prima facie' reason. An example would be that you say you do not a certain beverage because you do not like the taste. This reason is based on emotion rather than logic. You may have other reasons for not drinking this particular beverage, like the fact that you can get your intake of the vitamins the drinks provides from eating a particular vegetable instead, which you do like. Now you have made a *considered* reason for not drinking the beverage. You can get the same benefits elsewhere.

While an emotion may present a *prima facie* reason for taking action, you will need to work a little harder to come up with a *considered* reason.

Salesmen have used emotive arguments and loaded language for centuries to take advantage of people's propensity to take action immediately based on their emotional responses. This type of inappropriate use of the language has placed a considerable bias against it in general conversation. People do not like to feel they are being manipulated by the words you choose. It is equally impolite to use this language when speaking to the Cosmos. For this reason, you should avoid such emotive words and loaded phrases when communicating your desires to the Cosmos.

Consider how politicians use loaded language in their speeches and communications. They receive extensive training on how to use the language effectively. They are told what words to use, which ones to avoid and how to label opponents with emotive language.

Study loaded language and you may notice that loaded words or phrases come in pairs. There is always an overly positive and overly negative version of the same word. Think of 'abolitionist' versus 'pro-choice' or 'ministerial' versus 'public servant'. Think of how the word 'autonomous' has come to be automatically associated with 'good' these days. Anyone using speech that is 'undemocratic' could be easily labelled as 'bad'. If you want to be crystal clear in your Cosmic Orders, it is best to avoid loaded language. These words and phrases have double meanings that can muddle your message.

The Importance of Clean Language in Cosmic Orders

It is important to see problems in a functional sense, rather than as a personal attack. Your problems are, in a sense, the universe's way of helping you to create opportunities or grow to become a better person. However, do not get the idea that the Cosmos keeps its eyes on you, deliberately throwing difficulties at you just to test you. It is only that these problems often create opportunities for growth. Problems are like garden compost: they are rotten but they help you grow.

Unending Possibilities

When a problem arises, understand it is only the end of your dream if you let it stop you from trying. You can turn any difficulty into an opportunity either for growth or for profit. There is a fine line you walk when you run into problems. There may be an opportunity hiding within that helps you grow and creates abundance. If you are too wrapped up in the negative aspects of the problem, you may not notice the benefits.

In her famous bit, 'A Phone Call with God', Ellen DeGeneres thought it would be nice to just call up God and ask why we have fleas on this earth. These insects seem to serve no purpose other than to pester us and our pets. God responds by asking if Ellen realised how many people were employed by the flea collar industry, not to mention flea sprays. This bit was so well received because it speaks to a basic truth that we rarely think of when addressing common irritants in life.

Every problem should have a solution, so you should find another way to look at your difficulties. If the problem does not have a solution, then it is not a problem. Think of it as a train, that is taking you from point A to point B on a high speed rail. Find ways to use the problem to motivate and propel you closer to your goals.

You may have a difficulty that is large, complex and emotionally upsetting. In such a circumstance it would be natural to join a support group, sharing with others who have similar difficulties. Now you will meet new people that will enrich your own life. Not only this, but it will provide an opportunity for you to give to others, which serves to help both you and the group, Cosmically speaking.

It is best to find simple solutions to problems whenever possible, without enlisting the aid of the Cosmos in a Cosmic Order. Think about your problems and see what solutions are available to you before you try making a Cosmic Connection.

If you have doubts about Cosmic Ordering, stop reading, put down the book. I will not apologise in saying that you should not waste your time any further in this text. I am here to help those who genuinely believe they can use Cosmic Ordering to improve their lives. It is not my job to convert non-believers or form some cult with insincere followers, engaging themselves half-heartedly. This sort of participation only puts negative feedback into the equation for those who are truly interested and wish to explore Cosmic Ordering further.

Nor will I apologise for helping people get what they want in life. How can anyone say that you do not deserve the best in life? You deserve to have a better car, home, job, marriage, income, vacation and the like. This is at the heart of Cosmic Ordering. Not just having the good things in life you deserve, but going on to grow spiritually once you no longer need to waste emotion on the worries and anxieties that financial hardship brings. Once you have experienced these material pleasures, you will have a higher vantage point to see what lies beyond. When your desires go unfulfilled, they tug at you, always in the back of your mind, a curiosity, a question unanswered.

What I set forth here is not about any particular spiritual path to follow. I simply want you to understand and know the pleasures of the material world. I want you to enjoy the abundance available to you. Once you have this, you will more clearly understand what I mean.

To receive abundance, you must believe. Your difficulties will help you learn. They help you understand the inner workings of things. When all goes smoothly, you only see the surface. You will never change your understanding or viewpoint if there are no problems for you to experience.

I am intrigued with problems because although they often present pain in the beginning, they can start the growth of great peace, harmony and opportunity. Consider self-help organisations and how they first started with one person's problem. Now there are world-wide organisations helping millions. People pay large sums of money to get help with their problems. A company that finds a new product will hire employees to help sort out problems they encounter with a new product, refining things until it is right. Problems create ample opportunities for growth of all kinds.

Here is an important thing for you to understand. Never try to cover up your problems. Instead, own up to them and admit they are there. Putting on a false front to influence the way others see you is not helping anyone. First, they are likely to see through the front and think may think that someone who needs to cover up problems must have more problems than you actually do. Second, this will just eat you away inside, leaving your problems unresolved.

Not only this, but solving problems makes you the hero. When you resolve a question that others have struggled with, or simply never bothered to tackle, you receive recognition and admiration for your accomplishment.

Problems give you an opportunity to invent a new way of handling a situation, new products, new time saving procedures that make your life run smoothly. They can help you find happiness.

Problems can also give you just the right amount of challenge. They can put you in a positive mental frame so that you get more done, have an outlet for stress, and find success.

Think of the daily issues you have made efforts to improve with your Orders. There is gang violence, drugs, guns, lawlessness, home invasions, dishonesty and fear, just to name a few. If these problems could be solved for society, imagine what that would be worth!

There are times when you will want to change the negative aspects you see in you community. Social problems are a common concern, but most people do not realise there is something they can do about it. Only a small minority of the population causes the social difficulties, but that small population creates a great disturbance to the whole.

When you use clean language in Cosmic Ordering, you can more easily change unwanted personal habits, such as smoking, drinking and overeating. You can curb your desire for these negative influences by using correct and 'clean' language in your Cosmic Orders.

Cosmic Ordering is also effective for abating your concerns and fears. When you make the connection with the Cosmos, you can then run the Cosmic Order through your mind by natural means and clean language.

I cannot over emphasise what I have already related to you about 'Clean Language', as that is one of the key points in placing an Order. So I will reiterate. Avoid negative words. Do not fall into phrases like, 'My life is *rubbish*, and I *can't* make anything happen. *Nothing* good ever happens in my life, only *bad* things in life come to me. I want all that to change, please help me make good things happen.' Now take a look at the negative words highlighted in italics: rubbish, can't, nothing, bad.

We can rephrase this 'dirty' language by using clean, positive words like this. 'My life is always getting *better*. I *can* have *good* things happening in my life. The *good* things of life always *come my way,* in a safe and natural way. I *want* to *allow* that to *continue* to happen, as appropriate. Please make more of those things happen from now on.' Now you see the positive, clean words in italics: better, good, come my way, want, allow, and continue. You will also see some neutral words here, which can go either way, so you should just use them as appropriate for your situation. They are 'make', 'happen', and 'please'.

Let me show you how we can rephrase this even further to make the neutral words more active and make the Cosmic Order even more effective. 'Every day, my life is *improving*. *Good* things happen. *Good* things come my way. *Allow* that to *continue*, as appropriate. I can *continue* making those things *happen*.' Notice how instead of 'getting better' we used 'improving', a more active verb. Then notice how we changed from a passive position of asking the Cosmos to 'please make more of those things happen' to a personal action statement, 'I can continue making those things happen'. These are important clarifications that make your Cosmic Order more powerful.

Unending Possibilities

Also take note of the phrase: *continue* making those things *happen.* Do you see the way it gives an Order within the Order? Keep looking through the Orders in this book and watch for ways to incorporate similar phrases in your own Orders.

By now, I think you have the concept well in hand. I am certain you can improve the phrases in your Orders by using clean language. Once you have gained some practice and skill, you will be using clean languages even in daily conversation, not just your Orders.

Understand that failing to use clean language in Cosmic Ordering can actually hurt you. If you leave those negative words in, they will be taken literally by the Cosmos. You will simply get more of the negative things you are complaining about.

As a point of interest, I did not use clean language in the previous paragraph. If I were to do that, you would see something like this: 'You can have good happen to you when using clean language. This is the best way to enhance the good that you are already experiencing.' Take a moment to practice your clean language skills. Can you pick out the neutrals and improve them?

Safe & Natural Way
When you design the words for your Cosmic Order, make certain you include the words, 'in a safe and natural way'. For instance, if you are requesting good health, you could end up in on the operating table to ensure good health comes your way.

It may be better to be more specific and let the Cosmos know you would prefer to avoid drastic measures. This is where the phrase, 'in a safe and natural way', becomes useful. It allows you to maintain control over the ways in which your Order may be filled.

It is simply a way of avoiding the chance that things may go astray. If you want a week off work, you do not want to spend it stuck at home with the flu.

Cosmic Ordering: You Can be Successful

Reality and the Observer

Quantum physics has provided evidence of some astounding aspects of the universe and how it works. The most amazing of these experiments in recent times is the *double-slit experiment*. This is the one that shows how the entire universe exists by being observed.

The best way to describe how this was done is to picture a football shooting machine that puts out balls to travel across a space, which are then caught by a net. Shrink this machine down to the quantum level and see it shooting tiny electron particles instead of footballs. The electrons are shot through a vacuum, to hit a wide screen that will mark the position where they make contact with the screen.

Now pictures a second, smaller screen, with a vertical split in the centre, placed between the larger screen and the particle shooter. We will see how some electrons travel through the slit and strike the wide screen and how others are blocked by the smaller screen.

Because of the slit, we will see a vertical column on the larger screen where electrons have made their impression. Now let us try it with two slits instead of just one. Now the electrons will either pass through the slit on the left or the one on the right before they hit the larger screen. Logically, we should see two vertical columns, side by side, where the electrons pass through and strike the larger screen. However, the mysterious and wonderful outcome is that instead we see several vertical columns, a short distance apart from each other on the larger screen.

Now picture the screens under water, perhaps in a swimming pool. We have the larger screen in the distance, and closer up a smaller screen with double vertical slits. If we drop a ball into the water, directly in front of the double slit screen, the disturbance creates wave ripples in all directions. The impact wave will travel through the slits, breaking the wave into two smaller waves.

These new two waves are close together. As they travel out,

288

they will strike one another, cancelling each other out at some angles. The result will be two vertical columns, just as in the second experiment with electrons. The multiple columns show where the waves reinforced each other and the spaces between shows where they were cancelled out.

This leaves us with an important question. Why does the electron, which is made of matter, behave as though it is a wave when it passes through the two slits? Theorists believe that the electron actually splits in two, travelling through both slits at the same time. When it reaches the other side of the first screen, the two parts interfere with each other in the same way waves do.

The behaviour patter is referred to in quantum physics as *the principle of nonlocality*. This means the same object can exist in more than one place at one time. Because these electrons are not limited to a single location at a single time, they are omnipresent. To find out if this theory held up to reality, the scientists next placed a small device in front of the smaller screen to let us see exactly what is going on when the electron passes through the slits.

The results were beyond strange and could not be explained by understanding of physics held in popular science at that time. What the device showed was that when the experiment was observed by the device, the matter behaved differently. In fact, it behaved like matter again, instead of like waves or vibrations. This time, there were two vertical columns, as was expected in the first instance. So our interaction with these electrons makes them behave like the matter we understand them to be. If we turn our attention away, they behave like waves.

This demonstrates the basic truth that all things in the universe are actually energy. Our minds influence this energy so that it only appears as matter when we observe it. Because of experiments like these, quantum physics has come to see electrons and events and probabilities and potentials, not concrete entities. The means there are many potential outcomes, until someone observes, then the reality solidifies into reality. It is as thought our observation forces the universe to make a choice about what will be actualised.

Everything in existence is basically an unlimited field of quantum energy. It is an ocean of unending possibilities, just waiting to occur. Our observation or consciousness causes the probability wave function to collapse into the actual reality we observe in space and time.

Our consciousness takes energy and relays the experience as matter. It is the human energy that influences other energy. Because all energy is in actuality consciousness, it is consciously influencing itself. In other words, the observer is not on the outside looking in. The observer is part of the observation. In the same way, the experimenter is not outside of the experiment. The observer plays a part in creating the reality he looks at.

According to the Heisenberg Uncertainty Principle, we can not take any pure measurement until the reality is created by consciousness. That is to say that you cannot observe anything without causing it to change by your observation. It is the ultimate catch-22.

All things are energy and energy is of the mind. The mind forms and controls our reality. The power of our thoughts can shape reality. By the Law of Attraction, that which we focus upon with the most time and energy, we get. The simple act of observing creates the reality to be observed.

An old country doctor was celebrated for his wisdom. 'Dr Sage,' a young man asked, 'how did you get so wise?'

'Weren't hard,' said the doc. 'I've got good judgement. Now, good judgment comes from experience,' he continued. 'And experience - well, that comes from having bad judgement.'

19

Seventh Sense Secrets

Foolish people with all their other thoughts are always getting ready to live, but never living.

Your success will start when you begin to pursue it. To reach your goal or to attain success, you don't need to know all of the answers in advance. You just need to have a clear idea of what your goal is.

Don't procrastinate when faced with difficult problems. Break your problems into parts, and handle one part at a time.

Develop tendencies toward taking action. You can make something happen right now. Divide your big plan into small steps and take that first step right away.

Everyone who ever got where they are had to begin where they were. Your big opportunity is where you are right now.

A journey of a thousand miles begins with one step. Take it.

Remote Influencing

For a number of decades now, the United States government has secretly trained a select corps of military personnel in the art of 'remote viewing'.

The very same techniques and mental exercises used to train those remote viewers can be used by you. The seventh sense is dormant in you, now you can awaken it.

Ever feel someone staring at you? Maybe someone has looked up to catch your intent gaze before? There is a reason for this. It is not pure chance. In fact, when you focus your attention on another person, whether in your presence or half-way around the world, that person picks up subconsciously on those vibrations. There are physiological changes that occur in that person as well.

Just as when you focus on what you want to connect with it, you can connect with other people by focussing on them. Although theories have floated around for ages, only recently have serious studies looked into the matter. These researchers discovered the power of remote viewing, stunning those in the field.

Not only could remote viewers connect with the target, they could actually connect at times in the past, present or future. Experiments showed that these remote viewers could connect to an individual and specify the date and time that they wanted to connection to take place. Test showed physiological changes occurring in the targets, at the specified times, such as higher blood pressure readings.

To understand how this could be it is helpful to recall that each person affects every other person, all the time. If you take a slow stroll on a busy street, people back up behind you or are forced to walk around you on either side. My writing this has affected you as you are reading this.

At the heart of remote influencing is simply a way of affecting people remotely. We do it every day, sometimes without realising it. Perhaps you walk into a room and notice the intense atmosphere. You then learn there has been some bad news affecting those in the room. You have picked up on the tension and anxiety without anyone telling you about it. It can also work the other way around when people sense something wrong within you and avoid you. This is a form of non-controlled remote influencing. However, you can learn to do it in a controlled manner and use it to your benefit or the benefit of others. Using this method against anyone is highly discouraged because the negativity will likely come back to you tenfold.

When you master controlled remote influencing, you will be amazed how things seem to just go your way. Your unconscious mind will use subjective influence without you ever thinking about it consciously. The process eventually

292

becomes automatic.

When you have placed your attention within intense focus on a particular goal, you are using remote influencing to affect the outcome and bring about the desired result. When things go your way, it feels like good luck, but you should give yourself credit for your natural ability to influence your own life for the better.

The key to remote influencing is the same as abundance creation or any other technique to achieve your goals; mental imagery. You only need the ability to be able to visualise well, including your senses and inner feelings, but these skills can also be acquired with practice. When you are practicing this technique, watch for small changes in the person you are influencing and then build upon that success.

Learning to remote influence is much like riding a bicycle. The more you practice it, the easier it will become. In time, it will be as natural as breathing. The only reason this practice is not more widely used is because the initial step can be difficult.

However, once you are proficient in this practice, you will see that you need not even have a visual image of the person you wish to influence. You will not even need to be in that person's general proximity. Studies show that distance has no effect on the phenomenon. Similar traits have been seen in pairs of quantum particles, which react to one another no matter the distance between.

The first step in acquiring this skill is to learn remote projection. This practice, as with remote viewing, will require that you relax your mind and body fully. In remote viewing, you seek to tune into signals coming from outside of you. In remote projection, your goal is to project the object of your focus out. You are sending out a highly concentrated, controlled visual image. You will create a clear and precise thought, imbue it with energy, and then release it to your target.

In the first step, it is vital that you are crystal clear in your mind of exactly what you want to send out. Incomplete or fuzzy images simply dissipate. Releasing the image is the

293

second step. You shoot this highly compressed thought laser at your target, then immediately let it go and move you. You must not dwell on the thought. When you fail to let it go completely, it remains attached to you, not reaching your target.

The process described in the previous paragraph is the same method that was used in psychokinetic experiments. After sending off that imagery, you immediately go to thinking of something else. Typically, the psychokinetic effects occur after effort stops. Hold in your awareness that what you think about and how you feel truly changes the world!

There is energy in your thoughts. They can be measured as you have seen with EEG machines in medical testing. When you put great focus on your thoughts, the energy begins to resonate, growing in strength. When you direct this intent focus on another person, with absolute intensity, the energy impacts the target both physiologically and mentally.

In the same way, you can become a life designer, creating your own life situation by intentionally designing the life you want and focusing your thought with great intensity. As you train your skills to project, do not forget that your projections will be seen in your environment. Destructive projections will damage the world around you and come back to you in greater strength.

Think about someone how know who has a tendency to dwell on the negative, on fears and anxieties. The negative energy this person creates by dwelling on these thoughts often creates more problems for more fear and anxiety until he or she self destructs. When you learn to project your thoughts, it is vital that you avoid dwelling on negative thoughts. The reason you develop this skill is to improve your life, and the lives of those around you.

Projection Training
To begin your training, pick a person in a room that is filled with people as a subject. You do not want to let on to what you are doing in order to avoid influencing the outcome. Now

create a very clear mental image in your mind of the person scratching their nose. Because this can be an autonomous response, the person may not consciously realise he or she is doing it. Focus intently on your image and release it. Try this several times on several subjects until you see it work. When you do get a response, take careful note of the precise thought patterns and imagery you used so you can repeat your success. This exercise can be performed virtually anywhere; in a waiting room, on the bus, at a party.

You can also gain practice by sharpening your focus on a distant friend. See your friend picking up the phone to call you. Practice this repeatedly until you succeed. One success out of ten is very good for a beginner. The better you become at this, the higher your success rate will be.

Do not forget that this is a new skill. Just as with learning any new skill, time and practice are required. You learned many new skills in your life, so there is no reason to become discouraged when you are learning this one. As an infant, it took weeks to master walking. You mastered handwriting over the course of years, but you did not give up then and you should not give up now.

You may be trying to picture how you will use this technique in your life. Perhaps you know someone who is ill? You can remotely influence the healing process with this method. Your thoughts have the power to change another person's body cells from wherever you are. You focus intently on healthy, normal cells, and the loved one's cells become well. Always use the technique to help others and you will see positive results in your own life. Using the technique to harm others would result in serious negative consequences for you.

Treat the process with respect. This skill is potent and can change lives. When used with remote viewing and alpha/theta techniques, there is nothing you cannot do.

Another excellent way to use this method is to help those around you by sending them positive affirmations. Give them whatever it is they need right now; encouragement, joy, healing, optimism, love or self-esteem are just a few of the things you can project. Notice how their lives change as they receive your message. This will work best for you when you are a meditative state.

Telepathy and Mental Communication

We sometimes meet two people in life who are connected so closely, they seem to communicate without speaking. Two people can become even more closely connected, so that they can communicate without physical contact or speech. They can communicate telepathically and even feel each other's physical pain. You main have noticed this phenomena present in identical twins. The connection that creates this psychic link is a spiritual one. One person senses what the other is thinking or feeling. Not only can communications travel directly between two people; one may also receive messages from the other by way of the universal mind.

Communicating telepathically involves information travelling in both sending and receiving. Whether you are receiving the thoughts of another or sending them out will depend on your intention. Others will have difficulty picking up your thoughts if you hide from them. This is done by erecting a psychic shield that stops others from picking up on your intentions. Others can stop you from viewing theirs.

A strong presence of mind and great clarity of thought is required to penetrate a psychic shield. When two people are close enough spiritually, the sense of trust is strong and neither puts up a shield. They have a mutual empathy that keeps each always receiving from the other.

Telepathy requires empathy to work. This method of communication is beyond words and speech, comprised of the psychic energy in your thoughts, feelings and mental images. It is potentially possible to receive telepathic communication in words, but it is more often done through the mental imagery, feelings and desires you send or receive.

These messages are often received as an instant knowing,

called precognition. How you receive these messages will depend on several factors, such as whether the message is verbal or not, and your own dominant mental modality. You may also hear an inner voice, which is called clairaudience. You can see an image as with clairvoyance or feel an emotion, known as clairsentience.

Non-local telepathy involves communicating telepathically while the other person is out of sight. You may feel another person's emotions or see the image that the other person is seeing. You could sense the other person's intentions. When you receive these messages, there is a sense that the thought did not come from within your own mind. There is a feeling of clarity and certainty, similar to feelings of intuition. You simply know.

Any action or process on the psychic level works through your power of belief. You must truly believe you can send and receive such signals. There are three methods in telepathy, known as induction, visualisation and will.

Induction involves bringing up the emotion, mental image, or desire that resides in you. Truly feel and experience the thing within yourself first.

Next you visualise the message travelling to the other person and see the other person picking up that message and experiencing the same things you are feeling.

Finally, you must will it to take place. You must be certain that it happened just as you intended it. This method never fails. The outcome only depends on the laws that govern the spiritual connection, beliefs and attitudes of both you and the person you communicate with telepathically.

If your message seems to fail, or if it arrives unclear in the other person's mind, this is only because of problems with opposing intentions, beliefs, or the failure of both to trust fully. It may even be the interpretations you have attached to the signals within the communication create a failure within you to receive the message properly.

Sincerity is key to communicating telepathically. Honesty

and truth are necessary. These are the things that trust is built upon. A good telepathic connection allows you to comprehend each other's thoughts easily and clearly.

Counter-telepathy

If you wish to block certain thoughts and feelings from getting through, you could use counter-telepathy.

Counter-telepathy involves erecting a psychic shield by seeing it in your mind and creating the intent that the other person cannot read the thought. You could also try focusing on an opposing thought to send that message instead. However, be aware and cognisant of your thoughts at all times. If you have a negative thought about someone you have open telepathic communication with, they may pick it up and think that is what you really feel about them. It is important to be cautious about the thoughts you entertain after an argument or disagreement with such a person.

While such negative thoughts are bound to come up, you should counteract them with intense positive thoughts and send those well wishes to the other person, who you probably have a great deal of affection for.

This type of communication is most effective when we give up striving and do not try to force the matter. When you simply know that it works, then it works. When you think it might work, it will not work. Psychic communications are driven by subconscious beliefs, not conscious effort. IF you try to force things with your conscious mind, you are defeating your own efforts.

Your psychic messages will be made of the things you put the greatest attention to. When your focus is on positive, helpful things, you send the corresponding message. Negative things will send negative feelings, mental images and desires.

Dreams and Cosmic Ordering

While the brain is a physical entity, centred in reality, the mind is not of the physical world. Dreams occupy the space of the mind, or put more accurately, they occupy no space at all, since space is a facet of the physical world. Those images you see in your dreams do appear as forms, just not in this physical reality. The rules of space and time do not apply to them. They entail the material formation of spontaneous creations that normally could not take place in the physical world.

Even though we are only sometimes aware of dreams during sleep, they are actually a continuous and unending flow of images, feelings and thoughts. They are flowing in the subconscious mind when you are awake. The creations that are manifested from dreams do not have mass in our reality, but may have a similar quality to mass in another reality.

While in dreams, your personality is shaped and altered by actions that you could not take in the physical world. However, the events that take place in dreams can lead to changes in the physical world, dependent upon how their dreams are programmed within the conscious or subconscious mind.

Dreams can affect each other as well. Your neighbour's dreams may have an influence over yours. Two or more people have essentially the same dream, although often varying slightly in format. There have also been instances in close-knit communities where many people shared a similar dream. These are called mass dreams.

Mass dreams occur on a level just above the collective unconscious mind. Some people can actually tune in to these dreams and see what society is dreaming of collectively. This can give them knowledge of events to come since dreams format the future, both as individuals and collectively.

It is possible for the collective dream to be powerful enough that it creates significant changes to the future, whether it is for better or for worse. The dreams of a single powerful person can influence those of thousands. Such a person has the capacity to become a leader.

They normally come to be seen in a dream state initially, and then they are acknowledged in the material world later. You can use concentrated emotional attention to produce a form, subconsciously or consciously, and then send it off to someone else who could then perceive it. When this happens, the form becomes detectable by scientific equipment.

When you are dreaming, your consciousness is focused on a reality that is just as 'real' and enduring as the physical world we spend our waking hours in. There is a small amount of attention that remains attached to the physical world in order to maintain the life functions of your body.

The universe of dreams has a molecular structure, but does not take up space the way we understand it in the physical world. This is why dreams continue even when we are not aware of them. Your awareness of this alternate universe is limited to your sleeping mind. The things that occur in the dream world are just as important and meaningful as those in your physical reality. They are interrelated and affect each other. You can take advantage of this by easily programming your dream to have an immediate effect on the physical world.

Among the most effective and easy programs you can create with dreams can impact your health. By programming a dream correctly, you can induce miraculous healing within hours.

It is good that we do not usually remember our dreams. The incoming sensory information would create a mind overload, creating difficulties relating to the material world where we spend most of our hours. The ideas, thoughts and creations produced during dreaming are often created physically over a long time period. This will depend on the need for the item being materialised, emotional expectation you have attached to it and the depth of your yearning for it to occur. You can use programming in your dreams for particular things or events and allow it to be created over time, as long as you maintain focus on a single-minded goal.

Any specific dream creates an impact on the dreamer in the aspects of his or her physical, spiritual, electromagnetic, and psychological life. The physical image and environment is created according to the abilities and defects of the dreamer, in

300

line with the expectations he or she may have and the needs of the subconscious. In this way, the dreamer creates the dream, which in turn interact with the external environment, also of the individual's creation.

Notice how the dream world bears a close physical and psychological resemblance to your walking world environment. Those with difficulties in the material world will often attempt to resolve those conflicts subconsciously through dreaming, trying out different resolutions to the problem. In the conscious mind, these people are likely to be unaware of the dream solutions they have created. However, the correct answer eventually plays out in the real world, causing material world events to occur that will resolve the difficulty.

Dreams are also an excellent natural therapy connecting your psychic and material worlds. Dreams are often misunderstood. Few understand how we can manipulate our dreams to control our bodies and our environment.

Problem solving with dreams is really a simple process. You simply set the problem out in your mind, detailing all aspects of it. State the problem clearly to your subconscious mind and simply drift off to sleep. This sometimes happens by itself as you naturally contemplate an issue that has been giving you difficulty just before you fall asleep at night.

Your subconscious picks up the signal and uses dreams to solve the problem. During dreams, you can be presented with many alternative ways in which the problem could be solved and the potential outcomes of each solution. Just as you do consciously when considering alternatives, you subconscious mind chooses the solutions with the best probable outcome. In most cases, you will have no recollection of these dreams. Your first indication that it worked will be that the problem has been fixed. You many notice many unexpected events that dissolve the problem. It will feel miraculous as all the elements seem to fall in place of their own accord. This is how your dreams crate solutions in the real world, helping you to achieve the desired outcome.

Cosmic Ordering: You Can be Successful

You can also use dreams to resolve health issues. It is vital that you understand that the state of your current health and environment are of your own making. No one else is to blame for the way things are in your life right now. If you find yourself blaming others, break that habit.

There are no valid excuses for accepting ill health or an unsatisfactory environment. The belief system in your subconscious mind has created it all. Every aspect of your existence is the result of this belief system. You are not a victim of any circumstance outside of yourself. If you are a victim, it is because you made a victim of yourself with your belief and expectation system.

Communications that travel within your inner landscape are not affected by physical time. They are in psychological time, which is fluid and always changing. Psi time works during your sleeping hours when your consciousness is quiet and during meditation in the alpha/theta/delta states. This is why a dream can feel like it has gone on for hours or even days, but in real time they take only a few minutes or seconds. This is how Psi time is different from real time.

Dreams happen when there is a shifting in consciousness. You may wake up suddenly from a daydream and realise that you were separate from the physical world during that time. You were in another conscious state.

When dreaming, you may experience what feels like several hours passing in just an instant. However, you will not age by those several hours in the physical world. The world of dreams is free from the ego, so it has no need to create concepts into physical reality.

In an overnight state of dreaming, a destructive and negative thought can be altered immediately to create one that is more constructive and positive. You may experience this kind of dream when your inner self feels desperate, opening a deep channel in your subconscious to invoke the needed emotional healing. We have learned that such healing dreams can be easily evoked, even consciously.

The only requirement is that you ask for this kind of dream before you fall asleep. Perhaps you have an ailment that has been going on sometime and is beginning to wear on your patience. Then you wake up one morning, and the problem is instantly gone, as if it were never there. When this happens, it is almost certain that a healing dream caused to spontaneous change.

You can bring on these dreams through repeated self-suggestion just before falling asleep. These dreams can even reverse depression. If you have had a long-lasting sadness or depression and suddenly wake up feeling refreshed, cheerful and positive, it is quite likely because of a dream. You can induce such changes artificially by using the before sleep repetitive suggestions.

It is the same with anything. You can bring up dreams of wealth, happiness and success. Your dreams will eventually become the physical reality you desire. When you evoke such a dream, be sure to ask your subconscious to allow you full recall of the dream so you can use the feelings and joy in the dream to help push the creation of this reality along on the physical plane. You will marvel at the wondrous feelings of your desires fulfilled.

Dreams are really the ideal way to create the events and circumstances you desire. An event dream is more powerful and potent than any creative visualisation or affirmation. While it is helpful to continue using meditations in the alpha and theta states to create positive visualisations, one or two dream events can create the materialisation of your desires in only days, not just years.

The use of repetitive suggestions will allow you to reach parts of yourself that are outside the influence of your ego. While it is possible to change your personality through the use of the ego, dreams are infinitely more productive and effective. They are simply easier that will power alone.

You can also use suggestion through your dream to change the way you respond to events from the past that may haunt

303

you. Your suggestions shape your dreams, which then reshape your current reality and the future. Some dreams are so powerful that they can change a person almost instantly. There have been reports of serious illnesses vanishing in the night.

Your Dreams Can Come True
I use to have a Comfort Zone
Where I knew I couldn't fail
The same four walls of busy work
Were really more like jail.
I longed so much to do the things
I'd never done before,
But I stayed inside my Comfort Zone
And paced the same old floor
I said it didn't matter,
That I wasn't doing much
I said I didn't care for things
Like diamonds, furs and such
I claimed to be so busy
With the things inside my zone,
But deep inside I longed for
Something special of my own.
I couldn't let my life go by,
Just watching others win.
I held my breath and stepped outside
And let the change begin.
I took a step and with new strength
I'd never felt before,
I kissed my Comfort Zone 'goodbye'
And closed and locked the door.
If you are in a Comfort Zone,
Afraid to venture out,
Remember that all winners were
At one time filled with doubt.
A step or two and words of praise,
Can make your dreams come true.

Whether you are aware of it or not, you constantly give your subconscious mind suggestions during your waking hours. When you spend time dwelling on events as they occur, you are sending signals to you unconscious mind. By staying calm and relaxed, you avoid feeding negative energy to you subconscious and your dreams. Negative energy tends to fester and grow in your subconscious, creating dreams that are only unhelpful at best, frightening at worst.

When you want to remember your dreams, you only need to give yourself a pre-sleep suggestion. Tell yourself you will walk up right after your fist dream or two, or perhaps you could choose to wake up with full recollection right after your final dream. You do not want to wake up after every dream, which could seriously disrupt the restorative properties of your sleep.

Your subconscious is a powerful and useful tool. Take advantage of this blessing from the Cosmos each night. Before you head off to sleep, take a moment and ask yourself some questions so that your mind can work on them when you sleep. Meditate in any way that relaxes you right before bed to clear your mind and leave room for your unconscious mind to do its work.

For success to happen for you, you must have dreams and ambitions. Be sincere and honest with yourself about what your goals are and what it is you are really seeking in this life. Then, let your mind think big and dream big.

Mental Control of Physical Reality
When you dream, do you notice that your senses are just as awake as when your mind is? You can see, touch, smell, hear and taste. The objects feel solid, just as in the real world. Some dreams feel so real, we have difficulty distinguishing in our memory whether they are real or not. This is because your dreams are just as real as your waking state of reality. You often determine whether an event occurred in the physical world or the dream world by how it feels. It has a different

frequency.

You can be in a dream and remain conscious. This is known as a lucid dream. You have the ability to control the events in your dream however you choose based on your will and belief. This means of controlling your dreams works the same in the physical world.

Time is the difference in these two worlds. The mental plane instantly responds to your thoughts in either case, but the materialisation of those thoughts plays out in the physical plane more slowly. This happens because the vibrations in the physical world are finer. The gross forms of matter change more slowly. On the physical plane, things take time to come into being, but on the mental plane, they manifest immediately, the instant the thought forms. Your concentrated thoughts, maintained over time, will bring the thoughts into physical being.

Anything existing in your imagination or in a dream is your personal experience. When you picture a person or object in the dream world, you are creating a clone. This mental clone is just as real as the actual person in every way. However, if you imagine someone or something not existing on the physical level, it is your original creation. Over time, that mental creation can come into being on the physical world. You must concentrate your thoughts long enough to allow the needed actions to occur to manifest the original thought.

Remember that it is human consciousness that collapses the wave function, making particles in time and space. Thoughts typically manifest in the physical world in an indirect way. Your goals are first created on the psychic plane and action makes the thought materialise in the physical plane.

Back in the 19th Century two brothers had an idea which eventually became their passionate and consuming dream. Their relentless pursuit of that dream was rewarded with an accomplishment that changed world travel.

On Friday December 17, 1903 at 10:35 AM, the Wright brothers (Wilbur and Orville) achieved their dream. They flew 'the world's first power-driven, heavier-than-air machine in which man made free, controlled, and sustained flight.' This memorable feat took place at Kitty Hawk, North Carolina on a cold windy morning.

The dream started with an idea that was planted in their minds by a toy given to them by their father. In the words of the boys, 'Late in the autumn of 1878, our father came into the house one evening with some object partly concealed in his hands, and before we could see what it was, he tossed it into the air. Instead of falling to the floor, as we expected, it flew across the room till it struck the ceiling, where it fluttered awhile, and finally sank to the floor.' This simple toy made of bamboo, cork and stretched rubber bands, fascinated the Wright brothers and sparked their lifelong interest in human flight.

The Wright brothers were great thinkers. They enjoyed learning new things. Initially, they recycled broken parts, built a printing press and opened their own printing office. Their interest moved to bicycles and in 1893, they opened the Wright Cycle Company where they sold and repaired bicycles. But Wilbur (the older brother) had his mind set on something more exciting. He decided to seriously pursue flying.

The brothers spent many hours researching, testing their machines and making improvements after unsuccessful attempts at human flight. What started out as a hobby soon became a passion. With determination and patience they realised their dream in 1903.

The next time you hear or see an airplane or travel on one, remember where it all started. A simply idea conceived in the minds of two young men who did not finish high school. Believe it or not, they did not have a university degree in any subject. They were not scientists in the true sense of the word. In fact, many of their peers who did not witness their accomplishment, had trouble believing that two bicycle mechanics from Dayton, Ohio did what they claimed.

What idea or ideas are YOU working on? Have you said

307

you can't do this or that because you are not a scientist? Have you limited yourself by saying you are not smart enough? Or have you joined the majority in saying that everything has already been invented or discovered?

Since the introduction of the first generation of personal computers in 1981, we are able to do many things more efficiently. With a super computer between your ears and the personal computer at your finger tips, your dream can be achieved. First, give birth to that dream with an idea. A simply idea that ANYONE of us can conceive!

Cosmic Thoughts Influence Others

The best way to help other people is with your mind, not just your hands. Friends, family and loved ones come to you with troubling problems and negative feelings of not being able to cope. Perhaps it is only confidence they lack, or maybe they just need to feel they are not alone. If you feel that you are not in a position to help, that you have no power to influence the situation, you are wrong! The truth is that you have the power to help those in need. Otherwise, what would be the point of your loved ones coming to you in a time of need?

Having someone to talk to about problems does help to some extent. While it is true that simply sharing sorrow lightens the burden, there is much more too it. Your listening can help your friend organise his thoughts, making him more capable of seeing the problem objectively. When he has the opportunity to release those negative emotions to a receptive and caring friend like you, the negativity dissipates, allowing him to weaken the attraction to more of the same problem. It helps him to let go of his worrying. But there is much more that you can do to help your friend than simply being a good listener. Although remember, do not allow yourself to become an emotional dumping ground!

We often hear phrases like, 'lend a helping hand', and this is indeed the way most people think of helping someone else. Your hands can help; there are actions you can take or things you can give to help, but the biggest help you can give is with your mind! It is much more than simply trying to help the person solve the problem with your ego mind or speaking consoling and encouraging words. These things are good and useful, but they have little power when compared to the strength of the Cosmos.

Your psychic influence is the most powerful aid you can supply. You can use Cosmic thoughts to influence situations and the actions of others. The thoughts you focus on in your mind have the power to reach out to others and influence their minds. Your thought waves are just as real as sound waves or electromagnetic waves and the mind responds more easily to thought waves than any material thing or situation.

You can influence others in two ways. The first is visualisation. The other is affirmation. In using visualisation, you picture your friend taking the best, most positive actions he can for himself. See him carrying out actions to solve his problem.

Visualise your friend taking action with courage, full of strength and positive energy. You will see some amazing events occurring in his life after that. It is likely he resisted doing what he needed to repair his problems in the past. Your visualisation can give him the mental boost he needs. Often, when a problem is resolved, your friend will say that in retrospect he knew exactly what he needed to do and had no idea why he could not bring himself to take action before.

In using affirmations, you instead create and send a mental command to the person you wish to influence. You speak the command in your mind. You may affirm, 'You feel a renewed sense of power and confidence', or 'You hold the courage to take the actions you need'.

Affirmations can also be used by sending a thought to materialise in the real world. Think of statements like, 'My friend (Name) feels positive', 'He is taking action towards achieving his goal right now,' or 'He always succeeds in getting just what he wants.'

Cosmic Ordering: You Can be Successful

These are only examples and are generalised to demonstrate the point. You can make your statements much more specific to apply precisely to your friend's situation. Your mind controls not only your behaviour, but that of others as well. You can alter someone's behaviour by picturing him behaving in another way.

These visualisations and affirmations are the equivalent to Ordering. When you wish that a friend finds help or healing, you are asking The Cosmos for help. Ask and it shall be given unto you always. When you imagine the friend in success, you are asking. Your super conscious mind creates your thoughts in reality. However, understand that this super conscious mind works according to a sense of divine justice. If your thoughts are not aligned with the Higher Will, the influence will instead influence other minds to think opposing thoughts to negate or oppose the thoughts you send.

The power in righteous thoughts will always prevail over evil thoughts. While both can be given what they ask for, only one will actually receive the gift. One gift destroys the other, depending on the will of those involved. Evil only prevails when the righteous are passive mentally.

By understanding this, you see how positive thoughts actually work in daily life. When others influence you in a positive way, the results are positive. The reverse is true as well. When others influence you in a way that is harmful, the results are harmful. When you feel pressure or an impulse to take action that you know it does not benefit you, your ability to repel or succumb will depend on your ability to hold positive thoughts always in your mind.

Good thoughts attract good influence and repel damaging ones. This is also true for damaging thoughts. Your thoughts influence both your reality and the reality of others. When an entire group has negative thoughts towards one person, that person's reality becomes difficult and uncomfortable. That person will be in a constant battle over the inner conflicts that hold him back and the incoming conflict from the peer group.

Seventh Sense Secrets

The more the group sees success and wellbeing for the person, the more that person's reality will improve, gaining sustenance and support from the collective encouragement of the group.

It is common for others to think negatively about a person when that person has negative thoughts about themselves. The group is simply reflecting the negative thoughts back on the individual. It is like natural selection at work. Your negative thoughts are put back on you to discourage you creating more of them. Without awareness, however, you will only think more negative thoughts.

Our awareness of the higher aspects in our surroundings gives us the ability to control the reflection process with our minds. The external world cannot do anything but reflect the mind. However, the internal world within us allows us to choose if we wish to reflect or not. We can change our thoughts and thereby change reality. It is the power we are given as thinking beings. If you maintain negative thoughts about someone in a way that is disempowering and unhelpful, whether these thoughts are 'true' or not, the thoughts will perpetuate the other person's reality.

Begin changing your thoughts and you start changing the situation. When you make a conscious choice not to reflect the negative reality-forming thoughts, and to instead reshape reality into a more positive situation, you are exerting the strength of good over evil. Your reality has more strength than the other person's reality.

If you have the desire to help another person rid themselves of lack, limitations, or errors, it is best for you to avoid thinking about the person you want to help. You only need to feel the intention of wanting to help. This places you in mental connection with the other person. You should next force the negative beliefs in your mind away. Do not focus on the lack, limitation or error in the other person's life.

This is all you need to do. Once you have successfully done this, the person will be free. Understand that our own opinions about the other person's reality could be just what hold them

311

back. It is also true that the negative opinions of others could be holding you back from success.

This demonstrates why it is so vital to surround yourself with supportive, positive people who believe in the endless potential and abundance of your success. You must let go of all thoughts of lack and limitations if you are to do anything helpful for yourself or your friend. Instead focus on the endless possibilities and freedom of having the ability to create anything you desire in life.

When you think positive, empowering and helpful thoughts, the pay off is great. You, your friends and even the world will experience many benefits.

Give Momentum to Positive Thoughts

Because thought waves are both local and non-local, meaning in one place and also in all places at the same time, you have the ability to influence minds, even at great distances. You can influence others even when they are not in your presence. Reality takes form in accordance with your thoughts. The super conscious mind acts in accordance with your intentions. Always be a helping mind. Escalate the power of positive thoughts; give them momentum and always behave in alignment with your intentions. Always work to decrease the momentum of negative thoughts.

Understanding the Multidimensional Universe

We live in only one plane of many realities. The physical plane is our reality and the remaining realities are part of the mental plane.

In the seven states of matter, the highest state is that of the thought wave, which is in the mental plane of reality. The mental plane is the universal plane made purely of thought and mind stuff. This mental plane has multiple levels. These levels differ according to the vibratory frequency from one plane to the next. Finer vibrations produce higher planes.

When we think of higher, we tend to think of it in spatial

312

terms, but what we really mean it is closer to centre. Think of a globe, where the centre is the highest plane of reality and the outer atmosphere is the material plane we inhabit. The mental plane starts as the second plane, inwards of the material world. Within that is the etheric plane. All things in the material plane coexist in both physical and etheric states. Your body is both solid and vibratory. You live with the ethereal in the first and sixth states of matter. An electron exists as both a particle and a wave. Two things can only occupy the same space if they have differing space densities.

The material and etheric planes coexist in one space-time because they are out of phase with one another. However, the space-time of the material and etheric planes are in sync with one another.

OBE

During an out of body experience (OBE), your body remains asleep while your conscious awareness moves outside of the body. In this state, you are an etheric, energy body. Your consciousness is out of phase with the body and is in phase with the ethereal.

Your perception of the physical plane will be similar. You will see the same things around you, but in their etheric states. When awake and in your body, there may be a chair next to your bed. During the out of body experience, the same chair is there, but you will see it in its etheric state. All of the physical plane will exist for you in the etheric state.

This duplicity means that you can see your physical double while on the etheric plane. You remain connected to your body by a gossamer silver cord that keeps it living. This cord cannot be broken except by death.

Those awake in the physical world will see your body, but they will not see your etheric body. However, you will see the etheric bodies of others. You will not see the physical reality that you observe when awake; rather you will see their own perception of themselves. Someone with a poor self image may appear fatter or uglier than their physical body presents. Someone with a high opinion of himself or herself will present a more attractive image.

Some things from the etheric plane do not exist on the physical plane. Your imagination can easily create things on the etheric plane. It may take you time to learn to discern the imagined objects or beings. Angels and fallen angels may make themselves visible to you on the etheric plane.

If you hold your hands out and imagine an object in them on the physical plane, others on the physical plane typically will not see anything there. However, on the etheric plane, that object would look and feel just as real as anything on the physical plane to both you and others. Your thought projections are easily formed here. While on the etheric plane, you will see other's thoughts from the physical world manifested in the etheric plane.

The astral plane is the third plane. It does not exist in physical reality in any form. This is where the consciousness goes after death or when projecting astrally.

When on the astral plane, you meet other people who exist on that plane. The world there is entirely created from thought. You will see all manner of things created by the imaginations of you and those around you. This creates multiple levels, locations and dimensions on the astral plane.

Lower astral planes are comprised of those with negative energy like shame, guilt and condemnation. It is the negative energy that confines them. They experience terrible suffering and pain in a world of chaos and torment. Higher astral planes are home to those with positive energy like eternal love, joy and life. They cohabitate in peace among one another.

NDE

In a near-death experience (NDE), some have reported seeing themselves exit their bodies. Others have reported seeing a tunnel of light which they used to pass to the other side. Theses positive types of NDE are reassuring to many, but there are

314

also negative NDEs as well. Some have described horrible, frightening experiences, like entering Hell. In both types of experiences, people get a message that their time has not yet come and they feel pulled back to their bodies. People have different NDEs based on their expectations of how the afterlife will be. How they transition is irrelevant. In either case, they are passing to the astral plane.

The Dream Plane
The best way to describe the astral plane is to say that it is a plane of collective dreams where people interact in a land of fantasy.

The dreaming that we understand in everyday life occurs on a dream plane that is at the low end of the energy continuum. It is immediately below the collective human consciousness and personal consciousness (psyche). This is where the subconscious mind creates an astral ether, frequently based upon the thoughts in your waking consciousness, specifically those in your mind just before you fall asleep. This explains why it is so important to focus on positive, harmonious thoughts when you are drifting off to sleep.

The astral and etheric planes are different from the dream planes in that there is a shared reality in the first two. The dream plane creates an experience that only you are aware of. No one else has a direct experience of your dream. When you are on the etheric and astral planes, the reality you experience is shared with the other beings that exist in those planes. Shared dreams are the result of two or more people interacting in astral travel or in an out of body experience.

Others can influence your dreams by telepathic influence. Those existing on the astral plane can contact you through your dreams and communicate with you. Many report experiencing contact from a loved one who has passed.

The Fourth Plane
This is where the imagination dwells. You draw inspiration,

315

ideas and new solutions from the 'mental' plane. When you have a thought, it originates from the mental plane inside yourself. The thought then travels out towards the astral plan, then onto the etheric plane and finally reaches you on the physical plane. The things in your imagination have an effect in the physical plane.

This mental plane is spectacular! You will experience rivers of iridescent sound bordered by shores of pulsating rainbow light. Your thoughts take on the appearance of a kaleidoscope patterns, made of light and sound. You can walk on a field of ideas and look up at a sky sparkling with inspiration. There is no logic or reason on the mental plane. To attempt reason on the plane would lead to madness, for there is no way for a human to understand it. Existence on this plane requires an entirely open mind in which you simply accept all things and go with the flow.

Existing on the mental plane fills you with wonder and amazement. You can release the child in you and let it run wild, playing in a fairy wonderland. The objects and things here feel just as real as the things you touch on the physical plane. Time is greatly distorted and reality becomes kaleidoscopic. The astral plane is a lower heaven and the mental plane is the higher one. The soul exists on the astral plan and the spirit exists on the mental plane.

Celestial, Cosmic & Divine Planes

The celestial plane is the fifth plane and the Cosmic plane is the sixth. This is where we see beings in their most glorified forms. They are radiant, bright, shining and dazzling. It is the most positive and beautiful state of existence. Here all beings interact with great joy and the highest love for one another. There is no time. Reality is more solid than on the physical plane, being crisp and clear. In comparison, the physical plane is a vague and tired dream, filled with people who are only half alive.

The divine plane is the seventh plane and it is the source.

This is the highest mental plane, made of pure spirit or pure mind. On the divine plane, all things exist as pure consciousness and pure energy. There is no need for perception of form here, so it does not exist. There is no separation. All is one and one is all.

Your mind will remain differentiated from the universal mind, but it will be wholly integrated with all things. You will find complete and perfect everlasting bliss. Experiencing eternal life only on the mental plane is not necessary. You will be in a new glorified body that can change your vibratory frequency at any time, allowing you to walk through walls, materialise and dematerialise. You will be able to fly through all levels of reality unencumbered.

Because the levels of the mental plane are all made of pure thought waves and the physical plane is actually condensed thought waves, one could say the physical world is actually a dream that has been condensed. This physical world we inhabit is simply a dream that you can wake from. Then you can move on to another. The physical world is a dream world. The dream world is a physical world. All things are dreams. All things are reality. Therefore, dream is reality and reality is dream.

Indirect Manifestation

In the same way that awareness pulls Quanta or Energy together to create physical objects indirectly, thoughts also bring together different materials that are needed to create the object or situation on the physical plane via indirect mental manifestation.

In the physical world, things tend to manifest along the lines of natural growth patterns. Think of a seed growing into a seedling, then into a plant, starting with the roots and working up. Leaves form, then branches, then flowers and finally fruit. This all takes time and energy. Depending on the conditions, this growth can be accelerated or slowed. It can be warped or stunted. It can even be reversed.

If you imagine the car you wish to invent, you concentrate

317

your entire mind on it, using all your energies. Eventually, the car will be created. First you start with the original concept, then you add more concentration and thought to the idea. Your actions begin to flow in different directions that will bring the car into being. You create a design, and then find the people needed to bring it into production. The constant focus emits thought waves that bring the right people and circumstances to you to bring your car to fruition.

You and those around you work on constructing and refining the car until it works just as you imagined it would. Now your idea has become a reality. This is the growth pattern that our dreams and wishes follow to become reality. Concentration is the Greatest Secret of mind power.

The Three-Fold Law

The Three-Fold Law relates to the use of power and energy, for when used, power is returned to the sender, three times the level it was sent out.

Used in relation with the ethos, 'Do what thy wilt, though it harm none', take great care when preparing and using this that no harm should come to others because of it.

The nature of this three-fold return can perhaps be better understood when considering the cause and effect principle.

For example, someone comes to you in distress with a problem, you help by sending out positive energy and the problem is successfully resolved. This automatically makes you feel good about yourself and influences your thoughts; thus your state of consciousness is altered.

In turn your thoughts stir the emotions, which have a physical effect in the body by causing glandular secretions to enter into the blood stream. The resulting state of mind and body lifts your spirit, which is what makes you feel good. Thus with the act of a single good deed, you have been effected three times, in mind, body, and spirit.

This then is your three-fold response to the return of positive energy. Now consider your response had you sent out negative energy or something went drastically wrong?

The Law of Power

1. The Power shall not be used to bring harm, to injure or to control others. But if the need arises, the Power shall be used to protect your life or the lives of others.

2. The Power is used only as need dictates.

3. The Power can be used for your own gain; as long as by doing so you harm none.

4. It is unwise to accept money for the use of the Power, for it quickly controls its taker. Be not as those of other religions.

5. Use not the Power for prideful gain, for such cheapens the mysteries of Cosmic Ordering.

6. Ever remember that the Power is a sacred gift of The Cosmos, and should never be misused or abused.

7. And this is the Law of the Power.

On a positive note, I've learned that, no matter what happens, how bad it seems today, life does go on, and it will be better tomorrow.

I've learned that you can tell a lot about a person by the way he/she handles five things:

1. A rainy day
2. The elderly
3. The young
4. Lost luggage
5. Tangled Christmas tree lights

I've learned that, regardless of your relationship with your parents, you'll miss them when they're gone from your life.

I've learned that making a 'living' is not the same thing as making a 'life'.

I've learned that life sometimes gives you a second chance.

I've learned that you shouldn't go through life with a catcher's mitt on both hands. You need to be able to throw

319

something back.

I've learned that if you pursue happiness, it will elude you. But, if you focus on your family, your friends, the needs of others, your work and doing the very best you can, happiness will find you.

I've learned that whenever I decide something with an open heart, I usually make the right decision.

I've learned that even when I have pains, I don't have to be one.

I've learned that every day, you should reach out and touch someone. People close to you love that human touch - holding hands, a warm hug, or just a friendly pat on the back.

I've learned that I still have a lot to learn.

20

Reality Creating Mind Power

An old man was walking along the beach, when he came upon a part of the sand where thousands of starfish had washed ashore. A little further down the beach he saw a young woman, who was picking up the starfish one at a time and tossing them back into the ocean.

'Oh you silly girl,' he exclaimed. 'You can't possibly save all of these starfish. There's too many.

The woman smiled and said, 'I know. But I can save this one,' and she tossed another into the ocean, 'and this one,' toss, 'and this one...'

Use of Will

Opposing visualisations and images will muddy your clear true vision of wealth, whether those images come from inside you or an external source. Avoid talking of your past financial troubles. Keep them out of your mind. Avoid talking about how poor your parents were or how painful your early years were. When you dwell on an unpleasant past, you project an unpleasant future. You are labelling yourself as coming from a source of poverty and pain, associating yourself as the kind of person who will experience such things.

Once you have taken on a certain theory of the universe as correct, and rest all your dreams of happiness upon it, what will you gain by giving attention to conflicting ideas? Why should you give time and energy to ideas that are fading as you evolve, when you can cause them to fade more quickly by promoting growth rather than focusing on weakness? Evolution moves forwards, not backwards.

Consider the riches your world is in the process of receiving, not the poverty it leaves behind. Do not forget that the best way for you to help everyone in the world to gain wealth is to do so yourself by creative energy, not competition.

Do not look down upon the poor in a way that creates sadness for their condition. Instead, think of the great wealth they are receiving. Do not pity them for it will compound the situation. This inspiration grows just as the plant does and gains momentum as it grows.

Understand that you can create things by willpower alone, impress those thoughts on the formless substance and cause them to manifest!

Shifting Reality

Reality is always in flux from one minute to the next. It is fluid, not rigid. If you find yourself in a situation you do not like, remember the changing nature of reality. Your current experience is temporary and the truth at this moment can be altered entirely in the next.

Notice the way children can move instantly from one moment to the next in total acceptance of all that occurs. They have the power of being in the present. You were born with this power too; you only need to access it. Living in the now lets you look at every situation with a fresh perspective. Everything you experience will be the first time for you. You can use the powers of your mind fully and freely in the current situation.

Noticing how you associate events empowers you to make a choice between which associations will help you attain your gaols and which will hinder you. You can make a conscious decision when to link experiences together and when they should be thought of as separate. When you bring these associations into your conscious mind, you have more control. Otherwise they will be in your unconscious mind, potentially doing your goals harm.

It is a good practice to associate one positive experience

with another, rather than separate them as having different meanings. We can have a tendency to allow a negative event to diminish our feelings of joy from a positive one. When you separate the positive from the negative and then group the positive together, you give the positive events more force and power in your life. This helps you protect the joy from the positive experiences and even multiply it when it is associated with other positive experiences. These positive experiences build upon one another, creating a great sense of accomplishment, joy and well-being.

You can also use positive experiences to water down negative ones. You can use the positive situation to put a better light on the negative event, making it less damaging.

When we experience negative situations, one on top of the other, it is natural to associate these experiences and link them together. This can have disastrous affects on our happiness as we add power to the negativity. You must understand that these associations are made by choice. You can isolate each event or situation and view it as independent of the others. Do not make a bad situation worse by piling your troubles together.

When we reframe our thoughts about a situation, we stop giving it power and instead gain power over it. There is nothing wrong with allowing yourself to experience negative emotions following a negative experience. But to move on to acceptance is important.

After Acceptance Comes Allowing

You can begin allowing positive things to open up for you. Let yourself have positive thoughts again and take part in activities that make you feel good. All things have a rise and fall, increase and decrease, rest and flow.

If you are in the middle of a strong negative circumstance right now, recognise that you will move on to a positive circumstance that is just as strong soon. The pendulum swings both left and right. Maintain this awareness and have joy for the positive things to come.

Cosmic Ordering: You Can be Successful

It is natural for things to swing from one side to another. However, you can also take action to counter the swing, limiting its extremity. You can polarise your self on the end you prefer to be on. Choose to focus on positive experiences as much as you can. This will make your reality stay polarised towards the positive more often. Negative situations are inevitable, but your ability to accept and then allow will let you minimise the negatives and maximise the positives.

Remember that each moment is now and only now. It is a fresh start and new direction. Take advantage of this eternal truth whenever you encounter negative circumstances and you will become free of the circumstance more quickly. If your circumstance is frustration because of an absent opportunity, remember how reality shifts and be ready to pounce like a cat at a mouse hole. Your opportunity can come at any moment. This is how reality works.

Start Each Day Anew

The carpenter I hired to help me restore an old farmhouse had just finished a rough first day on the job. A flat tyre made him lose an hour of work, his electric saw quit, and now his ancient pickup truck refused to start. While I drove him home, he sat in stony silence.

On arriving, he invited me in to meet his family. As we walked toward the front door, he paused briefly at a small tree, touching the tips of the branches with both hands. When opening the door he underwent an amazing transformation. His tanned face was wreathed in smiles and he hugged his two small children and gave his wife a kiss.

Afterward he walked me to the car. We passed the tree and my curiosity got the better of me. I asked him about what I had seen him do earlier.

'Oh, that's my trouble tree,' he replied. 'I know I can't help having troubles on the job, but one thing's for sure, troubles don't belong in the house with my wife and the children. So I just hang them on the tree every night when I come home. Then in the morning I pick them up again.'

He paused. 'Funny thing is,' he smiled, 'when I come out in the morning to pick 'em up, there ain't nearly as many as I remember hanging up the night before.'

Be Efficient in Action

Being efficient in action means doing all you can in your current place. Use your thoughts and willpower as I have directed you to advance towards your goals. Advancing requires that you not only live in your current space, but do it fully so that you overflow your boundaries. You must be larger than your present place. You can only do this by leaving nothing undone that you can achieve. The world will only evolve when all people do more than fill their present circumstances.

People who do not fill their present places weigh down the rest of society, industry, government and commerce. These people are carried by others at great cost. They retard progress for others by failing to fill their own places. This type of thinking is from an old age and lower stage of development. It brings degeneration rather than regeneration. Society cannot advance if every man and woman does not fill his or her entire space. Evolution takes place when there is abundance and excess of life. Society's evolution follows the same laws.

An elderly carpenter was ready to retire. He told his employer-contractor of his plans to leave the house building business and live a more leisurely life with his wife enjoying his extended family.

He would miss the pay, but he needed to retire. They could get by. The contractor was sorry to see his good worker go and asked if he could build just one more house as a personal favour. The carpenter said 'yes', but in time it was easy to see that his heart was not in his work. He resorted to shoddy workmanship and used inferior materials. It was an unfortunate way to end his career.

When the carpenter finished his work and the builder came to inspect the house, the contractor handed the front-door key to the carpenter and said, 'This is your house, my gift to you.'

What a shock! What a shame! If he had only known he was building his own house, he would have done it all so differently. Now he had to live in the home he had built none too well.

So it is with us. We build our lives in a distracted way, reacting rather than acting, willing to put up less than the best. At important points we do not give the job our best effort. Then with a shock we look at the situation we have created and find that we are now living in the house we have built. If we had realised that we would have done it differently.

Think of yourself as the carpenter. Think about your house. Each day you hammer a nail, place a board, or erect a wall. Build wisely. It is the only life you will ever build. Even if you live it for only one day more, that day deserves to be lived graciously and with dignity.

The plaque on the wall says, 'Life is a do-it-yourself project'. Your life tomorrow will be the result of your attitudes and the choices you make today.

Create Impressions of Increase

Your present actions must pertain to the business at hand, whether you change that business or not. You get the business you seek by utilising and taking action upon your present business. Perform your daily work in a way to moves your present business toward the one you strive for. Do all things in a certain way. Where your business brings you into contact with others, by personal contact or correspondence, all your communications must convey to all minds the impression of increase.

Every human activity has its basis in the need for increase. We seek more food, better clothes, more comfort, greater beauty and pleasure; increase in something, more life.

This natural desire for increase in wealth is not bad or

shameful; it is simply the way of all things; to become more abundant. This basic instinct in the nature of all things attracts all people to anyone who can help them sustain more as well.

Increase radiates from your creative centre. Know this without a doubt and relay assurance of this to every person you come in contact with. It does not matter how small the interaction, whether you are selling chewing gum to a child or negotiating the sale of a large corporation. Always convey the impression of increase to the other person. Show advancement in every thing you do, impressing upon others the idea that you are advancing, increasing and making strides. This principle applies even to those you meet socially, with whom you have no business dealings.

The best way to convey this impression is to hold the absolute faith that you are taking the path of increase. Let this idea inspire you and fill every part of your inner landscape and actions. Keep the firm conviction in all your dealings that you are one who advances and gives that advancement to all who have contact with you.

It is also important to impress upon others how they can gain increase simply by associating with you. See the value you provide to others that is greater than the cash value you receive from the transaction.

As your success grows, be cautious to avoid the way of modern business. Much of the business world acts as an army of soldiers, marching after the almighty revenue, laying waste to all they encounter. They scramble for power and dominance over others. This lust for power is harmful to all. Avoid the temptation of seeking authority in your business. Do not think of yourself as above anyone else or that you need to show off your wealth in lavish displays.

Minds that seek to master others are competitive, not creative. The only person you should seek mastery over is yourself. Master your surroundings and your fate. You need not hold authority over any others. Such attempts lead to competition and struggle. The environment begins to conquer you, leaving your attainment of wealth to chance, rather than your own scientific control.

Setting Goals by Programming Your Mind

Although I covered this subject in an earlier chapter, this is about programming your mind for success. Now you can put it to good use, leading the way to succeeding. The best possible way to do that is to teach your mind to set goals.

The most effective tool at your disposal for crafting and programming your thoughts and goals is your mind. Having your goals planned out will make it much easier to shape your life. Still, many fail to set goals using their minds, which must be done if you are ever to take action towards achieving your goals.

Failing to set goals has a negative effect on your mind. You will be vulnerable to mistakes and setbacks that could be avoided with proper goal setting. These mistakes can stop you from reaching your dreams. In addition, your failure to set goals stops you from laying out a clear plan and purpose.

Purpose is necessary to motivation. If you do not have strong emotional reasons behind your actions, you will only take the right actions for a short while then stop. Rather than enjoying the work, you will be slaving away through an unhappy chore. Without goals, there is no purpose. Without purpose, there is no sense of achievement or fulfilment in your actions.

When this happens, your mental image of your goals becomes muddied. You will find yourself without direction and filled with uncertainty. You may even wonder why you chose this path in the first place, which leads to the worst of all failures; giving up.

Dreams with no purpose or direction are a recipe for disaster. Your unfocused mind will flounder, drowning in the sea of opportunities, unable to choose the most advantageous options. You may run this way and that, but will not be certain if any of those directions are the best way. You will end up on the most difficult of all journeys, with undesirable results.

Be Precise

It is important that you come to a decision about precisely what it is you truly and deeply want. You must know this with absolute certainty. It is not enough to just know what it is you want; you must also know why you want it. Making this decision means evaluating what you do not have now that you want and consider the benefits of having it. If you had it right now, what would you get? This is the fundamental process of programming your mind to identify and understand what your core desires are.

Write down your goal in clear and specific language. Include details that will give you a clear and bright image of what you truly and deeply want. Studies prove that those who write down their goals are far more likely to achieve them.

Speak your goal repeatedly and continually to yourself many times each day and any time you begin to feel the sharpness of your desire fading. This serves to reinforce the goal in your mind and underscore its importance. It will renew your purpose and help you keep that clear and precise image of your goal.

There are many affirmations you can use to help you along, but you can author some of your own if you wish. Use statements that encourage you to keep an open connection with the Cosmos like, 'I am now open to receive', 'I now give and receive freely,' or 'My greatest good is arriving NOW.' Other affirmations can help you to keep your focus off obstacles. You can try, 'My life is easy; I have abundance in all my needs', 'Money comes to me easily and without effort', 'I move forward and expect my greatest good,' or, 'I seek and receive a bountiful supply.' It is also helpful to remind yourself of all you have now with affirmations like, 'I now have a surplus and my needs are all met,' or 'I have limitless abundance.' You can also try, 'This universe supplies plenty for all of us,' or 'I now live in a rich and loving universe that always supplies me with all that I need.'

Now that you have set your goals with a clear mind and laid a clear path, there is another vital step you must take to get you on the road to success.

You must take your goals, dreams and aspirations and fit them together. Consolidate your dreams into a master plan. This way, you can maintain a sharper focus on just one or a few goals. When your mind is focused, you can then train it to stay entirely focused on the master plan so you will resist trying to change the plan too much. It is good and natural to 'tweak' your plan as needed, but too many changes can send you off in the wrong direction.

Keep in mind that staying focused means that once you choose your master plan or goal, you always know the direction you must travel. It will be your compass on the road to success. Follow the compass and do not stray too far from your original destination.

When your mind clearly understands the path and direction, your actions naturally follow. Everything you do will reaffirm and underscore your desires, bringing them effectively into reality.

Cautious Observations

You may hear people scoffing at the concept that there could be a scientific way to acquiring a limitless supply of wealth. They have fixed ideas that money is limited. They blame governments and society for poverty. Such people insist that only government and societal change can bring about true wealth for the masses. While it is true to an extent that governments keep the masses in poverty, it is the mindset of the masses that is really to blame. Each person has a choice about his and her own beliefs. When they do not choose to act a certain way, they remain poor.

When people have faith and keep an advancing mind, they can become rich. They can make progress just as well as anyone else. A fixed purpose and clear vision will overcome any obstacle. People can decide to act in a certain way any time they choose, under any administration or government. They can make themselves rich and when they accomplish this in large numbers, it will be the impetus for change in government. They will know their personal power and have the strength to change the laws that govern them.

If you experience failure, then you have not asked for enough. Think bigger, understand that there are no limits and demonstrate your faith in the universe. Talent or knowledge has nothing to do with it. You will not fail for lack of these things. If you act in the certain way I have shown you, you will secure all the knowledge and talent you need to accomplish your goals.

If a dog were your teacher
These are some of the lessons you might learn...

When loved ones come home, always run to greet them
Never pass up the opportunity to go for a joyride
Allow the experience of fresh air and the wind in your face
to be pure ecstasy

When it's in your best interest
practice obedience
Let others know when they've invaded your territory
Take naps and stretch before rising
Run, romp and play daily

Thrive on attention and let people touch you
Avoid biting, when a simple growl will do
On warm days stop to lie on your back on the grass
On hot days drink lots of water and lay under a shady tree
When you're happy dance around and wag your entire body

No matter how often you're scolded
don't buy into the guilt thing and pout

Cosmic Ordering: You Can be Successful

run right back and make friends

Delight in the simple joy of a long walk
Eat with gusto and enthusiasm
Stop when you have had enough
Be loyal
Never pretend to be something you're not

If what you want lies buried
dig until you find it
When someone is having a bad day
be silent .....
...sit close by.

...and nuzzle them gently.

21

Zapping Negativity

Inner Voices: Constructive & Destructive

The ego mind rarely rests. Often in the background, sometimes in the foreground, the inner voice of your ego can guide or misguide you. It can motivate you or stop you dead in your tracks. This inner voice has many facets that can be considered different parts of your personality, speaking to you on what you should or should not do.

Think of a little angel on one shoulder and a devil on the other, whispering in your ear. Whether you hear a kind nurturing voice, a critic or the gentle quiet voice that comes from deep inside, these voices serve two main purposes, they help you go forward or hold you back.

Your inner voices can either help or not. They can give you positive or negative feelings. They will either be constructive or destructive. Either they help you bring about the results you want or they bring results that are mediocre at best.

The best way to manage your inner voices is to choose which ones to listen to. You may be getting absolute gibberish. Just ignore them. However, these voices can represent your intuition as well, leading to creative breakthroughs. The point here is to help you handle the negative voices that may lead you astray by asking the right questions.

When you hear the inner voice, and decide you do wish to listen, analyse the thought to see where it leads. Determine if it is positive, constructive, and useful. Will it lead to effective results or will it be negative, destructive, and useless?

To figure out if the inner voice is helpful or not, you must first understand that what you call your inner voice would be more accurately termed as your inner 'perceptions'. It is made of signals in your consciousness coming from a source other than your five external senses. You may experience your inner voice in many forms. It can be emotions, bodily feelings, voices, visual images, memories and other forms.

When you isolate an inner voice, put it into a category. Determine if it is an auditory perception akin to sound or a visual perception with an associated image. It may be a kinaesthetic signal, a feeling that comes with your body. It may also be an emotion or intangible feeling floating in your mind.

Take a moment to ask the deeper parts of your mind why it has sent this signal. What is this message's purpose? Is there something you need to know? Next, ask if the voice springs from your Highest Self, the deep seated centre of your being, the part of you that is perfect and formless like the universe itself. Is this your source of greatest wisdom? Determine if it feels 'right' and listen to yourself. Are you comfortable with the voice?

Begin asking yourself some questions that will tell you where the voice is leading you. Consider what will happen if you listen to the voice. What will the result be? Then consider what the result would be if you do not listen. Consider the implications. You should also think about the message in relation to how the message reached you. Does the content match the form of delivery?

There are times when your inner voice feels negative but is actually providing you with a constructive message. Constructive criticism is a good thing. Your constructive inner voice will not always send you sunshine and rainbows.

Instead of focusing on how the inner perception feels, focus on the practical outcome. When discussing positive and negative inner voices, you should understand that the result is the important aspect; how you use these signals to move forward.

So when you consider your inner voice, you should also consider some other factors. For instance, how will you know if the voice is constructive, neutral or detrimental? Consider what signs or clues will help you come to a decision. Think about how you can and why you should decrease negative voices and increase the quality and quantity of positive ones each day. Have you diminished the quality and quantity of your destructive voices already?

These questions serve a greater purpose. They will help you to decide which voices you will pay attention to. Simply ignoring negative messages saves you an enormous amount of brain energy and time. Do not entertain every single thought that pops into your head.

The questions also help you to categorise the inner voice to its appropriate category to help you decide if it is constructive or deconstructive. They will also help you reduce negative voices and increase the positive ones. By selecting to focus your attention on constructive thoughts, you give them more energy and prevalence in your mind.

Ask yourself these questions for each thought for a few days to give yourself practice at sifting through the thoughts that enter your mind. You will notice that more positive and constructive thoughts come to you, drastically improving the quality of your thinking and self exploration.

Effective Questions to Gain a Position of Power
Allowing negative feelings to dwell inside you is a common source of failure for many. There is of course the other extreme of what some would call a Pollyanna, someone who is always positive and happy, even when all goes wrong.

Negative emotions do have some value and necessity in your life. Grief helps you come to grips with the loss of a loved one. Guilt helps you make better moral decisions or bring you to apologise for a wrongdoing. In proper doses, these types of negative emotions are necessary and healthy.

The problem arises when you let these negative emotions take up too much time and energy. If you cannot let go of them, or 'move on', even though you desire to, you are caught in a trap.

In some cases, even being like Pollyanna, applying excessive positive thinking, does not help. No matter how often you assert your affirmations or simply try to ignore the negative emotions, they simply return time and again. There are some ways to handle persistent negative emotions to break the pattern and release you from the trap.

The first step in finding a way out of the trap is to analyse the root cause of the negative feelings. Find the foundation they are built on so you can remove the support for the negative feeling and let it crumble.

In most cases, the trap of negative emotions will begin with an event. This spark for the negative emotions is often an event that is beyond our control. This means you need not give energy to it. Events that you have no control over have nothing to do with you. They are not your fault. Focus instead on items that you can influence, the factors that you do have control of.

When you shift your focus to items you can control, you are immediately changing to a more positive thought pattern. Now, you are adding to your sphere of influence, expanding it. This will give you more things to have control over, making you more effective.

Just as the Cosmos adds to your abundance, the more you focus on what you can control, the more things there are that you are in control of. The more control you have, the more effective you are.

Sometimes, negative emotions result from events that are already within your control. This is a good thing. It means that you can fix it. To do so, you must first determine why you failed to attain what you sought after, triggering that negative emotion.

Asking yourself effective questions can help you learn from the mistake and make more constructive decisions next time. These questions allow you to figure out why you failed.

Use 'Why?' to help you follow the breadcrumbs back to the source of the problem. This type of inner probing means asking 'why?' again to each answer you receive to the question. You may ask why you failed and respond that you did not put forth all your effort. Then, 'why didn't I try harder?' and answer, 'I was just not that into it.' Your next question would be to find out why you were not motivated. Maybe this was not the right path for you. Maybe it is the right path but you have other blockages preventing you from taking the path with enthusiasm. As you ask each deeper *why*, you will come closer to the heart of the matter and learn the true reason for the failure. You can them make an informed decision about how you will proceed in the future.

Although it happens rarely, we do sometimes feel negative emotions for no apparent reason. There may be no trigger, simply a sudden bout of the blues. Use the why method to dig deep and find where the emotion is coming from. It is likely due to a past anxiety or trauma that you have not yet come to terms with.

In some cases, there is no quick fix to a negative emotion. No amount of affirmation or positive thinking will help here. At these times, you must ask even deeper questions to come to the heart of the matter.

Clearing Negativity

The clearing process is the first step in learning to resolve persistent negative emotions with deep roots. It is a group of effective questions you should ask yourself to get to the source of your negative emotions. Firstly, you must identify your negative emotion. Ask how you feel. Then ask again how you REALLY feel. Is it the feeling you have identified, or is it something else? Is this emotion simply another in disguise? Determine if you want to feel this emotion. Ask why you do or do not want to feel that way.

Consider the consequences that would result if you allowed yourself to feel the negative emotion for an extended period. Are those the consequences you want? Consider the positive consequences of banishing the emotion. Do you want those positive consequences? Think about the pleasure and happiness you would feel from the positive consequences. Consider what you would gain by freeing yourself from those negative emotions. Understand that they may be the reason for any current failures you are experiencing. Ask about the possibility that ridding yourself of these emotions would finally help you attain success. These practical questions lead you to a decision. You can decide to be happy.

Resolving Negative Emotions

The second step in resolving persistent negative emotions involves another group of probing effective questions. Reword the same group of questions to consider how you really want to feel and consider why you need to have those positive emotions. Consider how you can attain more positive feelings. Think about what would happen if you had those positive emotions right now. How would it feel, both to have the positive emotions themselves and to feel the pride of overcoming your negative emotions? Can you feel those emotions right now?

Take some time to consider what you have in your life right now that can help you feel positive feelings right now. Think about those that you love, who love you, who make you feel more secure and happy. What can you be happy about right now? Think about the importance of maintaining this happiness and how you can keep it going. What would happen if you could keep this positive emotion going right now?

When you perform these exercises, you are basically emptying yourself of your negative emotions by feeling them deeply and making a decision to feel or not feel them. You then fill yourself back up with healthier feelings. This technique provides you with a feeling of power and control over your own feelings, rather than feeling weak and trapped by them.

Recognising an Energy Saboteur

Energy saboteurs are everywhere. They can be family, friends, acquaintances or strangers. They may or may not know that they sabotage your energy. You can recognise energy saboteurs or vampires by paying attention to your feelings. You may notice that some people make you feel tired or drained in their presence. 'Psychic vampires' drain energy from those who do not know how to shield themselves, however you do not need to spend great amounts of energy shielding yourself from these attacks. They are typically rare elements in your life. It makes more sense to take some small protective measures to avoid such infringements. Spending all your time shielding yourself from psychic vampires would be obsessive-compulsive and damaging to your emotional health.

Banishing rituals are helpful and simple. They can be practiced regularly, although more advanced rituals can be developed for selective use. Banishing rituals can also benefit you by strengthening your natural psychic shielding abilities.

You can learn how to create magickal shields so that they are easy to erect through visualisation, or you can establish them more permanently. Some prefer to create easily-made amulets or charms around the home that can be recharged when needed. When used regularly, these techniques will increase both the efficacy and clarity of the practitioner's mind. They create boundaries and protective 'magic' that can help give you more clarity and focus to keep negative influences at bay.

Quickly use Visualisation to Banish Negative Vibrations

Create a mental picture of your crown chakra sending out powerful energy in the form of white light. Visualise the white light flowing out of your crown chakra in all directions, surrounding your person, all the way down to your feet. See the white light washing the bad vibrations away. This quick method can help you before a job interview or before placing a Cosmic Order. It is easy to do and highly effective.

Protect Yourself from Psychic Attacks

There are several methods you can employ to protect yourself from psychic attack. When possible, limit contact with those who drain your energy or make you feel negative emotions. You can distance yourself physically, or simply reduce your contact with such people.

When in the presence of a psychic vampire, you can separate yourself mentally from the attack by aligning yourself with the present moment. When under psychic attack from an energy vampire, simply change the topic of conversation. Inject your positive energy and influence and hold onto that positive energy regardless of resistance from the other party.

Notice your own responses and determine how you might be attracting the negative person into your life. Have you been unreasonable or generated a problematic relationship from your inner unresolved problems?

If all else fails and you cannot resolve the negative influence, you must be ready to detach from the relationship.

Remember to accept yourself and be happy with who you are. Needy relationships often crop up when you lack confidence, contentment or security with who you are. When you resolve these issues, you will have a greater capacity to select friendships that are healthy and nourishing.

Our senses give us all that we need to pick up on the energy fields around us. Everyone has this gift. When under psychic attack, you will know it because your contact with the other person makes you feel tired and drained. You may even feel ill when the negativity rubs off on you, bringing on depression or a poor mood. When any relationship makes you feel this way, you are under psychic attack.

What You can Do

Meditation and visualisation can be used to clear negative energy. The same protective glow that you use to protect your mind, body and spirit can be used to shield yourself from others' negativity. There are also some more practical steps you can take, but it is dependent upon the nature of your relationship and the extent of the difficulty.

Zapping Negativity

Overcome Fear

If you have strong fears or phobias, the Rewind Technique (Fast Phobia Cure or V/K Dissociation technique) is an effective way to treat PTSD (post-traumatic stress disorder), panic disorders and phobias. It is called the *Rewind Technique* because the sufferer actually rewinds the unpleasant experience that led to trauma, effectively undoing the event.

The theory behind this process says that it works by reprocessing traumatic memories in the higher cortex. This allows the emergency responses associated with the event in the amygdala to be reclassified as non-threatening. In this way, there is no longer a pattern-match to trigger the anxiety or panic.

This technique was pioneered by the same scientists who came up with NLP. They initially called the process Visual-Kinaesthetic Dissociation Technique (V/K Dissociation). The technique was refined by Joseph Griffin and Ivan Tyrrell from the Human Givens Institute who subsequently named it *The Rewind Technique*.

Before this technique became available, it was believed that the only way to deal with phobias and post-traumatic stress disorder was to recreate the phobia or anxiety situation in order to de-condition the anxiety response. This method has since been discredited.

The Rewind Technique asks the sufferer to replay the painful memory using imagery, but not in the way we do when suffering from flash backs. The method disassociates the experience with pain so that the mind can recode the event as a non-stressful one. This method is much quicker and more effective than the traditional talk form of therapy. The process helps those with a good ability to visualise even more.

Let us consider the example of Joe, a gentleman who worked as an assistant manager at a store. It was his job to take deposits to the bank. One afternoon, Joe was accosted by a man with a gun who demanded Joe hand over the bank deposit.

Joe was immediately frozen and gripped with fear. He

handed over the money bag with shaking hands. The event occurred so quickly, Joe barely had time to even register the details of the perpetrator's face. Joe could only see the pistol in the man's hand. Thoughts of his wife and child ran through his mind while he said a quick prayer in hope that he would survive the event.

While Joe was shaken up badly, he was not hurt physically. However, as time went on, Joe noticed recurrent thoughts about the robbery. He began having nightmares. He was anxious at work and often felt panicky each time he had to make a deposit run. He was afraid he would be robbed a second time and this fear began to overwhelm him as it grew more frequent and intense. Joe knew he could not go on this way and needed help.

I was able to help Joe by telling him about the visual/kinaesthetic dissociation technique (v/k-d). I explained how the process would require him to replay the visual memory of the robbery, but not in the same way he had been reliving the event. Because Joe was good at visualising, I thought this technique would be especially helpful for him.

First, I asked Joe to explain what happened to lead to his anxiety. I then asked some questions about how he saw the event in his mind. This part of the process is important because when people are still coming to grips with a trauma, they remember the details differently than those who have successfully managed trauma.

Joe's memory of the event put him in the event as if it were happening to him all over again. The gun seemed gigantic to him. The colours were vivid as he saw the red getaway car. The gunman seemed to be right on top of him. In the movie Joe played in his mind, the incident did not happen in real time, but ran slowly. All the drama in this movie triggered intense fear for Joe.

Joe was most affected by certain images in the robbery; the robber, the gun, and the red get-away car. Joe ranked his level of anxiety on a scale of 1 to 10 at 8. This information is important because it will help to determine how successful the therapy has been for Joe.

Next, I guided Joe through a visualisation. I asked him to imagine he was in a small theatre, looking at a blank movie screen. I then instructed him to picture himself on the screen in black and white, without any sound. Next I asked him to retract himself out of the visual image by walking up to the projection booth and watch himself as an audience member observing the image of himself on the screen.

These changes in perception, taking colour and sound out of the image, are important to diminish the intensity of the scene he will replay. When he stepped outside to become an observer, Joe immediately removed himself from the situation.

By putting himself in the projection booth, Joe creates even more separation. From up in the booth, the scene will look much smaller and not as threatening. Now Joe will be able to view the event in a similar way to those who have already overcome an unpleasant memory.

I instructed Joe to replay the robbery on the screen, keeping in mind the new perspective. Joe played the scene in his mind and I watched closely for signs of disturbance. It was important that Joe keep distanced from the event and not revert to his old painful way of replaying the scene.

When Joe finished replaying the movie in his mind, he noticed he had successfully stayed in the projection booth, disassociating himself from the event. He watched himself in the audience, seeing the movie in black and white play silently. This was the first time since the event that he was able to think about it without fear.

I then helped Joe with the second half of this process. I asked him to replay the movie again, but this time he was to leave the booth and go back to his seat in the theatre. I asked him to walk up to the screen and step back into the picture, on the last frame of the movie.

Joe was then to revert the movie to colour and visually rewind it back to the start over a span of two to four seconds, much like viewing a DVD and holding the rewind button. We went over this several times until Joe could rewind the movie within the four-second time frame.

When Joe was done, we repeated the first and second parts of the treatment several times. This therapy helped Joe to accomplish some important changes. He managed to reduce the intensity of his fears from an 8 on a scale of 1 to 10, to a 3. This means he reduced his level of anxiety by over 50 percent in only one session. In addition, Joe managed to alter the way the event was coded by his mind. He no longer saw the event as something happening directly to him. The gun no longer appeared out of proportion. The lighting was less dark and foreboding. Joe now recalls the scene as if it was on a DVD.

In additional therapy sessions using the same technique, we put attention to other concerns, such as his discomfort with making bank deposits and the anxious responses he encountered when he saw a red car like the one the robber used. Each aspect of the trauma was treated the same way and the results were excellent. Joe does not have nightmares or flashbacks any more. The thoughts and fears about being robbed again or shot have subsided.

We finished therapy with Joe's anxiety level between 1 and 2. We discussed the factors that might be distressing him and he explained that the store had not hired any security and the area where his store was located was prone to crime. In fact, crime had been on the rise. Given the nature of the area where he works, and his employer's lack of security support, his level of anxiety seemed appropriate.

Joe realised that he would need to find employment elsewhere. Although he enjoyed his work at the store where he had been employed for seven years, his concerns about the every-increasing crime in the neighbourhood and the lack of store security compelled him to find a safer job. Even after Joe was robbed, the store owners refused to hire additional security. It was reasonable for Joe to seek employment elsewhere given the situation; any prudent person would have

344

done the same.

Not long after, Joe found a job in a better neighbourhood with better pay. This change created a drop in his anxiety level to zero. He no longer had any fears or intrusive thoughts, even when making bank deposits.

Joes's case shows how NLP for traumatic incidents can help. If there are several related events, each incident and their respective aspects must be addressed and treated. NLP effectively desensitises fear-based reactions to experiences, resolving the symptoms associated with traumatic stress.

The Rewind Technique is one of the fastest ways to use the basic human principle that separating yourself from an event by remembering it calmly; the associated emotions from the experience are removed. The memories will no longer trigger fear and stress. The 'fight or flight' mechanism in the amygdala is reconfigured to see the event in a narrative sense, allowing you to detach from the event and respond from the neocortex, the calmer reasoning part of the brain.

Depending on the choice of language, this can be referred to as a hypnotic technique, but the techniques are no different. It is simply a way of utilising the human trance state.

The technique allows a traumatised person, while in a state of safe relaxation, to reprocess the memory, making it as ordinary as any other unpleasant memory. The memory is no longer threatening and will no longer trigger a terror response. It works by allowing the memory processing to be transferred to the neocortex from the amygdala.

Events are processed first in the amygdala where the sensory memory is formed. The processing is then passed to the hippocampus where it moves on to the neocortex where it can be translated into narratives. However, events that feel life-threatening can create an overload of sensory information. These sensory memories become trapped in the amygdala instead of moving on the hippocampus and neocortex.

When these memories are struck in the amygdala, no meaning can be associated with the trauma memory. No narrative can be formed with which to put the event in perspective. It can only be experienced again and again as a sensory memory, resulting in feelings of fear or panic. By allowing the memory to be processed in the neocortex, the rewind technique lets us reason with the event and put it into proper perspective.

This technique can eradicate unnecessary fears, leading to a clearer mind. This results in a cleaner connection to the infinite and more successful Cosmic Ordering. If you suffer from irrational fears, you should seek a qualified practitioner to resolve these issues. You may also find help from various audio CDs that use this technique.

Taming Fear with the Law of Attraction

Fear has an affect on your desires. It can stop you in your tracks, making life difficult. Fear is debilitating. Think about why fear is there. It has a useful function when you are in a situation where there is imminent physical harm. It lets us use caution to protect ourselves from danger. However, that part of our personalities can be over zealous. It may tell us to protect ourselves when there is no danger. In the end, you must use your reason and inner thoughts to decide if the fear is justified or if it is only stopping you from achieving your desires only because it can. The Law of Attraction will bring more fearful thoughts back to you if you focus on them too much. You can tame fear before you take action so that the Law of Attraction will bring back only positive results for you.

How to Rid Yourself of Fear

When you have fear, take a moment to reflect on exactly what makes you feel afraid. Where is the source of this emotion? Check to see if it is validated. For example, if you are getting ready to jump out of a plane without a parachute, clearly there is a good reason for fear. This fear is validated by your survival self, to protect your physical being. The survival self sends you a message of fear and hopes you will listen.

Zapping Negativity

Now think about this scenario. You are beginning a new job and you fear people will not like you and that you may not perform well. Can you validate this fear? In a sense, yes, things could go quite badly, especially if you have been putting a lot of energy into your fears and self doubts. But is it reasonable to feel this fear? Is your physical person in harm's way? In this instance, your survival self is sending a message of fear, but it is misplaced. You need to tell your fear that it has no business in this situation.

So, when you begin to feel fear, first pause to check if the fear is valid and physically threatening.

Pay attention to what you do want and you will get what it is you want. Just as fear brings more fear, joy brings more joy. Love brings love and the universe brings your feelings back to you with more of the same.

Do not let fear rule your life; make it your servant. Think about how it is useful to your physical safety and how it has no business butting into your normal daily affairs. Fear makes the object of the feeling seem ominous. Consider what there really is to be afraid of. Are there past experiences that are making you afraid now? If you learned from the past experiences, then you are now in a different situation and the fear no longer applies.

Perhaps you are afraid of getting hurt. This is a normal reaction, but to allow it to dominate you is senseless. Wouldn't it be better to take a chance? It very well could be that the thing or person you fear that will actually bring great joy and beauty into your life. If you never try, you may miss a wonderful opportunity.

Gain control over your fear by questioning its validity. If your fear has a valid, physical reason to be there, then listen to it. However, when your fear is based on a past event that caused pain or on your self doubt, just go ahead and do it anyway, and tell your survival self it is overreacting.

Your survival self will take a step back as long as you are persistent. You can trust that the universe will give you what you want. You must only stay focused on your desires and trust that you will get them. Allowing fear to rule just tells the universe that you do not have faith in its benevolence. Use the Law of Attraction with trust and faith.

Simple Process for Overcoming Doubt

The first step to overcoming doubt is to clearly and accurately define the problem. What self-limiting belief is causing the disturbance in you? Avoid being too general in this. Describe the limiting belief along with the supporting beliefs that allow it to exist.

The next step is to use a statement to encapsulate the basics of the limiting belief. Go through each supporting belief (sub-limiting belief) and do the same process with each one: 'Although I (write the limiting/sub-limiting belief here), I sincerely, deeply and completely forgive, accept and love myself.'

Next put the negative belief into the following three questions. Read these questions a few times to help you to remember them more easily. This way you can practice the exercise any time fear rears its ugly head.

The first question is, 'Can I let this {limiting/sub-limiting belief} go?'. Next ask, 'Would I let this {limiting/sub-limiting belief} go?. Finally ask yourself, 'When (will I let this {limiting/sub-limiting belief} go)?'

Letting Go of Anger Harmlessly

For many, anger is a common problem that blocks Cosmic Ordering. When not handled in a healthy way, it grows and festers, causing more negative emotions and outcomes. Instead, we must release anger in a healthy way. Otherwise, you will see the negative consequences in your life in the form of consequences, people, experiences, situations, and events that can damage your life.

Cause and effect rule the universe. This concept is not so simple as it may sound. In actuality, the universe is not only a

348

Zapping Negativity

Newtonian system; it is also a churning, bubbling, random quantum mixture. All these random, unstable, constantly changing things are easily influenced. They are not fixed and can be affected by your emotions.

Your actions affect you and every person and everything around you. The results of your actions travel out, spreading through the entire universe. Each action is like a pebble thrown into still water. You see the ripples travel out to the edges of the pond, then bounce back, travelling back towards the source of the disturbance. Your actions can come back to affect not only you, both those near you as well.

The affects of our energy travel in two directions. One affects all and all affect one. The golden rule, do unto others as you do would have them do to you, only touches the surface of the reality. Perhaps it should say, 'Do unto others and you are doing unto yourself.' Cause and effect: what goes up comes down; each action has an equal and opposite reaction.

What comes back to you can be either good or bad, depending on your perspective. It depends on your decision, when you choose your intentions. Think about yourself becoming angry because of an event or action from another person. Let us say you become extremely, inconsolably angry. Maybe you are just angry at the entire world. In any event you are mad, really screaming, jump up and down, out of your skin angry. The first impulse is to direct that anger toward the thing or person that made you angry, whether or not that person or thing holds any responsibility for it. You are looking for a punching bag, for a target to take your aggression out on.

It is healthy and good to express your anger in ways that do not cause harm to others, or at least cause very little destruction.

Well, I will show you another, powerful way to exert your anger that will neutralise it and help you use to be constructive. This method removes your anger and begins a chain of events that affect you and everyone around you in a positive, nurturing way. It will feel miraculous. It is like turning a lion

349

into a lamb.

This is how it works. If you get very, very angry, no matter the reason, and wish to vent that anger on something or someone else, and you know this venting may set off a harmful series of events, stop in your tracks. Instead, do something exceptionally good, kind, charitable, and helpful for someone else. Do it with selflessness and altruism, so much that you actually feel pain in giving this away.

Here's an example. One day, you happen to be angry at your boss because he took credit for work that you worked very hard on. Now think of someone, anyone at all, maybe even a stranger, who you know needs help and is worse off than you. Help this person in a way that gives so much of yourself that it hurts.

The essence of this practice is simple. When you feel that you have been treated unfairly, simple reverse it by forming an opportunity for abundance to flow into your life. Your altruism to the point of pain is an outlet, releasing the harmful feelings. Simply kill the anger with kindness, just as you could overcome a nasty person by being excessively kind to him or her. The reward for choosing this course will be an incredibly satisfying, fulfilling and abundance experience. You could make these rewards even greater by giving to the person who did you wrong until it hurt. If you instead reacted with anger or revenge, the response from the Cosmos could be cataclysmic.

Chuck was a US Navy jet pilot in Vietnam. After 75 combat missions, his plane was destroyed by a surface-to-air missile. Chuck ejected and parachuted into enemy hands. He was captured and spent 6 years in a communist Vietnamese prison. He survived the ordeal and now lectures on lessons learned from that experience!

One day, when Chuck and his wife were sitting in a restaurant, a man at another table came up and said, 'You're Chuck! You flew jet fighters in Vietnam from the aircraft carrier Kitty Hawk. You were shot down!'

350

Zapping Negativity

'How in the world did you know that?' asked Chuck.

'I packed your parachute,' the man replied.

Chuck gasped in surprise and gratitude. The man pumped his hand and said, 'I guess it worked!'

Chuck assured him, 'It sure did. If your chute hadn't worked, I wouldn't be here today.'

Chuck couldn't sleep that night, thinking about that man. Chuck says, 'I kept wondering what he had looked like in a navy uniform: a white hat; a bib in the back; and bell-bottom trousers. I wonder how many times I might have seen him and not even said "Good morning, how are you?" or anything because, you see, I was a fighter pilot and he was just a sailor.'

Chuck thought of the many hours the sailor had spent at a long wooden table in the bowels of the ship, carefully weaving the shrouds and folding the silks of each chute, holding in his hands each time the fate of someone he didn't know.

Who's packing your parachute? Everyone has someone who provides what they need to make it through the day. When your metaphorical plane falls from the proverbial sky, you need many kinds of parachutes - you need your physical parachute, your mental parachute, your emotional parachute, and your spiritual parachute. You call on all these supports before reaching safety.

Sometimes in the daily challenges that life gives us, we miss what is really important. We may fail to say *hello, please,* or *thank you,* congratulate someone on something wonderful that has happened to them, give a compliment, or just do something nice for no reason. As you go through this week, this month, this year, recognise the people who pack your parachutes.

Choices Determine Obstacles

Everything we do in life has its own set of obstacles, difficulties, setbacks and negatives. These are natural parts of the growing process and occur with anything we do in life. What separates the achievers from the non-achievers is how they view these problems.

More importantly, achievers have a different set of questions they use to make decisions. Sometimes they are not even aware of it. In observing the successful and those who seem to flounder, I have made some fascinating realisations. I have seen a natural phenomenon in the patterns of life, some of which occurred in my life, and others that I have seen in the lives of others. These observations are some basic truths that can help you understand how your choices determine your obstacles.

The first truth is that infinite possibilities, probabilities and variables exist. At any point in time when a decision is about to take place, there are almost unlimited possibilities for the outcome. Cause and effect does not follow a straight line, rather it is like a complicated mesh of possibilities. One event or cause can produce many different outcomes or effects. The effect can come from almost any combination of causes.

The second truth is that every experience has both objective and subjective elements. A prudent person maintains a balance by using both subjective and objective labels to categorise the experience. This is why you should use objectivity in judging and labelling setbacks, but you must also view it subjectively and actually feel how it weighs you down.

Now why on earth would you every want to let yourself feel bad? Because those negative feelings serve a purpose. They help you to learn from your mistakes and avoid repeating them. The negative emotions your experience produces create a stronger memory so that you will not be caught in an endless cycle of making the same mistakes over and over. Put these negative emotions to good use and really feel them. Then, let them go. Once you have allowed yourself the subjective experience, it is time to look at the situation from an objective angle. The trick is balancing how much subjectivity you allow before moving on to objectivity.

When we use an objective viewpoint, we can separate ourselves from the negativity and see the problem for what it really is; feed back from the Universe telling you that you are on the wrong track. It is merely the effect that resulted from the cause of our action or failure to act. You then see how this is a natural consequence, an intended outcome (lesson you needed to learn), just as things are supposed to be. From this objective viewpoint, we can easily leap to action to set ourselves on the right track. We are light and free, not weighed down by the subjective experience any longer.

The thoughts that come to mind at this point are of new action, things we can do to fix, change or reverse the failure. We do this, by looking back on the first truth and the patterns of cause and effect. Remember that any given cause can have any number of effects. Any effect has a combination of multiple causes. Your intentions, those things you wish to bring about, are effects. You simply need to try another combination of causes.

When you fail to achieve the effect you intended, then the cause utilised was not ideally effective. Not good, bad, wrong or right. For a cause to be truly effective, it must correlate with the initial intention. Understand that the cause was somewhat effective, because it did product a reaction. Not only this, but that reaction is productive and useful in teaching you the best way to make your cause ideally effective.

So, if the effect you intended is not the effect you realised, then you simply need to change the cause. Remember, true failure only comes when you give up trying.

Here are some of the effective questions that have helped achievers become who they are. Ask yourself at each point along the way how your undertaking or enterprise can be improved. How can it be better or worse? These questions help you to remain flexible and open to the opportunities that will present themselves.

When you are planning your venture, map all the steps that will take place towards your goal. Make alternate plans. In fact, do not just make a plan B, but make a plan C and a plan for contingency. The level of complexity for your plan will often depend on how complex the undertaking is and in the value of the reward you seek.

There was an important job to be done and Everybody was sure Somebody would do it. Anybody could have done it, but Nobody did it. Somebody got angry about that because it was Everybody's job. Everybody thought Anybody could do it, but Nobody realised that Everybody would not do it. It ended up that Everybody blamed Somebody when Nobody did what Anybody could have done.

These meta questions will help you learn from problems and mistakes so that you can apply improvements to your plans and modify your plan of attack. First ask yourself what is really going on to cause the problem. What is the essential truth behind the situation? Consider that the feedback you are getting could be inaccurate. Maybe the advice or instructions you received from others is wrong. Ask your self if other people are correct. If they are right, to what extent? What is your opinion? Are you entirely correct and how will how know that is the case? Take a moment to decide if you are viewing the situation with emotions (subjectively) or with logic (objectively). Think about ways to view the situation more objectively. Take a moment to ask yourself if you have fully released yourself from the subjective experience. Is it time to go back and allow yourself to feel it fully? Think of why you must now see it more objectively. What will happen if you are already viewing the problem more objectively?

Now consider what alternatives there are for achieving your goal. How else can you act or behave to complete your goal? Mentally follow the paths of these alternatives to see how they can lead to success. What are the good and bad points about each potential path? What will you gain or lose if for each one?

Think about how you can keep open-minded and stay open to other alternatives that align with your goals and beliefs. Ask why you must stay open-minded this way. What would it be like if you are already open-minded and remaining open to alternatives that will align with your goals and beliefs? What other questions can help you work out your plans.

Cure Negative Thinking

In the landscape of your mind, there is a beast that lurks, waiting to pounce. It's time to tame this and make it your friend. Negative thinking is not always to be avoided. When you ignore negative thoughts, they grow like weeds. This is especially true for those prone to negative thoughts. It is true that old habits are hard to break. It is even more difficult when those habits are deep seated and intangible.

I like to use the word 'cure', but this is really a treatment. It is a set of actions you can take to allow negative thinking. That's right; I'm going to show you how to NOT stop thinking about your negative thoughts. Instead you will manipulate these negative thoughts, allowing them the space to be and gently nudge them into a better direction.

The first thing to do is embrace those negative thoughts. They are part of you, and therefore sacred. They are a normal and natural part of your being. Remember that all parts of you are there for a purpose. You only need to direct them towards the appropriate ends to stay healthy. Even anger is good and useful. Even the craving for material gain is a good and natural feeling that I recommend you embrace. Denying any feeling means you are snubbing a part of yourself. Accepting and allowing these feelings is a way of loving yourself for who you are.

So the best thing to do is embrace and allow the negative feeling. Accept it and then stop. Do not feed any more energy to the negative feeling by falling deeply into concentration on the negative thought.

The next step is to ask constructive effective questions that will help you find a way to deal with the situations in a practical way. Try asking what you can do about the situation causing the negative feelings. Is there a remedy available? Consider your options and determine which options will be most effective. What is the best way you can use your available

355

resources (energy, time, thoughts, and materials) to improve or perfect the circumstance?

Third, redirect your thoughts. Think a good thought about another person and let it go. Believe believing that your good thought will be rewarded and it will come back to you tenfold. If you have trouble believing that you deserve the best in life, you must change this condition of self-punishment.

Simply continue to direct your thoughts towards another person other than yourself. It can be anyone; a friend, an acquaintance or a loved one. The technique is even more effective if you think about someone who has little stake in your emotional and social lives. Even better, try to think loving thoughts about someone you dislike intensely (not hate, mind you). May be there is someone who does not seem to like you no matter how you approach him or her. Offer kindness and forgiveness to that person where appropriate and let it go.

Thought Killing Clichés

Avoid allowing others to kill your thoughts by using cliché. These sayings often tell us to give up or accept what we have accomplished even though it is not our ultimate goal. They may also hold us back with things that tend to make us fearful of risk like, 'A bird in the hand is worth two in the bush.' Consider someone who is considering an investment and his is told this cliché by a friend. If he takes this to heart and never investigates further, he will never know if it was a good opportunity or not. The cliché terminated his thought.

Clichés are simple, thought-killing, vague statements that are used to dismiss thoughts rather that let them thrive and grow. They are used as substitutes for true thought. Consider these clichés, translated into their true meaning, and you will see how senseless they are. 'I'm a work in progress,' really means, 'I'm still not dead'. 'Life is a journey,' really means, 'I will go places and do things in my life.' 'It is what it is,' means, 'It exists.' 'It will be what it will be,' means 'It will change or it won't.'

356

Zapping Negativity

See how devoid of thought these clichés are? They are nothing more than obvious expressions like, 'The sky is blue.' You do not need anyone else to tell you that! So why do we use such trite, useless expressions? Because they allow us to avoid truly engaging with the person we are speaking to. There is no need to probe deeply into feelings that may create discomfort or friction. Maybe it is just because these phrases are repeated so often that they come readily to mind with only the slightest provocation.

Using these clichés will help you to give up the effort of thinking on your own. The do the thinking for you, coming to a conclusion without any careful contemplation in the interim. The more you use these mind-numbing phrases, the more difficult it is to avoid them.

When you use one, you give up your precious awareness, your thinking, feeling and self. You accept the cliché as the proper outcome, stagnating your own thoughts. There is no analysis or discussion. The conversation is done before it has even begun. These thought killers are used by totalitarian regimes to control the masses.

When you hear the phrase, 'Everyone is entitled to his own opinion,' you know the conversation is over. If you are having a complex discussing of a deep seated problem and you hear, 'Such is life.' The discussion has died. When you are engaged in deep debate over good versus bad and you hear, 'We will have to agree to disagree,' the debate has just been lost to both parties. Clichés reduce, define and minimise the situation at hand.

Empowering versus Limiting Beliefs

There are essentially two beliefs that will decide whether you succeed or fail in your goals. Your beliefs will either be empowering or they will be limiting. The names of these beliefs make their meaning clear; empowering beliefs are positive and limiting beliefs are negative. Let us look at these more closely to be sure we understand them fully.

Cosmic Ordering: You Can be Successful

Beliefs that propel you forward and open your perspective are empowering. They determine how successful you can be. Those with empowering beliefs cannot be stopped from attaining their goals. Their minds tap into their full potential if only to prove they are right and that they can succeed. They use every resource available to help them achieve their goals.

Unfortunately, these empowering beliefs are only known to some. Most people hold themselves back with self-limiting beliefs. These beliefs create mental blocks. They are the negative beliefs you keep in your mind, having negative effects on your actions, making you shut off potential opportunities and the possibility of achieving your goals. These beliefs affect who you understand yourself to be. Think about your own self-limiting beliefs and how they affect your actions.

There was once a king who had a wise advisor. The advisor followed the king everywhere, and his favourite advice was, 'Everything happens for the good.'

One day the king went hunting and had a little accident. He shot an arrow at his own foot and was injured. He asked the advisor what he thought about the accident, to which the advisor replied, 'Everything happens for the good.'

This time the king was really upset and ordered for his advisor to be put in prison. The king asked his advisor, 'Now, what do you think?'

The advisor again replied, 'Everything happens for the good.' So the advisor remained in prison.

The king later went on a hunting trip, this time without the advisor. The king was then captured by some cannibals. He was taken to the cannibals' camp where he was to be the evening meal for the cannibals. Before putting him into the cooking pot he was thoroughly inspected. The cannibals saw the wound on the king's foot and decided to throw him back into the jungle.

According to the cannibals' tradition, they would not eat anything that was imperfect. As a result the king was spared. The king suddenly realised what his advisor said was true. The advisor also escaped death because had he not been in prison, he would have followed the king on the hunting trip, and would have ended up in the cooking pot.

Self-limiting beliefs can cause a great deal of damage. They lead to procrastination and laziness. They can destroy your dreams and dampen your hopes. These beliefs bring your morale down, and often damage the morale of those around you. Self-limiting beliefs cause you to lose focus on what it is you desire, making you deviate from the path of success and ultimately to give up trying.

There are certain self-limiting beliefs that are particularly harmful, such as believing something is too hard or impossible to achieve. You may fear that you are not good enough, that you are destined for failure or that you are not capable of greatness. It could be that you fear rejection. The worst of these is believing you cannot succeed in a particular field even though others have had success. If they can do it, so can you. If you want to be successful, it is of vital importance that you defeat the self-limiting beliefs within you.

Wishing to encourage her young son's progress on the piano, a mother took her boy to a Paderewski concert. After they were seated, the mother spotted a friend in the audience and walked down the aisle to greet her.

Seizing the opportunity to explore the wonders of the concert hall, the little boy rose and eventually explored his way through a door marked 'NO ADMITTANCE'.

When the house lights dimmed and the concert was about to begin, the mother returned to her seat and discovered that the child was missing.

Suddenly, the curtains parted and spotlights focused on the impressive Steinway on stage. In horror, the mother saw her little boy sitting at the keyboard, innocently picking out 'Twinkle, Twinkle Little Star.'

At that moment, the great piano master made his entrance, quickly moved to the piano, and whispered in the boy's ear, 'Don't quit. Keep playing.'

Then leaning over, Paderewski reached down with his left hand and began filling in a bass part. Soon his right arm reached around to the other side of the child and he added a running obbligato. Together, the old master and the young novice transformed a frightening situation into a wonderfully creative experience. The audience was mesmerised.

That's the way it is in life. What we can accomplish on our own is hardly noteworthy. We try our best, but the results aren't exactly graceful flowing music. But when we trust in the hands of a Greater Power, our life's work truly can be beautiful.

Next time you set out to accomplish great feats, listen carefully. You can hear the voice of the Master, whispering in your ear, 'Don't quit. Keep playing.'

Doing Away with Self-limiting Beliefs

A well known speaker started off his seminar by holding up a £20 note. In the room of 200, he asked. 'Who would like this £20 note?'

Hands started going up. He said, 'I am going to give this £20 to one of you - but first, let me do this.'

He proceeded to crumple the £20 note up. He then asked. 'Who still wants it?'

Still the hands were up in the air.

'Well,' he replied, 'what if I do this?' He dropped it on the ground and started to grind it into the floor with his shoe. He picked it up, now crumpled and dirty. 'Now, who still wants it?'

Still the hands went into the air.

'My friends, you have all learned a very valuable lesson. 'No matter what I did to the money, you still wanted it because it did not decrease in value. It was still worth £20. Many times in our lives, we are dropped, crumpled, and ground into the dirt by the decisions we make and the circumstances that come our way. We feel as though we are worthless; but no matter what happened or what will happen, you will never lose your value.

'Dirty or clean, crumpled or finely creased, you are still priceless to those who love you. The worth of our lives comes, not in what we do or who we know, but by ...WHO WE ARE.

'You are special – don't ever forget it.'

Your self-limiting beliefs are weighing you down, keeping you from achieving your goals. They are the primary cause of mediocre performance and your personal disapproval regarding your capabilities. Sometimes, we need to just set our doubts aside and get the job done.

Manipulate Beliefs with Creative Visualisation

Now that you have cleared your self-limiting beliefs, I will take time to help you understand how empowering beliefs work. However, I first want you to picture a tractor-trailer truck moving on a highway. Think about what gives that truck the force that moves it. Obviously, it is the engine. However, the engine is not the only part at work here. The engine is not all of the truck. The truck needs wheels, a chassis, fuel and many other things to do the job.

A belief is just like the truck's engine. The engine is your mind and your thoughts. The other parts are your proofs that your thoughts are correct and worth believing. A belief works in exactly the same way, and we can use the above as an analogy! The belief can be likened to the truck; the thought is akin to the engine. The synergistic affect the other parts on the periphery of these beliefs and thoughts, say, like the wheels, the chassis, fuels and other parts of the truck, play an important role in helping you move that belief into action.

To complicate matters, all these rudimentary parts, including the engine (thought), are providing you with belief in other people or events. As long as it is compatible with the engine (your thoughts), you will take it and never consider other options.

So what do we do to change the problem engine and customise the vehicle so that it runs at maximum performance?

Cosmic Ordering: You Can be Successful

Put simply, you choose the parts that go into the ideal engine. You decide how you will customise the vehicle. You can build your own belief system and let it drive your success or limit you. Altering your belief system is easier than you think.

You first must have ample reasons to change you way of thinking. This will create the strong emotional reasons you need to effect change. Then you must examine each piece of evidence that encouraged or supported the faulty belief. You will give other evidence to show the faulty belief is inaccurate. Once you have stripped down the parts of your belief system, you are ready to install new gear.

Now install your new equipment; put in your new, positive beliefs. Support your new beliefs with the proofs from your life. Now you have taken an old engine that was making your life limp down the proverbial road of life and made it into a mean, green, destiny driving machine. But the work is not over yet.

Finally, you need to write your new beliefs down to reinforce them. Understand that there are no beliefs that are 100 percent true. When you write your beliefs on paper, you can review them and consider changes that will make them more compatible with your overall belief system.

Your beliefs rely on your thoughts, and the mind can be fooled. Remember this and use it to make more useful and empowering beliefs. If you acknowledge a belief is not serving you well, you can just change it.

In summary, you just find enough motivation to change, disprove old beliefs, take on new ones, support your new beliefs with evidence and then write them down. Simple.

Boosting Creativity

Now that you have cleared your limiting beliefs and empowered your mind with new, more positive beliefs, you are ready for the next step. You will now learn how to use your creativity more efficiently so that you will generate more and better ideas. Understand that your ideas are the bedrock of any process for creative thinking. If you have no ideas, how will you create a unique, inspired and imaginative solution to bring you your desires?

You sometimes may feel you are not a very creative person, that ideas do not come naturally to you. The truth is that ideas and inspiration are everywhere, surrounding you. They are like little kids waiting for you to notice them and acknowledge their presence. It is up to you to discover these ideas and use them to further your cause.

Look around you for inspiration; not just with your eyes. Listen to sounds, taste the air, smell it, touch the objects around you and open your mind to intuition. Absorb the stimuli all around you and take them deeply into your mind. As ideas crop up, make mental pictures of them that you can then enhance and shape.

A water bearer in India had two large pots, each hung on the end of a pole which he carried across his neck. One of the pots was perfectly made and never leaked. The other pot had a crack in it and by the time the water bearer reached his master's house it had leaked much of its water and was only half full.

For a full two years this went on daily, with the bearer delivering only one-and-a-half pots full of water to his master's house.

Of course, the perfect pot was proud of its accomplishments. But the poor cracked pot was ashamed of its own imperfection, and miserable that it was able to accomplish only half of what it had been made to do.

After two years of what it perceived to be a bitter failure, it spoke to the water bearer one day by the stream, 'I am ashamed of myself, and I want to apologise to you.'

'Why?' asked the bearer. 'What are you ashamed of?'

'I have been able, for these past two years, to deliver only half my load because this crack in my side causes water to leak out all the way back to your master's house. Because of my flaws, you have to do all of this work, and you don't get full value from your efforts,' the pot said.

The water bearer felt sorry for the old cracked pot, and in his compassion he said, 'As we return to the master's house, I want you to notice the beautiful flowers along the path.'

Indeed, as they went up the hill, the old cracked pot took notice of the sun warming the beautiful wild flowers on the side of the path, and this cheered it some. But at the end of the trail, it still felt bad because it had leaked out half its load, and so again the pot apologised to the bearer for its failure.

The bearer said to the pot, 'Did you notice that there were flowers only on your side of your path, but not on the other pot's side? That's because I have always known about your flaw, and I took advantage of it. I planted flower seeds on your side of the path, and every day while we walk back from the stream, you've watered them. For two years I have been able to pick these beautiful flowers to decorate my master's table. Without you being just the way you are, he would not have this beauty to grace his house.'

Don't be afraid of your flaws. Acknowledge them, and you too can be the cause of beauty. Know that in our weakness we find our strength.

22

Activating the Mind's Eye

Activating your third eye is *more important than any other* technique I have shown you in Cosmic Ordering.

We often think of our physical bodies when we think of ourselves, but the primary truth is that we are spirits. We only occupy these physical bodies so that our spirits can interact with the universe on this material plane. Our bodies allow us to experience material things that our spirits cannot. The body is a vehicle for transport.

Most of us forget we are truly spiritual beings. We easily become overrun by the tactile experiences of this realm. As spirits, we knew none of this. We had little concept of space, time or limits. We were called towards this physical plane, travelling through many doors, making adjustments as we entered each plane of existence.

Finally, we entered our bodies at birth. As infants, we enter and leave the body easily, still learning to identify with this flesh capsule that contains us. Eventually, we become addicted to the tactile experiences this world offers; warm embraces, smiles from our mothers, tasting mothers milk, seeing light, hearing music, growing.

As our bodies grow, our spirit adjusts to the vehicle, learning to move, walk, speak and interact with other body-clad spirits. This learning requires that we focus on our physical senses, learn to understand what the signals mean and become better operators of these body machines.

Although we understood seeing as spirits, in a body, the experience is different. We see through two holes that limit what we can see. We learn to use our eyes from the signals coming in from bright toys and television. Eventually, we forget about spiritual seeing. However, we can relearn how to see as spirits. We can activate the third eye in a passive observing way.

You might have read or heard about the experience of *Shape-Shifting* or *Mirror Gazing*, which is a way of looking at differing aspects of yourself, a step in using the third eye. Your third eye is a gate leading to other planes of existence. It is a metaphysical and esoteric idea that refers partly to the brow chakra (Ajna).

The third eye is a symbol for enlightenment and higher consciousness. It is often referred to in association with precognition, clairvoyance, visions and out of body experiences.

The Ajna Chakra is linked to the pineal gland and is the chakra of awareness, light and time. Sometimes called the mind's eye, the Ajna Chakra sits between your eyes, expanding to the centre of your forehead, then separating to the left and right sides of your body.

In actuality, the third eye is only your dormant pineal gland, located between the two hemispheres of your brain. Pinealocytes, or pineal gland cells, work the same way as the light receptors in your physical eyes. This gland creates DMT (dimethyltryptamine), known to induce dreams, mediation, visions and near-death experiences.

Calcite Microcrystals

In 2002, scientists studying the pineal gland found that microcrystals existed within the gland. This discovery showed a new form of biomineralisation in the brain. While other calcifications had been noted in the pineal gland before, these tiny crystals were distinct and entirely separate from the previously seen mulberry-type hydroxyapatite concretions.

Scientists developed a procedure to help them isolate the crystals from the organic matter found in the pineal gland. Under electron microscopes, they were able to observe cubic, hexagonal, and cylindrical forms of the crystals. While the facets of the crystals were rough, edges were found to be sharp. These crystals were comprised wholly of carbon, and oxygen.

By studying the crystals with near infrared Raman spectroscopy and selected area electron diffraction, they found that they were made of calcite. Except for the inner ear, this is the only known part of the body to contain this substance.

It is believed that these crystals are responsible for the second harmonic generation properties in the pineal gland. This is the process in which photons interact with others in a way that combines their waves so that the energy is doubled. The resulting wave frequency halved, thus it is sometimes called frequency doubling.

These crystals have a complex structure. Although the individual molecules are symmetrical, the overall structure has broken symmetry, a property that has been tied to piezoelectricity, a way in which crystals are able to store and then discharge energy. This may be how the pineal gland responds to light waves and electromagnetic energy to effect physiological changes in conjunction with the adrenal gland.

Because there are two distinct types of crystalline compounds in the pineal gland, scientist theorise that they have two distinct biological functions. Research continues to look into these crystals, what their function might be and how they interact with electromagnetic fields.

Piezo Cosmic Ordering Actuating

The word 'piezo' is derived from the Greek piezein, which means to squeeze or press. This is an advanced technique I have developed for connecting to The Cosmos. It uses the principles explained in 'Calcite Microcrystals' above.

This is a very, very advanced method so I will not go into detail here as it does need a qualified practitioner in attendance due to the initial electrical surges that are created from the first connection.

I mention here it so you can understand the reason for my

367

explaining about piezoelectricity.

Perceptions from the Third Eye

You may have noticed some miniature particles in your eyes. Usually, we do not notice them because we typically focus 1 – 2 meters in front of our eyes. However, when we are very relaxed, we can focus very close to the surface of the eye. You may notice a sort of 'coloured static' that can distort bright objects and add colour to your surroundings. This is not just a subtle perception but a physical effect.

The third eye is responsible when you feel a presence at the peripherals of your vision, causing you to turn your head and look. A real person or thing may be trying to gain attention from you.

On the physical plane, your attention stays mainly in the centre of your visual range. In the peripherals, there is less focus, so your inner eye may substitute for the vision difficulties at that part of your eye. When you catch a presence from the corner of your eye, it is often your third eye that formed the perception.

I believe that almost everyone has experienced a perception from the third eye. However, most people fail to recognise the significance. Their belief systems reject such experiences and label them as 'imagination'. This text is intended to help you regain awareness of your third eye and learn to accept it as part of your physical reality, not as a paranormal concept.

Preparation for Third Eye Activation

The pineal gland of the average person has been dormant since early childhood and has become atrophied as a result. A healthy and active pineal gland is about the size of a small grape. In those with atrophy from disuse, the gland is about the size of a raisin.

These common practices will help you to open and prepare yourself for activating (or should I say reactivating) the third eye. It is important that you read through these exercises carefully and thoroughly since problems can arise if you fail to do them correctly.

Correct Breathing

Before beginning these exercises, I strongly recommend that you learn how to breathe properly. The simple breathing that takes you through the day is uncontrolled and not sufficiently relaxing to accomplish the mind state required. It may be hard to believe you can breathe the wrong way! Correct breathing is important to keeping both your body and mind healthy. Breathing equals life. Even the word, 'spirit' comes from the word 'spirare', meaning to breathe.

Breathing is the basis of many fundamental actions; just as one is 'inspired' by great ideas, 'aspires' to do great things and 'expires' with the final breath. This root word has been applied to such important things because of the vital place it held in our ancestors' culture. In one minute, we take about 12 to 18 breaths. That means we take 18,000 to 26,000 breaths in a day!

It is easy to think you should be an expert at breathing by now, since it comes so naturally and you practice it constantly at every moment of your life. However, my experience shows that you cannot make such an assumption. Interestingly, at one time in our lives, we all breathed correctly.

Mother Nature tells us just what to do, starting us off with diaphragmic breathing. Notice the way babies breathe when lying on their backs. They breathe with their bellies, rising like a beach ball, and then falling back down. This is the physical sign of correct diaphragmic breathing.

On to the anatomy lesson; your diaphragm is a muscle, shaped like a dome, located in your midsection. It sits over the stomach and intestines and under your heart and lungs. Think of it as division, a layer that separates your lower torso from your upper. In proper breathing, the in-breath causes it to become inwardly concave, as the diaphragm pulls down, pulling air into your lungs. On the out-breath, the diaphragm pushes up, forcing the dome to become outwardly concave.

Cosmic Ordering: You Can be Successful

How actively your diaphragm is engaged in breathing determines the level of oxygen and carbon dioxide you take in and let out. This is an important fact to remember. Even if you take only a little more oxygen in every time you inhale, that extra oxygen is multiplied by 18,000 to 26,000 breaths a day. The benefits of this extra oxygen will help you physically, mentally and emotionally. Try this exercise to observe your breathing and evaluate your breathing pattern.

First, find a quiet place to sit where you will be undisturbed. Take a minute or two to settle in. Next, horizontally place your hand about one inch above your navel. Now close your eyes. Just breathe normally, without making any effort to engage the diaphragm specifically. Notice the movement of your tummy as you inhale and exhale. In correct breathing, your hand will move significantly as you breathe in and out.

Breathing from the abdomen is the right way. If you are breathing from your chest, your breaths are shallow and inefficient. Unless your have medical reasons to breath through your chest, you should focus on breathing through the abdomen. Now do an exercise to see how correct breathing feels.

Sit in your quiet place and close your eyes. Place one hand on your hest and the other on your belly. Now your tummy should move outward when you inhale and inward when you exhale, making your hand that is on your belly move much more than the hand that is on your chest. If you are having difficulty making that happen, here is how to correct it.

Breathe in slowly and deeply, and then breathe out the same way. Your next breath will come on its own without effort from you. Your tummy will naturally move outward on the next inhale and inward on the exhale. If you lose focus or your breathing reverts to your chest, just start again. Take a slow, deep breath in and gently blow it out. Do this as often as needed. It will only make it easier for you to maintain this type of breathing in your every day life.

Activating the Mind's Eye

A note of caution: In rare cases, people can become anxious when they focus on the breath. If this makes you anxious, then only do these exercises under an expert's guidance. For people with this type of anxiety, 'Take a deep breath,' is poor advice indeed. A person who is prone to this kind of anxiety may become more aroused and anxious by breathing deeply. The breathing can alter the CO_2 level in your blood. In those with anxiety problems, this level may have already found its optimum balance. For such people it is better to breathe slowly but not deeply.

Breathing too deeply when you are prone to anxiety may cause hyperventilation. The CO_2 level in the blood regulates how quickly the body takes in more air. A low level of CO_2 can excite the nervous system. When this gas is released too quickly, constricting of the arteries and blood vessels results. This reduces the blood and oxygen flow to all parts of the body, even the brain. This can cause the fight or flight response to kick in, creating tension and anxiety. Such low levels of oxygen in the brain can also be tied to depression and other changes in brain wave activity.

Thoh Mantra

This mantra is performed with a particular tone and chant. By doing this exercise for three days, it becomes permanent and need not be done again afterwards. The mantra 'thoh' is pronounced, 'toe'. You must chant the mantra with the correct vibration. It should not be too low or too high, but within the alto range. Try a few mid-range tones until you find the one that feels right. You will know the right tone when you hit it.

Sit up so that your back is straight. Inhale through your nose and hold the breath as long as you feel comfortable. Allow your lower jaw to drop a bit, so there is a gap between your top and bottom teeth. Put the tip of your tongue in that gap and place a very light pressure there. It will feel the same way as when you pronounce the 'th' sound. Once you have found this position with your tongue, exhale slowly through

371

your mouth saying t-h-h-o-h-h in a single long outward breath. You will say the word one time on each exhale. Your tongue will remain touching your teeth and you will feel a vibration in your tongue and teeth as you say 'thoh'. You will also feel air moving past your teeth and tongue. Practice this five times in a row.

When done properly, you will notice a sensation of pressure in your jaw and cheeks. You should also feel a vibration in your third eye. This sensation can feel odd at first, but you will become accustomed to it very quickly. Simply keep going. You must do this exercise for three consecutive days, spaced 24 hours apart.

Inner Changes

Among the first experiences you will notice is a sensation of pressure, or even a headache in the centre of your forehead. You may feel the sensation emanating from within, from approximately one inch beneath the surface of your forehead. This is a good sign that your pineal gland is activated and functioning again in a healthy way.

Some report a migraine headache lasting several hours. The level of pressure or pain you notice will depend on the level of atrophy that has taken place in the pineal gland.

Once the pressure or headache passes, you may awake one morning feeling a throbbing or tingling in the centre of your forehead, similar to a goose bump sensation. The sensation can be quite intense. You will have this sensation throughout your day. This pulsing or throbbing is the final physiological sign showing that your third eye has been activated.

How it Helps

You will notice some great benefits once your pineal gland is active. You will learn and remember things more quickly and easily. Your creativity will be enhanced as psychic talents develop and strengthen. You will gain the ability to see auras and hear psychic messages. The following exercise will help you further activate and strengthen your pineal gland. You may notice some bodily discomfort as your physiology adapts.

Activating the Third Eye Further

This exercise should only be done well after you have performed the 'Thoh Mantra' exercise. You should wait at least 10 to 14 days before trying this exercise to give your body time to adapt and open to the flow of energy. You will notice a great feeling of pleasure and even euphoria from this exercise. Most people enjoy it greatly and have no trouble performing it once a week, as is recommended.

First, inhale deeply and hold the breath for a count of five, then let it go. Do this three times to help you relax and become focused. Next, put all of your attention on your third eye. You will feel a sensation like those you felt when awakening the third eye in the Thoh Mantra. There will be sensations of pressure or awareness in the centre of your forehead, where you third eye rests.

Now inhale deeply and hold the breath as long as is comfortable and then release the breath while vibrating the word 'May', pronounced just like the month. Let the word come out all at one time, gradually and slowly; m-a-a-a-a-a-a-a-a-y. You may adjust your pitch while you do this.

Inhale again and repeat the mantra four more times in an alto tone. As with Thoh, you will know when you have struck the correct pitch. You will feel it in your head.

The next part is VERY IMPORTANT. When you vibrate the word 'May', notice the feeling of the energy that goes into your head. It will enter first into the third eye, and then travel towards the centre of your brain, then reach the crown chakra on the top of your head. Keep your focus on the third eye, then the centre of your brain and finally the top of your head. Do this through each chant.

In summary, breathe in, and then exhale while vibrating 'May'. Focus on your third eye, then the centre of your brain, then the top of your head as you vibrate the word 'May'.

373

Repeat four times, for a total of five.

This exercise has pleasurable effects. You will notice a sensation of lightness immediately after. You might notice the sensation of energy tingling inside your head or covering your head entirely. There is likely to be a slight pressure at the top of your head and you will feel intensely euphoric. This state of bliss can last for hours of even days. With practice, it becomes permanent, giving great assistance to your void meditation, clairvoyance and other psychic powers.

Activation with Quartz Crystal

If you have a piece of clear quartz you can try the following activation exercise as an alternative. Simply place the piece of quartz upon your forehead in the location of your third eye. Ideally, you would use a pyramid shaped piece of clear quartz. The crystal will bring clarity of mind and open your third eye. If you receive insights while practicing this exercise, focus on that insight. You may have visions of the past, present or future. You might receive answers to questions you have been contemplating. Practice this for 5 to 10 minutes, twice a day for three days.

Activation with Candle

You can also use a candle to activate your third eye by watching a flame for about one or two minutes and thinking calm thoughts. Feel comfortable in your own skin and focus on peaceful thoughts. Do not stare at the candle so that your eyes become watery, but simply look at the flame and let your thoughts and body calm. You will do this to establish a state of mediation that is different than that the common practice of meditation because here you keep your eyes open. Practice this exercise for a few days until you feel your pineal gland activating.

Activation with Eye Contact

Watch your pet's eyes and relax, establishing a deep peace

within you. Animals reflect human emotions and thoughts. You can learn much about your own inner peace through deep contact with your pet.

Activation with Mirror Watching

Look at your face in a mirror. Watch it at a distance, saying, 'That is now my face. It is part of my self, my physical body, my vehicle.' Keep attention on your own face for one or two minutes, ideally with dimmed light to help keep your eyes comfortable.

Activation Tips

Headaches are often a natural result of reactivating this dormant gland in your brain. It is normal to have some pain when using a part of your body that you have not used from a long time. It takes time for your brain to grasp the new information coming in. You might also have a blockage of energy in the third eye chakra.

One way to help manage headaches from activating the pineal gland is to put one hand on your heart chakra and the other on your forehead. Then take the hand from your forehead and put it on the back of your head. This may relieve the discomfort, especially after your first time. You are likely to have a headache for a day or two, but it should not be too uncomfortable.

It is also helpful to avoid alcohol when meditating. Alcohol has an affect on your solar plexus and also can influence the throat chakra where some of the subtle energy of the alcohol is absorbed.

Total Activation

Fully activating your third eye with the Kundalini is a key step. If your third eye remains partly isolated, you cannot achieve the full potential. However, when you open your other chakras and begin to perceive subtle realities, you get pictures accompanied by feelings and emotions that can help you gain a deeper understanding of your psychic impressions. When you use your consciousness to work with your base chakra, heart chakra and crown chakra, you may even experience miracles.

In addition, fully activating your third eye helps you to balance all other chakras. This is the Kundalini, the path to true enlightenment of the spirit residing within the body. There are no short cuts to enlightenment.

Introduction to the Ajna Chakra Meditation Technique

Chakra Meditation is a way to activate and balance a chakra. This will improve the workings of all things in that region of the body and refine the personality traits associated with the area. Some will experience the opening of psychic powers linked to a particular chakra as well.

The literal meaning of Ajna Chakra is 'To Command'. It is referred to as the 'Guru Chakra' because when it is activated, it connects you to your 'Inner Guru'. The Ajna Chakra has also been called the 'Eye of Shiva' or 'The Divine Eye', since the awakening of this chakra implies the attainment of a higher state of wisdom and meditation.

Each of the chakras can be activated in many ways. This guided meditation will focus on using the physical trigger point of the chakra, or kshetram, as a place to focus our concentration to activate the chakra. Each chakra is linked to a specific sound or Beej Mantra that can be used to activate them. The Ajna Chakra is activated by the Beej Mantra of 'Om', which is pronounced 'aum'.

Ajna Chakra Meditation

It may be helpful for you to use a stopwatch or other timing device in this practice. You must first find a comfortable sitting place. You may sit cross-legged on the floor, sit on a chair, or lean against a wall. Set your timing device for 20 minutes.

Sit up so that your spine is elongated. Lengthen your neck by gently bringing your chin back and in, as a solder stands at attention. This will align your spine with the back of your head.

376

Now take five deep, slow breaths through your nose. This serves to relax you and oxygenate your blood.

Keeping your head aligned, look up at the imaginary point located in the centre of your forehead, immediately above your eyebrows. This positioning of the eyes is called 'shambhavi yoga mudra'.

Next, close your eyes while maintaining the mudra. Be certain you are relaxed on not straining too much. Now rest your hands in any way that is comfortable. Many prefer to place their hands on their knees. Remain as still as you can.

Now breathe in deeply and begin the chant in a slow, soft and stead voice. Speak the mantra 'Om'. A single chant of the mantra should last for the duration of the exhalation. Begin with the long 'oh' sound and follow with the 'mmmm' sound for a shorter period. When all of the air is exhaled from your lungs, inhale again fully before exhaling the next 'Om' mantra.

Picture in your mind the 'Om' coming from the point in the mudra, emanating out through all of your body.

Continue this practice throughout the 20 minute meditation. If your eyes become tired from the shambhavi yoga mudra, let go of the pose and continue with the chant. Reapply the mudra when your eyes feel sufficiently rested.

When your first meditation has been completed, rub your palms together, warming them. Place them on your eyes while slowly opening them. This will bring relaxation and comfort to your eye muscles.

Tips for Ajna Chakra Meditation

Many variations of this meditation exist. Here is a variation that only requires you chant 'Om' silently, allowing you to practice your meditation in almost any situation. Follow the steps in the previous guided meditation, but instead of chanting 'Om' aloud, chant the 'Oh' sound to yourself silently as you inhale and visualise the sound flowing from your forehead to the Ajna Chakra. Then silently voice the 'Mmmm' part of the mantra as you exhale, seeing the sound come back through your forehead from Ajna Chakra. The remainder of the meditation is the same.

Using a Bindi for Ajna Chakra Meditation

Some people practice Ajna Chakra Meditation unknowingly by wearing a bindi. This is the traditional red dot that you may see people wear in the centre of their foreheads. Bindis were designed to stimulate the Ajna Chakra through its physical trigger point, or Kshetram. Wearing a bindi is not just a fashion statement; it is a way to raise your consciousness.

There once was a king who offered a prize to the artist who would paint the best picture of peace. Many artists tried. The king looked at all the pictures. But there were only two he really liked, and he had to choose between them.

One picture was of a calm lake. The lake was a perfect mirror for peaceful towering mountains all around it. Overhead was a blue sky with fluffy white clouds. All who saw this picture thought that it was a perfect picture of peace.

The other picture had mountains, too. But these were rugged and bare. Above was an angry sky, from which rain fell and in which lightning played. Down the side of the mountain tumbled a foaming waterfall. This did not look peaceful at all.

But when the king looked closely, he saw behind the waterfall a tiny bush growing in a crack in the rock. In the bush a mother bird had built her nest. There, in the midst of the rush of angry water, sat the mother bird on her nest - in perfect peace.

Which picture do you think won the prize? The king chose the second picture. Do you know why?

'Because,' explained the king, 'peace does not mean to be in a place where there is no noise, trouble, or hard work. Peace means to be in the midst of all those things and still be calm in your heart. That is the real meaning of peace.'

23

Q & A

Many years ago in a small Indian village, a farmer had the misfortune of owing a large sum of money to a village moneylender. The moneylender, who was old and ugly, fancied the farmer's beautiful daughter. So he proposed a bargain.

He said he would forgo the farmer's debt if he could marry the farmer's daughter. Both the farmer and his daughter were horrified by the proposal. So the cunning money-lender suggested that they let providence decide the matter. He told them that he would put a black pebble and a white pebble into an empty money bag. Then the girl would have to pick one pebble from the bag.

1) If she picked the black pebble, she would become his wife and her father's debt would be forgiven.

2) If she picked the white pebble she need not marry him and her father's debt would still be forgiven.

3) But if she refused to pick a pebble, her father would be thrown into jail.

They were standing on a pebble strewn path in the farmer's field. As they talked, the moneylender bent over to pick up two pebbles. As he picked them up, the sharp-eyed girl noticed that he had picked up two black pebbles and put them into the bag. He then asked the girl to pick a pebble from the bag.

Now, imagine that you were standing in the field. What would you have done if you were the girl? If you had to advise her, what would you have told her?

To find out the answer turn the page, but do try and think this one out before doing so. Use that creative part of your mind to come up with a solution to the quandary. Now look.

Cosmic Ordering: You Can be Successful

Careful analysis would produce three possibilities:

1.   The girl should refuse to take a pebble.
2.   The girl should show that there were two black pebbles in the bag and expose the money-lender as a cheat.
3.   The girl should pick a black pebble and sacrifice herself in order to save her father from his debt and imprisonment.

Take a moment to ponder over the story. The above story is used with the hope that it will make us appreciate the difference between lateral and logical thinking.

The girl's dilemma cannot be solved with traditional logical thinking.

Think of the consequences if she chooses the above logical answers.

What would you recommend to the girl to do?

Well, here is what she did ...
The girl put her hand into the moneybag and drew out a pebble. Without looking at it, she fumbled and let it fall onto the pebble-strewn path where it immediately became lost among all the other pebbles.

'Oh, how clumsy of me,' she said. 'But never mind, if you look into the bag for the one that is left, you will be able to tell which pebble I picked.'

Since the remaining pebble is black, it must be assumed that she had picked the white one. And since the money-lender dared not admit his dishonesty, the girl changed what seemed an impossible situation into an extremely advantageous one.

Moral of the Story
Most complex problems do have a solution. It is only that we don't attempt to think. Start your day with this thought provoking story and have a nice day

Q & A

Q: When is the best time of day for placing a Cosmic Order?

A: While there is no 'right' way, I believe the best time is to do it in the early hours of the morning. Many people place their Orders first thing in the morning or just before bed at night. However, the popularity of these times means there is a lot of Cosmic chatter coming from your vicinity at these times. By placing Orders in the early morning hours, before sunup, you are sending your message at a time when the airways are clear and your message will be less prone to muddling or unwanted interaction with other messages.

Early morning hours are also quite peaceful, positive and clear. This is the optimal environment for placing a Cosmic Order. Busy times and places are full of chaotic energy that can impact you and your Cosmic Order. If you are unable to work on your Order in the wee hours, you may practice at dawn, when the astral realm is least dense and the most clear.

Q: Is a particular time of month best for placing an Order?

A: While a full moon is the optimal time to place a Cosmic Order, you can also place them any time from the end of the first quarter moon until just before the next full moon ends. It is best to avoid placing Orders in the first quarter after the full moon. The waning moon changes the density of the astral plane. The moon plays an important role in Cosmic Orders and the density of the Astral Plane. In addition, moon cycles affect mental and spiritual work.

Q: Is writing down Cosmic Orders necessary?

A: No and yes. It is not necessary that you write down your Cosmic Orders, but it is a powerful technique for solidifying and reinforcing your wishes and thus is strongly recommended. The heart of Cosmic Ordering is connecting to the Cosmos;

however you manage to do that.

Q: How important is it to speak Orders aloud?

A: Affirmations are important to voice externally, increasing their effectiveness. However, Cosmic Orders can be spoken internally. If you feel more comfortable speaking Orders out loud, then you should do so. Whichever method works best for you is acceptable.

Q: What role do bio-rhythms play in Cosmic Ordering?

A: A biorhythms is a natural cycles of growth and decay in all living things. These rhythms occur throughout our lives. This is why you feel very good one day and not so much the next. You may wish to search online for a biorhythm checker that can help you determine the stage in your biorhythms right now. You can then select a time when your cycles are most conducive to Cosmic Ordering. I prefer to place my Orders when my mental cycle is at or near peak, since it makes it easier for me to create and direct my requests.

Q: What can I do about my stubborn habits of cynicism and negativity so that they will not hold me back in my Cosmic Ordering?

A: Unfortunately, there is no easy way. You are already asking the right question. You know that you have negative influences that you need to work on. It is unlikely that stubborn negative habits will change overnight since they have taken a lifetime to create. Use effective questions to help you find the root of your negativity and the motivation you need to overcome these habits.

Q: Those closest to me have no belief in Cosmic Ordering. I am afraid to talk to them about my enthusiasm and interest because they may ridicule me. What should I say to them?

A: There is nothing wrong with keeping Cosmic Ordering to yourself for now. You are still learning and working on developing your own beliefs and faith. Opening yourself to a source of doubt can block abundance creation for you. In addition, telling others about your self-development does not serve any purpose.

Q: My family and friends know about my Cosmic Ordering and make negative statements to me about it and ridicule me. How can I handle these statements?

A: Ideally, you would avoid such people at all costs, but you simply cannot do that with family. Think about it this way. If your brother made fun of you for having green skin, what would your reaction be? It would have no affect on your sense of self at all and you may be concerned about his mental health. You KNOW that your skin is not green. Your faith in Cosmic Ordering is the same. When you KNOW the truth of it, no comment can affect you. However, it is probably best simply not to bring the subject up while you are gaining that true knowledge and faith. Don't feed the fire by trying to convince others. You can always try the best conversation killing cliché, 'to each his own' and move onto to your own work.

Q: In what situations should I avoid using Cosmic Ordering?

A: There are definitely times when it is best to stay away from Cosmic Ordering. Such times may be after the death of a loved one or the break up of a relationship. Times of emotional weakness are best managed by allowing yourself to heal and regain your strength. It is also best to avoid Cosmic Ordering if you have a diagnosed case of depression and take medication for your condition.

Q: Should I use Cosmic Ordering if I take tablets for depression?

A: For those who have controlled depression over a long period of time through medication, it may be okay as long as you have no depressive symptoms. However, understand that prescription drugs can have a negative impact on activating your pineal gland. Your efforts may be best used with manifesting techniques such as a manifesting board or placing affirming reminders throughout your environment.

Q: Is it okay to place an Order for another person without their knowledge?

A: In my experienced, beginners should NOT attempt this. You do not know what is best for others and it is not your place to do so. This type of controlling can damage your ability to manifest in your own life. If you have become experienced and adept with Cosmic Ordering, you are more likely to know how to place an Order in a safe way. For the scope of this book, which is intended for those seeking to learn Cosmic Ordering, third-party Orders should be avoided.

Q: Should I take advantage of offers from web sites that sell Cosmic Ordering secrets that say they can make me rich in only a few days?

A: Such claims are not substantiated. There is no way to be made rich in just a few days from buying an e-Book or similar product. The information you will get is nothing secret, in fact the information is readily available for free at your local library. Cosmic Ordering is a science and an art form. Such things take time. Get rich schemes have been preying on the gullibility and desperation of the masses for ages. Do not be taken in by them. While these things can help you to experience some immediate changes, you are not likely to be rich in just a few days.

Q: How long will it take to change my life?

A: At this point, it is a good bet your life is already changing. You have read this book from beginning to end and have learned much about Cosmic Ordering. The speed at which this process gains strength will depend on your positive attitude and ability to develop positive reflexes. Start with smaller 'Step Orders' and use Cosmic Ordering every day to gain more practice. Do not reserve it for emergencies, when your mind will be cluttered with worry. The process can be slow or quick, but it is all up to you and your level of commitment and belief.

Q: Is using target dates in Orders a good idea?

A: Certainly you should, but be sure to understand when such Orders fail, you must analyse the process to find out what went wrong and fix it. This is actually one of the best ways to perfect your skills. You can put a date on every Cosmic Order to help you to see what goes right when they do happen and what goes wrong when they do not. Some of the most common obstacles have to do with doubt, interference or unrealistic requests. For instance if you ask the Cosmos to deliver your perfect mate within a day, you may be asking too much.

Q: I feel like my Orders have dried up. What can I do?

A: You simply need to avoid placing Orders for the time being and reread this book. Everyone needs to refresh their minds at some point. This is normal and common and has even happened to me. Clear your chakras and give your self a mini-vacation to relax. Start again with small Orders and build yourself back up.

385

Cosmic Ordering: You Can be Successful

Q: I think about my Orders all the time. Is that good?

A: Well, yes to an extent. As long as those thoughts contain positive expectations and affirmations that your desires will be fulfilled, it is good to have it on your mind often. However, obsessive thoughts of yearning and desire are Order killers. Avoid obsessing. It is the antithesis of positive expectation, based in fear and worry. If you cannot stop obsessing about a topic, avoid Cosmic Ordering. You do not want to get back more reasons to obsess!

Q: Can I use affirmations in Orders with deadlines?

A: There is no reason why not. They work together to bring about the desired outcome. The way your phrase your affirmations will be important, however.

Q: I placed and Order and want to place it again until it comes about. Is that a good idea?

A: No and double no! Repeating Orders is the best way to get them ignored. Use affirmations and strategic reminders instead. Manifesting boards can also help you maintain focus on your desire without pestering the Cosmos.

Q: Is it okay to Order for a lot of money?

A: Yes, as long as it is done indirectly. What you really want is an opportunity to become wealthy that you can take advantage of. Place an Order for the means to make money. Do not expect the postman to show up with a fat envelope of cash. Instead, expect ways to make extra money to appear in your life. Maybe your boss will allow you to work extra hours. Perhaps you will finally have the courage to ask for the raise you deserve. However the opportunity comes, your firm belief and willingness to act will bring wealth to you.

Q & A

Q: Should I tell others about my Cosmic Orders?

A: Sharing with positive-minded people is an excellent way to help manifest your desires. This reasserts your Order and affirms your commitment. It is up to you whether you share your Cosmic Ordering techniques or not.

Q: Is shared Ordering a good idea for a group of friends or family who want the same thing?

A: Yes! As long as all parties have absolute belief, this method can be very powerful. Your combined energy will go a long way to manifesting the desire.

Q: How else can I manifest my Order?

A: Visualisation helps Cosmic Orders to come about. You can take it another step by using articulated visualisation. This means not only seeing an image of your fulfilled desire, but including your five senses in the visualisation.

Q: Once I receive my Order, is there anything special I should do?

A: Never forget gratitude! Always be thankful, but never surprised, for everything you have in life. You do not need to take any special action or throw a party. Just be grateful, thank the Cosmos and move on to the next Order. One excellent way to give back and ensure the success of other Orders is to share with those in need. Do something nice or helpful for someone else. While tithing is one way to do this, do not feel you must give in this way. Cosmic Ordering has nothing to do with religion.

Q: Does Cosmic Ordering require a lot of my time every day?

Cosmic Ordering: You Can be Successful

A: There is no need to spend all of your day on Cosmic Ordering. It is best to let it happen naturally. You will need to spend a little extra time in the beginning as you learn to use Cosmic Ordering, but it eventually becomes simple and quick. Ordering will become a reflexive action that you take whenever there is something to manifest in life. Try not to get too serious about Ordering. I know it is about what is most important to you, but taking yourself too seriously is not healthy either. Do not obsess or let your life revolve around it. Just have fun!

Q: What is the difference between Cosmic Ordering and the Law of Attraction?

A: The Law of Attraction is a theory. Cosmic Ordering is a practice putting that theory to work.

Q: Isn't Cosmic Ordering basically a form of religion and prayer?

A: No! While both Cosmic Ordering and prayer are forms of communication, prayer is a way of sharing thoughts or words with a religious entity and is often based in the Christian faith. Prayer is associated with guilt and the Christian way of confessing sins. While prayer can be a good and useful practice for finding solace in hard times, it is not a powerful means of bringing about change in your life. How many prayers for world peace have gone unanswered? Well, how many stars are in the night sky? Cosmic Ordering is a scientific system and means for communicating to the divine what you want. It is not simply a way to talk to a religious deity.

Q: Is there a web site where I can find out more about Cosmic Ordering and related items?

A: cosmicordering.net & cosmicorderingexperience.com

Other Titles - Mirage Publishing

A Prescription from The Love Doctor: How to find Love in 7 Easy Steps - Dr Joanne 'The Love Doctor' Coyle

Burnt: One Man's Inspiring Story of Survival - Ian Colquhoun

Cosmic Ordering Guide - Stephen Richards

Cosmic Ordering Connection - Stephen Richards

Cosmic Ordering: Chakra Clearing - Stephen Richards

Cosmic Ordering: Rapid Chakra Clearing – Stephen Richards

Die Laughing: War Humour from WW1 to Present Day - George Korankye

Hidden Secrets: Attract Everything You Want! – Carl Nagel

Internet Dating King's Diaries: Life, Dating and Love – Clive Worth

Life Without Lottie: How I survived my Daughter's Gap Year - Fiona Fridd

Mrs Darley's Moon Mysteries: A Celebration of Moon Lore and Magic – Carole Carlton

Mrs Darley's Pagan Whispers: A Celebration of Pagan Festivals, Sacred Days, Spirituality and Traditions of the Year – Carole Carlton

Rebel Diet: They Don't Want You to Have It! – Emma James

The Hell of Allegiance: My Living Nightmare of being Gang Raped and Held for Ten days by the British Army – Charmaine Maeer with Stephen Richards

The Real Office: An Uncharacteristic Gesture of Magnanimity by Management Supremo Hilary Wilson-Savage - Hilary Wilson-Savage

The Tumbler: Kassa (Košice) – Auschwitz – Sweden -Israel - Azriel Feuerstein (Holocaust survivor)

Wisdom of the Heart – Flora Rocha

www.miragepublishing.com

Submissions of Mind, Body & Spirit, Self Improvement and How To manuscripts welcomed from new authors.